The Expanding Role
of ESOPs in
Public Companies

THE
EXPANDING
ROLE OF ESOPs IN
PUBLIC COMPANIES

Edited by Karen M. Young

QUORUM BOOKS

New York · Westport, Connecticut · London

Library of Congress Cataloging-in-Publication Data

The expanding role of ESOPs in public companies / edited by Karen M.
   Young.
     p.   cm.
   Includes bibliographical references.
   ISBN 0-89930-527-X (lib. bdg. : alk. paper)
   1. Employee ownership—United States   I. Young, Karen M.
HD5660.U5E97   1990
338.6—dc20   90-32646

British Library Cataloguing in Publication Data is available.

Library of Congress Catalog Card Number: 90-32646
ISBN: 0-89930-527-X

First published in 1990

Quorum Books, 88 Post Road West, Westport, CT 06881
An imprint of Greenwood Publishing Group, Inc.

Printed in the United States of America

The paper used in this book complies with the
Permanent Paper Standard issued by the National
Information Standards Organization (Z39.48-1984).

10 9 8 7 6 5 4 3 2 1

Contents

Tables

Figures

Preface

The number of employee stockholders has increased dramatically in the last few years. This has come about primarily as a result of employee stock ownership plans (ESOPs) being set up by public companies. Why has this proliferation occurred? How are companies actually structuring these plans? Are the new shareholders central or incidental to the process? And what role do and should they play? Information about these questions along with other technical and empirical material about public company ESOPs is presented in this book.

When I was putting material together for the book, one person I contacted told me that "the public market for ESOPs is dead because of what Congress is doing." What Congress has now done (see Chapter 9) is try to curtail expenditures of public monies where there is little or no return to those footing the bill. Someone should be keeping a close watch when ESOPs borrow money to the tune of $24 billion, as they did in 1989, with Uncle Sam, Aunt Sally, and Cousin Lem picking up the tab. In the words of former U.S. Senator Everett Dirksen (R. IL), "A billion here, a billion there, pretty soon you're talking about real money." Again, someone should be paying attention when at a roundtable gathering for public ESOP companies the talk all focused on EPSs, LBOs, and A-1s. Not one person mentioned employees, public support, or moral concerns.

That is not to say ESOPs should not be used and used wisely by any company. But it is to say benefits should and *must* accrue to all constituencies, not just a select few. The whole notion of employee stock ownership plans centers around broadening the benefits of capital accrual. This book, like ESOPs themselves, encompasses a spectrum from the scientific to the sublime. I beseech you to read not the parts you already know about but the parts you do not already know about.

I want to thank the contributing authors. Their vast knowledge and willingness to share some of it will add greatly to the understanding and appreciation of the complexities of employee ownership through the ESOP. The views of the authors expressed in their individual chapters are their own. They are not necessarily the persuasions of the other contributors or The National Center for Employee Ownership (NCEO). My gratitude goes to Anna Jeans, at Ludwig & Jeans, for patiently explaining the governmental filing processes when establishing an ESOP. I also thank NCEO staff members Gianna Durso, Martin Jimenez, Lauren Segarra, and Sue Steiner for their help in the preparation of these materials. I especially want to thank my colleague and husband, Corey Rosen, for reading this manuscript and making comments and mostly for just being there.

The Expanding Role
of ESOPs in
Public Companies

1 ⸻

An Introduction to Employee Stock Ownership Plans

COREY M. ROSEN

Not too long ago, a busy executive threw off the Burlington sheets from his bed and stumbled downstairs to make some Quaker oatmeal. After brushing his teeth with Colgate, he put on his Hart, Schaffner, and Marx suit, jumped into his General Motors car, filled it up at the Arco station, and drove to the airport to catch a Delta flight to Chicago. At his business meeting, he munched on some Dunkin' Donuts donuts, leafed through some Xerox copies, and sent some material back to his office via Federal Express. On his way home, he picked up a *Chicago Tribune*. Arriving home tired and weary after a hard day, he found a stain on his new shirt, and so he tossed it in the Maytag with some Tide and went to bed.

Our theoretical executive did all that in products made by public companies which borrowed more than $24 billion in 1989 to fund an employee stock ownership plan. Not too long ago, our fanciful business person would have had to make do with products made by non-owners. Prior to 1974, employee ownership was almost unknown. And until just recently, it was limited primarily to private companies. Employee ownership has grown at a rapid pace in the last several years, however, thanks to a combination of tax benefits, a growing perception that employee-owners make better employees, and increasing familiarity with the concept among financial professionals. Today, we at The National Center for Employee Ownership estimate there are over 10,000 ESOPs covering 11.5 million employees. ESOPs control over $40 billion in assets, almost half of which was borrowed by public companies in 1989 alone.

Now that ESOPs have become a center of attention, they are also the subject of much greater scrutiny. Are they really a means to create a more equitable distribution of wealth, as Congress intended? Do they actually enhance corporate performance, as many ESOP promoters believe? Are they really appropriate for every company? Or are they just another elaborate tax dodge benefiting managers and investment bankers more than employees?

These questions have come into particular focus with the surge in ESOPs in public firms. There are several reasons for this. First, public firms have borrowed huge amounts of money to fund ESOPs, thus increasing the amount of tax loss associated with ESOP incentives. Second, public companies get a lot more attention than private companies in the financial press. Reporters like to write about public firms because readers like to invest in them and because information about them is so much more readily available. Perhaps most importantly, however, the recent public-company ESOPs have been a sharp departure from normal ESOP practices. In most private companies, ESOPs either are a new benefit for employees, provided at no loss of other benefits or wages, or they replace an existing benefit plan but at a much higher level of contribution. In the recent public-company ESOPs, the plans almost always replace existing contributions to employee benefit plans on a dollar-for-dollar basis. About one-third of the public-company ESOPs are used as takeover defenses. While public companies represent only 10% of all ESOPs, they represent about 30% of the covered employees and about half the total borrowing, so this new pattern is very significant.

It is also very troubling to some in Congress, who believe the taxpayer should not provide tax subsidies to corporations that simply allow them to provide the same level of benefits at a lower after-tax cost. Nor are they pleased that ESOPs are sometimes being used to protect existing management, or that relatively few of the new public-company ESOPs provide meaningful opportunities for employee participation in decisions affecting their work. The result has been legislation that cut one ESOP tax benefit, and a continuing investigation into others.

The outcome of this legislation will have a substantial impact on the use of ESOPs in public companies. In assessing the performance of ESOPs, however, it is important to keep in mind that public companies are only a part of the overall ESOP phenomenon. Overall, ESOPs do, in fact, seem to be performing well. They often do provide employees with substantial capital ownership, and they can help a company perform much better. For many companies, an ESOP is an ideal solution to problems of business continuity, employee benefit planning, or raising capital. But the beauty of ESOPs is largely a reflection of the motives and practices of the companies that embrace them. When paired with participative management practices and a corporate philosophy stressing the centrality of ownership, they shine. When partnered only with a desire to capture the fleeting glory of the moment's tax breaks, they quickly fade into little more than a public subsidy of financial cleverness. As Congress is now demonstrating, there is little appetite for continued subsidy of that.

The rest of this book will explore in detail how public companies have used

ESOPs. To place this in context, this chapter provides a more general discussion of how ESOPs are used, how they have performed, and what is needed to make them work well.

HOW EMPLOYEE OWNERSHIP PLANS WORK I: RULES AND REGULATIONS

ESOPs are a defined contribution employee benefit plan—technically a stock bonus plan that can borrow money. They can be used for a variety of purposes and can give employees anywhere from 1% to 100% ownership of a company. The NCEO estimates that about one-third of the ESOPs own or will own a majority of the stock, and the typical plan is designed to own about 30–40%. ESOPs can be found in every size and kind of company, from small retailers to industrial giants. Contrary to popular impression, ESOPs are only rarely used to save failing firms, such as at the widely publicized Weirton Steel Corporation near Pittsburgh, or to prevent hostile takeovers, such as the ESOP at Lockheed. We estimate that fewer that 4% of all ESOPs are set up for these two purposes. Moreover, according to the U.S. General Accounting Office (GAO), only 3% of all ESOPs require concessions. The GAO also found only 8% of all ESOPs are set up in place of pension plans.

To establish an ESOP, a company sets up a trust fund, into which it contributes new shares of its own stock or cash to buy existing shares. Alternatively, the ESOP can borrow money to buy new or existing shares, with the company making cash contributions to the plan to enable it to repay the loan. Regardless of how the plan acquires stock, company contributions to the trust are tax-deductible, generally up to 15–25% of covered pay.

ESOPs are governed by detailed rules designed to insure that employee participants are treated fairly. Shares in the ESOP trust must be allocated to individual employee accounts. Normally, all full-time employees over 21 with at least 1,000 hours of service in a year participate in the plan, although a company can exclude employees covered by a collective bargaining agreement (provided it bargains in good faith about whether these employees will be included). In some cases, however, ESOPs can include only employees in a certain line of business of the company, provided the effect is not to discriminate in favor of higher paid people (such as making the managers a separate division). ESOPs can also base allocations on matches of employee contributions to a savings plan (such as a 401(k) plan), provided certain complex rules assuring equitable participation by lower paid employees are met.

Allocations are made either on the basis of relative pay or some more equal formula. As employees accumulate seniority with the firm, they acquire an increasing right to the shares in their accounts, a process known as vesting. Stock either must be 100% vested after five years, or must start vesting at 20% per year after three years until full vesting occurs at seven years.

The ESOP trust is governed by a trustee, usually appointed by management.

The trustee can be an "insider," such as a company officer, or an "outsider," such as a bank trust department. The trustee oversees the ESOP to assure it operates for "the exclusive benefit of the employee." Because of this legal responsibility, many ESOP advisors suggest that it is safer to have an outside, independent trustee.

When employees leave the firm, they receive their stock, which the company must buy back from them at its fair market value (unless there is a public market for the shares). Private companies must have an annual outside valuation to determine the price of their shares. All ESOP transactions must take place at this appraised price. Valuations are normally done annually (more if there are interim major transactions), and assess such factors as earnings capacity, hard assets, goodwill, market and industry conditions, and other factors that make a business worth more or less.

In private companies, employees must be able to vote their allocated shares on major issues, such as closing or relocating, but the company can choose whether to pass through voting rights (such as for the board of directors) on other issues. If the employees do not vote the shares, management usually directs the ESOP trustee as to how the shares should be voted. In public companies, employees must be able to vote on all issues.

HOW ESOPs WORK II: TAX BENEFITS

ESOPs can be used in a number of tax-advantaged ways. When the ESOP does not borrow money, contributions of stock or cash to buy stock are deductible up to 15% of the payroll of the plan's participants. The size of the contributions is at the discretion of the company. If the ESOP is part of a "money purchase pension plan," up to 25% of pay can be deducted. At least 10% of this, however, must be contributed annually on a non-discretionary basis. If the ESOP borrows money, the principal portion of the loan is deductible up to 25% of the annual payroll of plan participants. All the interest is deductible as well, provided more than one-third of the ESOP benefits do not go to "highly compensated" people.

In all these cases, there is a maximum annual contribution of the greater of 25% of pay or $30,000 that any one individual can get any year. The $30,000 figure will be indexed for inflation according to a complex formula. These limits include not just ESOP contributions, but contributions to other qualified benefit plans as well (such as profit sharing and, using a somewhat different formula, pension plans). These deductions can be combined with other ESOP tax benefits to provide the following variety of attractive uses for ESOPs.

To Buy the Shares of a Departing Owner

Owners of privately held companies can use an ESOP to create a ready market for their shares. Under this approach, the company can make tax-deductible cash contributions to the ESOP to buy out an owner's shares, or it can have the ESOP borrow money to buy the shares (see below). Once the ESOP owns 30% of all the shares in the company, the seller can reinvest the proceeds of the sale in the securities (stocks, bonds, debentures, etc.) of other domestic operating companies and defer any tax on the gain. This benefit applies only to sellers who have held the stock for three years prior to the sale.

ESOPs could qualify the seller for another important tax break as well. A sale of stock to an ESOP qualifies for capital gains tax treatment. By contrast, if the company redeems the stock by buying it back directly, the gain on the value of the shares is taxed as ordinary income. Under current law capital gains and ordinary income are taxed at the same rates, but if capital gains tax rates are lowered, selling to an ESOP could provide an important benefit.

Using an ESOP to buy out an owner, of course, will only work in a company with earnings adequate to buy the owner's equity. The price of that equity must be determined by an outside valuation. About half of all ESOPs are set up to buy out an owner in this way. This use of ESOPs is one that almost always is "win-win." Many profitable, closely held businesses are difficult to sell and end up being liquidated; many others are sold to competitors or investors more interested in the firm's markets, technologies, or assets than in keeping it open. In most of these cases, an ESOP would at least be a realistic option. By selling to an ESOP, jobs are retained and capital ownership is spread.

The actual mechanisms to purchase the shares can be through borrowing, or through periodic cash contributions, both of which have other uses and are described later. Note that if the rollover treatment is chosen, spouses, children, siblings, and parents, as well as any 25% shareholder-employees, cannot receive an allocation of shares in the ESOP on those "rolled-over" shares. They can get allocations, however, from shares contributed to the ESOP not subject to the rollover.

To Borrow Money at a Lower After-Tax Cost

When an ESOP borrows money, it can buy new or existing company shares. The company then makes tax-deductible contributions to the ESOP to repay the loan, meaning both principal and interest are deductible. By buying new shares, the company can finance new capital, acquisitions of other firms, or other growth. Or the ESOP can simply buy existing shares. Dividends paid on ESOP shares can be used to repay the loan as well, and any dividends paid are counted over and above the 25% of pay limitation. Moreover, banks can deduct 50% of the interest income they receive from loans to ESOPs, provided the ESOP owns 50% of the company's stock and employees can vote their allocated shares purchased with the loan monies on all issues. In practice, this has resulted in ESOP loan rates about 10% less than what a company would otherwise receive. About one-third of all ESOPs use the leveraging feature.

The interest exclusion initially applied to all ESOP loans. This limitation came in response to a huge increase in ESOPs in public companies, most of which were relatively small in percentage ownership, but large in dollars borrowed. These public-company plans, unlike most ESOPs, were usually substituted for existing benefit plans, leaving employees with no net gain. General congressional support for ESOPs, however, remains strong.

The loans do not have to come from commercial lenders. Sellers can make the loan, for instance, provided they do so on an arm's-length basis. Only commercial lenders qualify for the interest deduction, however.

To Create an Additional Employee Benefit

A company can simply issue new or treasury shares to an ESOP, or contribute cash, deducting the value of the contributions for up to 15% of covered pay, or 25% if 10% of that is in a money purchase pension plan in which the company pledges to contribute at least 10% of pay every year. Employees get a benefit at no up-front cash cost to the company. Or a company can contribute cash, buying shares from existing public or private owners. While almost all ESOP company executives say that creating an additional employee benefit is one reason they set up their plan, we estimate that about one-third of the ESOPs are set up primarily for this purpose.

ESOPs IN PUBLIC COMPANIES

The most rapid growth in ESOPs has occurred in public companies. Although they comprise only about 10% of all ESOPs, they accounted for 90% of the ESOP borrowing in 1989. Public company plans tend to be very different from other ESOPs in several respects. First, they tend to buy less of the company, typically 5–15%. Second, they usually replace a company contribution to a 401(k) or profit-sharing plan. Most of the time, these company contributions were used to match employee contributions to an existing defined contribution plan. Sometimes, the contribution to the ESOP is made at a higher level than was being made to the existing plan; sometimes the previous contributions are replaced dollar-for-dollar. Only a few public companies just add the ESOP as another benefit, largely out of concern that existing shareholders will object to providing "free" and dilutive stock to employees. Third, the plans almost always are leveraged, whereas other ESOPs are leveraged only about half the time.

Most of the public-company plans also take advantage of the ability to deduct dividends paid on ESOP shares when these dividends are used to repay an ESOP loan. A company typically will have the ESOP borrow money, which is used to buy, and retire, common shares. Dividends paid on these shares are not deductible. The company then creates a new class of preferred shares to contribute to the ESOP, equal to the principal portion of the loan. These shares pay a high dividend rate. The company can now deduct the dividends it pays on these shares, and take advantage of the lower interest rates available on ESOP loans. Suffice it to say here that the combination of the lower rates on ESOP loans and the dividend deductibility was what attracted public companies to ESOPs. The loan provisions were passed in 1984; the dividend deduction provision in 1986. By late 1987 public companies were beginning to explore how ESOPs could save them money; by 1988 the tidal wave of public company ESOPs had started.

Public companies also frequently use "immediate allocation loans." Available to all ESOPs, these loans actually do not go through the ESOP. Instead, the company borrows an amount of money and, within the first year after the loan transaction, contributes an equal amount directly to the ESOP in the form of company stock. This contribution is deductible in the first year up to 15% of covered payroll, and lenders qualify for the same tax incentive as with a conventional ESOP loan. Often, companies will take out a series of these loans over a period of years. The benefit here is that companies can be more certain how much stock they contribute each year, whereas with a straightforward leveraged ESOP, how much stock is allocated to employee accounts each year depends on the changing value of the shares. The disadvantage is that companies must have very large payrolls relative to the size of the loans to make these kinds of transactions practical.

OTHER USES FOR ESOPs

ESOPs can be used in a variety of other ways as well. Firms can divest subsidiaries to their employees, rather than putting the division on an uncertain market. Employees of distressed firms can sometimes use ESOPs to buy their companies. We have counted about 60 such buyouts since ESOPs started. Most of the early ones were closed or sold within five years, but those occurring since 1980 have a much better track record, with about 90% still in business. As experience with employee buyouts has grown, employees have become much better advised on how to make them work.

ESOPs AS AN EMPLOYEE BENEFIT

The only stated legislative purpose of ESOPs is to broaden the distribution of the ownership of wealth. By that measure, ESOPs seem successful. We estimate that ESOPs now control about $40 billion in assets. While that is but a small portion of the roughly $2 trillion in corporate assets in the United States, it is a vast increase from what workers would have had otherwise.

Looked at on an individual level, ESOPs do provide substantial ownership opportunities for employees. According to a 1985 study we performed, the typical employee in the typical ESOP can expect to receive a benefit equal to twice annual pay over 10 years in the plan and six times annual pay after 20 years. ESOP companies typically contribute 8–10% of pay to their plan, with stock values increasing 10–12% annually. By contrast, according to government data, companies that have qualified deferred benefit programs typically contribute only about 4% of pay to all their plans combined.

ESOPs, as mentioned, also usually do not replace other benefit plans, at least in private companies. Only about 8% replace pension plans, while about 35% replace profit-sharing plans. Unfortunately, we do not know if these predecessor plans were contributing equivalent amounts of pay, although ESOP consultants agree that they generally were much more modest than the ESOP.

ESOPs AND EMPLOYEE MOTIVATION

During the early 1980s we conducted an exhaustive investigation of how employees react to being owners. We surveyed over 3,500 employee-owners in 45 companies. We looked at hundreds of factors in an effort to determine whether it mattered to employees that they had stock in their company, and if so, when.

The results were very clear. Employees did like being owners. The more shares they owned, the more committed they were to their company, the more satisfied they were with their jobs, and the less likely they were to leave. Naturally, some employees in some companies liked being owners more than others. More than any other factor, employee response to ownership was first to how much stock they received in their accounts each year. After that, employees responded more favorably if they had ample opportunities to participate in decisions affecting their jobs, worked in companies whose management really believed in the concept of ownership, and not just the tax breaks, and were provided regular information about the company.

By contrast, the size of the company, the line of business, demographic characteristics of the employees, seniority, job classification, presence or absence of voting rights or board membership, percentage of the company owned by employees (as opposed to the size of the annual contribution), and many other factors did not have any impact. Employees looked at the ESOP and asked "how much money will I get from this?" and "am I really treated like an owner?" If they liked the answers to these questions, they liked being an owner.

OWNERSHIP AND CORPORATE PERFORMANCE

Knowing the answer to whether ESOPs motivate employees seems to provide the answer to whether ownership improves corporate performance. Not so. In most companies, labor costs are under 30–40% of total costs. Motivation on its own, presumably, makes employees work harder. We often ask managers just how much more work they think they could hope to get from more motivated employees, based on an eight-hour day. Fifteen minutes is a typical response. That comes to just 3% more time—3% times even a high estimate of 40% for labor costs results in just a 1.2% savings.

That can be a lot of money, of course. It is also not what distinguishes the really successful companies from the mediocre ones. The star performers are those that react to their environment in creative, innovative ways, providing better value to their customers than competitors. How is that achieved? Through processing information and acting on it intelligently. In most companies, the information-gathering is limited to a group of managers. The generation of ideas is similarly limited. So is the decision-making. The assumption is that only these people have the talent, and perhaps motivation, to carry out these tasks.

In fact, no one has more daily contact with customers than non-management employees, at least in most companies. No one is closer to the day-to-day process of making the product or providing the service than the employees. And employees often do have useful ideas they could share with management.

So for a company to use employee ownership effectively, it needs to do more than motivate people to work harder at what, after all, may not be the most efficient or effective thing to do. Instead, it needs to enlist employee ideas and information to find the best ways to do the most important things. To do that, companies need to get employees involved. Managers should seek their opinions. Employee task forces, ad hoc and permanent, should be established to solve problems. Quality circles and employee involvement teams can be set up. Individual jobs can be enhanced and supervision limited. Suggestion systems can be implemented. This all may seem like common sense, and it is. It is not very common practice in most companies, however.

It is also not as common as it should be in employee ownership companies, because it requires such a major change in corporate culture. About one-third of all ESOP firms, according to the U.S. General Accounting Office, have some degree of employee participation. These firms, the GAO reported, show a strong improvement in productivity when they combine their ESOPs with participative management practices. In a study by the NCEO published in the September/October 1987 *Harvard Business Review,* we found that participative ESOP firms grow 8–11% faster with their plans than they would have without them. In both studies, no other factors had any influence on the relationship between ownership and performance. A recently completed study by Professors Michael Conte and Jan Svejar, on manufacturing firms with ESOPs, supports these results. Only participation can translate the motivation of ownership into the reality of a healthier bottom line. Participation is not enough on its own, either, as hundreds of studies have shown. One reason is that few participation programs last more than five years in conventional companies. By contrast, we have not found a single ESOP company that has dropped its program.

Chapter 8 discusses management practices in ESOP firms that contribute to improving the companies' performance.

CONCLUSION

Employee ownership is not all that its most ardent advocates claim. A significant number of plans provide only modest, or no, net benefits to employees. Nor does employee ownership automatically improve performance. That takes considerable work and effort. Employee ownership is an even further cry from what its critics proclaim, however. It is not mostly about takeover defenses, nor does it usually require employees to give up pensions or wages to participate. Compared to most of the fixes for the economy, such as investment tax credits, research credits, industrial policy, safe harbor leasing, and one management fad after another, employee ownership seems to be a permanent and important change in how we approach business (and one much less costly to the taxpayer). Many foreign countries, from Poland and Russia to Costa Rica and Argentina to England and Canada, are working to accommodate employee ownership within their legal structures. With all its admitted faults, it is the only idea on the horizon that combines ideals of social equity with the promise of economic efficiency. That alone makes it worth every penny we put into it.

Nonetheless, as the discussions in this book demonstrate, we need to review ESOP law periodically to assure that it is providing incentives for what we want to accomplish. The growth of ESOPs in public firms has departed significantly from the pattern of ESOPs in general. Policy makers will differ on how they judge these developments, but they clearly need evaluation. This book is a step in that direction.

2

The Structure and Implementation of ESOPs in Public Companies

INTRODUCTION

This chapter presents the results of research into the structure and implementation of employee stock ownership plans in public companies. Historically, ESOPs were implemented primarily in small private companies as a way to simplify business continuity and provide an employee benefit plan, but in 1988 and 1989, public companies began to realize that ESOPs could be a useful tool for them as well. This study focuses on ESOPs in public companies for two reasons. First, the public-company ESOP is relatively new and therefore unresearched. Second, the larger size of public-company ESOPs sharpens questions regarding ESOPs' role in spreading capital ownership.

The general goal of this research was to examine the ways in which public companies are actually structuring their ESOPs, but a secondary goal was to answer the question, "Do public-company ESOPs add to employee financial security, or are they being used strictly as a tool of corporate finance with limited benefit for employees?"

The study results show that while public companies certainly are taking full advantage of the tax incentives and corporate control benefits of ESOPs, they are also providing a higher level of benefit to employees in about half the cases and maintaining the same benefit level in most of the rest of the cases. The data also show that companies are giving the employees a meaningful percentage of the company, with the average ESOP holding being approximately 15% of company shares. The full results of the study are presented in Table 2.1 at the end of this chapter. Key findings are discussed below in detail, but before presenting the results, it is necessary to provide a foundation.

THE HISTORY AND GROWTH OF ESOPs

Between 1974 and 1986, under the guidance and urging of attorney Louis Kelso and Senator Russell Long (D. LA), the U.S. Congress wrote over a dozen laws granting special tax advantages to employee stock ownership plans. The purpose of these benefits, as expressed in the legislation, was to promote the wider ownership of capital. That is a goal the most diverse political positions can, and have, endorsed. With supporters from Jesse Jackson to Jesse Helms, widening the ownership of capital is a goal that has bipartisan support.

Many ESOP advocates feel that in addition to spreading share ownership, employee ownership is a good workforce motivation and could improve company performance. This appears to be true in many cases, especially those companies that combine ownership with a participative management style, but this benefit was not part of congressional intent per se. The main goal was to correct the extremely skewed pattern of ownership of wealth in the United States.

Before 1986, there were two types of ESOPs: tax-credit and payroll-based ESOPs, known as TRASOPs and PAYSOPs, and the now standard tax deduction ESOP. Private companies tended to implement the vast majority of tax deduction ESOPs, while public companies implemented a number of the now defunct TRASOPs and PAYSOPs and had little interest in conventional ESOPs. The tax credit plans allowed only minimal ownership transfers to employees and were eliminated in 1986.

In 1986, however, Congress added an additional benefit, allowing companies to deduct from gross income the dividends paid on ESOP shares if they are passed through to employees or used to repay the ESOP loan. The deductibility of dividends made public companies begin to take notice of ESOPs. Another ESOP benefit that seemed to spark public-company implementation of ESOPs was the use of ESOPs as a takeover defense, as was highlighted in the case of *Shamrock Holdings Corp, et al. v. Polaroid Corporation et al.* In a highly visible court battle, Polaroid's ESOP was instrumental in defending against Shamrock's hostile takeover attempt. Since then, there has been remarkable growth in the number and size of ESOPs in public companies.

The incentives for implementing an ESOP vary from company to company and from the public to private markets. As noted above, the incentives regarding private ESOPs have remained quite stable, and private-company ESOP implementation has had a smooth growth curve. Public-company ESOPs, however, experienced a surge after the Tax Reform Act of 1986. It is difficult to separate the motivations behind this growth, but whether public companies adopted ESOPs for tax or corporate control reasons, it is clear that they began adopting them in astounding numbers.

ESOP BORROWING

The amount of money borrowed through ESOPs in 1989 was $24 billion, nearly four times the $6.5 billion total amount borrowed in 1988. This increase was due almost exclusively to public-company leveraged ESOPs. NCEO data show that in 1988, 80% of the total ESOP debt was held by private companies. In 1989 that ratio flip-flopped, so that 85% of the borrowing was done by public companies. In addition, the size of the transactions increased sharply. In 1984 the Weirton Steel Corporation ESOP was the largest in terms of dollar amount borrowed at $320 million. By 1989, just five years later, there have been five transactions over $1 billion, with a $4 billion transaction at United Airlines in the works.

This new use of ESOPs has made Congress quite concerned. Congress began to ask if public-company ESOPs should continue to be subsidized by the American taxpayers. There was a perception that the large public companies were manipulating ESOPs for their tax incentives without providing any real capital ownership benefit to employees. The question boils down to whether or not the benefits of ESOPs outweigh the fact that the U.S. Office of Management and Budget estimates ESOP borrowing will cost $1.6 billion per year, while the Congressional Joint Tax Committee has put the cost at $2.6 billion per year.

PURPOSES OF THE RESEARCH ON PUBLIC COMPANY ESOPs

In order to understand this phenomenal growth better, The National Center for Employee Ownership performed a detailed study of the ways in which public companies structure and implement their ESOPs. The study incorporates telephone and written contacts with a thorough press search of over 8,000 publications. NCEO culled any reference to employee ownership in public companies, and given the quantity of press coverage for public-company ESOPs, the data search should be quite comprehensive. In some cases, complete data were not available, so NCEO followed up with written contacts and some telephone calls. However, the study does rely primarily on published sources. This research is critical in order to evaluate the success or failure of ESOPs in fulfilling their mission to expand the ownership of capital. The study focused on the questions that appear to be most worrisome to Congress.

RESULTS OF RESEARCH

ESOP Leveraging

First, the study examined just how many public companies are taking advantage of low-cost ESOP loans. In a leveraged transaction, the ESOP borrows money to purchase company securities. Typically, the company assets or a company guarantee are used as collateral. Alternately, the company itself borrows the money and then makes an "immediate allocation loan" to the ESOP.

The prediction was that most public companies would leverage their plans simply because the tax benefits are so good. Companies can deduct both principal up to 25% of covered payroll, and interest payments from corporate income tax. In addition, there are the benefits from the interest income exclusion rule. This provision allows companies to borrow at rates below prime because lenders can deduct from taxable income 50% of the interest received from ESOP loans, where the ESOP owns 50% of the stock and employees have full voting rights. Keep in mind that the plan does not own 50% of the stock in most public companies. This translates to low-cost capital for the company, because lenders frequently pass some of their tax savings on to the leveraged ESOP in the form of lower interest rates on the loan, typically 85–90% of prime. Not surprisingly, study data showed that 42 of 52 tracked companies did leverage their plans using one of the two methods outlined above. The number may be even higher than this because some companies that made "immediate allocation loans" were not said to be "leveraged" in the print articles because of the variant method used.

Implementing the ESOP

The next issue examined in the study was the type of stock issued to the ESOPs in public companies. There are basically three types of securities— common, preferred, or convertible preferred—and each has advantages and drawbacks. Common stock has the advantage of being readily understandable to the employees and can give holders a larger share of equity gains (and losses). Preferred and convertible preferred stock have the advantage of higher dividends and a preference in liquidation, but holders share less in the equity gains and losses of the company.

In order to take full advantage of the benefits of leveraging an ESOP, a company can choose to issue to the ESOP some type of preferred security. Because of their higher dividends, which are now deductible, the company can repay more of the ESOP debt out of its earnings of its shares rather than the cash flow of the company. But preferred securities can complicate the establishment of an ESOP. A company may need to register the new form of stock, and the unusual nature of preferred, especially convertible preferred securities, can lead to employee communication difficulties.

In fact, employee communication issues can crop up at many points of the transaction, and they should always be dealt with as clearly and directly as possible. The transaction for a leveraged ESOP is fairly simple, and the company should make clear to its employees at least the outline of the plan. Basically, there are three ways of getting shares to the ESOP, and the method chosen should be based on the company's resources and needs.

First, a company can simply issue new shares from the treasury, but this may have an unwelcome dilution effect. Second, the company can repurchase shares from the market, but this will decrease the number of shares outstanding. Or third, the company can issue the new preferred shares to the ESOP and use the proceeds from the sale to buy back an equivalent number of common shares from the market. The company is able to pay the dividends on the ESOP shares with pretax dollars and save the cost of paying dividends on the old common stock. This method has the additional benefit of slightly reducing the number of outstanding shares, because the preferred shares have a higher price. A company may be concerned about an increase in the number of shares outstanding because the dilution decreases the price/earnings ratio. This issue and buy-back method appeared to be the most common among the firms in the study, although it was not specifically tracked.

The Preference for Preferred

The study did track the type of stock issued, specifically to determine whether public companies issued preferred shares in order to take full advantage of the dividend deductibility. Ralston Purina, best known for its pet foods, implemented an ESOP by selling 4.51 million shares of convertible preferred stock to the trust. It then used the $500 million in proceeds to repurchase shares of common from the market. By doing so, Ralston Purina was able to establish its ESOP without increasing the number of shares outstanding. The ESOP implemented by Ralston Purina is a clear example of how a company can take advantage of the features of convertible preferred securities in a combination issue and buy-back transaction.

In a similar transaction, Citizens and Southern, a bank holding company, bought back $125 million worth of common shares from the market in conjunction with selling the ESOP 2.95 million shares of convertible preferred stock. The shares, if converted, would represent about 5% of outstanding shares. Thus different types of corporations can take advantage of this type of transaction.

The study results show that of the 30 companies for which stock data were available, 19 issued the ESOP either preferred or convertible preferred securities. These results show that most public companies do take full advantage of the dividend deductibility in repaying the ESOP loans.

Substitutions and Combinations

To address concerns that ESOPs are merely substituting for other, safer pension plans, the study then looked at the question of whether public companies actually use leveraged ESOPs as replacements for standard benefit plans. Companies might do this in order to use the tax advantages to provide employee benefits at a lower cost to the company. For example, Merrill Lynch announced the termination of its old pension plan and the implementation of an ESOP effective January 1, 1989, and the company expected a $220 million after-tax gain. Clearly, Merrill Lynch had cost-cutting on its mind and was expecting the ESOP transfer to boost gains. National Standard, a wire products and specialized machinery manufacturer, terminated its pension plan and converted $4 million of the plan assets to an ESOP as part of a debt reduction scheme. The company estimated that the transfer would provide them with about $12 million in excess assets.

Another way companies use the ESOP as a replacement plan is when the ESOP replaces benefits other than the standard pension plan. The ESOP at McKesson Corporation does not replace an existing pension plan, but the company now expects that employees will use their ESOP benefits to pay for post-retirement medical care, saving that cost to the company. This shows that there is more than one way to use ESOPs to replace other benefit plans.

ESOPs can also be *combined* with other plans to allow the company to pre-fund and reduce the cost of employee benefits. They do this by contributing stock to employee accounts instead of cash. It is only relatively recently that the sophisticated financial tools were developed to take full advantage of this by combining ESOPs with 401(k) plans.

A 401(k) plan is a deferred savings plan into which employees can place some of their pretax earnings. In some companies, the employees' deferred income is all that goes into their accounts, but in some cases the companies provide a partial match to the employee contribution to encourage savings and investment. It is the company match portion of the plan that provides for the combined ESOP 401(k) structure.

In the combined structure, the company matches employee contributions with payments on an ESOP loan. About 65% of the matches in public company 401(k) plans, according to data from the Employee Benefit Research Institute, are already in the form of company stock, so the employees may not see much of a difference in plan investments. With a leveraged plan, the company pre-funds its matching contribution. Thus the initial costs can be high, because a great deal of stock is purchased up front and paid off over what is typically a 7- to 15-year period. If the after-tax cost of the stock is lower than the increase in the value of the shares, however, the company will gradually see its costs decline. Companies can thus provide the same level of benefit to the employees with a lower cost or increase benefits for the same cost.

Companies typically match the 401(k) plan at about 50 cents on the dollar, and may increase that to 60 or 70 cents in an ESOP match. United Technologies (UTC), for instance, implemented an ESOP in conjunction with the company's employee savings plan. It plans to match employee contributions at 60 cents to the dollar in its combined ESOP and 401(k) plan. NCEO survey data indicate that in 25 of 49 tracked companies, the ESOP added to or restructured existing plans. Of those, it is estimated that 20 linked 401(k) plans and ESOPs in a manner similar to the method used above.

Whether the companies use the ESOP as a replacement or a restructuring device, it is clear that it can save the company money. PPG Industries, a manufacturer of glass, paint, and chemicals, estimates that it will be able to provide the same level of employee benefit for 30% less cost to the company. NCEO data indicated that 27 of the 49 companies tracked appeared to be either replacing another qualified employee benefit plan (partially or wholly) or creating a combined structure with an ESOP. This was a difficult issue to track, because of the ambiguity of some of the terms in the print articles, and some plan descriptions in Table 2.1 may cross with other types.

Financial Benefit to Employees

From the employees' standpoint, it does not really matter if the plan is a replacement or an addition. What matters is the bottom-line financial benefit they receive. In some cases, even with a straight replacement, the company passes the savings along to the employees in the form of higher benefits. Key Centurion Bancshares' ESOP was a replacement plan that actually increased benefits to employees. On the other hand, some plans that are in addition to existing plans can keep benefits neutral or even decrease them. For example, Aristech Chemical increased employee share ownership but made other cuts that kept financial benefits neutral or even decreased them a bit.

To clarify this issue, NCEO looked at the actual level of financial benefit to employees to determine whether companies that used ESOPs as a replacement benefit were providing the same level of benefit or whether the ESOPs actually increased the bottom-line benefit to employees, thereby spreading the ownership of capital.

This is a difficult issue to track accurately because of reluctance on the part of the company to divulge this type of information. Superficially, it seems that companies would not want to alienate labor by saying that benefits have decreased. Also, they might want to say that they had increased financial benefit to employees, so that they look like good corporate citizens. But there is a countering factor. They also have to keep the employee benefits "reasonable," so that outside shareholders do not become concerned that employee benefits are too high. In addition, the Delaware court in the case of *Shamrock Holdings v. Polaroid Corporation* said that ESOPs are a sounder defense if they are shareholder neutral. Thus there is pressure on most public companies to report that the ESOP is neutral in terms of employee financial benefit. Under these circumstances, it is interesting to note that 20 of 41 tracked companies indicated an increase in employee benefits, 20 reported that employee benefit levels had remained constant, and 1 company reported a decrease.

ESOPs as a Takeover Defense

The low-cost capital and employee benefit plan cost savings make ESOPs attractive to many companies, but the ESOP use that claimed the spotlight recently is as a takeover defense. In the Polaroid case, the company's ESOP clearly played a significant role in deterring Shamrock Holdings' hostile takeover bid, leading other companies to investigate that type of defense for themselves. Shamrock contested the ESOP, saying that it was primarily a tool for the entrenchment of management. A Delaware court ruled, however, that the ESOP provided significant employee benefits, had the potential to improve the company's productivity, and was "shareholder neutral" due to wage cuts employees took to pay for the program.

Thus the court ruled the ESOP was within management's "business judgment prerogative." The court also noted that Polaroid had been considering an ESOP before Shamrock's announcement (although initial plans for the ESOP were significantly lower than the 15% level sufficient to prevent a takeover under Delaware law). Shamrock cast doubts on the timing of the ESOP introduction, but the court did not find this issue overriding.

Articles used for the survey often mentioned the ESOP as a takeover defense, but many companies denied that the ESOP had anything to do with takeover rumors. Implementing a defense could hurt the company's stock price, as shareholders see less of a possibility for an outside bidder. The diverse reactions can be shown by example. Colgate Palmolive was not the visible subject of takeover rumors at the time of the ESOP, but it had been for years before then. A Goldman Sachs analyst believes that the ESOP would not be a major hurdle, and the company denies that the ESOP is related to the takeover. Nevertheless, the ESOP does put 11% of the company in the hands of the employees, and the company had been the subject of takeover rumors in the past. Similarly, Oryx Company claimed that the reason for the ESOP was to increase employee holdings but "acknowledged" that it would make an unfriendly takeover more difficult. Oryx has been a target of takeover rumors, including several mentions in the press.

On the other side of the coin, FMC Corporation was straightforward in its admission that the ESOP is designed to make the company less vulnerable. Procter & Gamble, long the subject of takeover rumors, also admitted that its ESOP was designed with deterrent qualities.

The legality of ESOPs as a takeover defense has never been fully tested in federal court. In addition, there are no doubts as to whether or not an ESOP is useful as a takeover defense in most situations. First, the employees must be expected to vote their allocated shares with management, or the transaction giving them a large block of stock will not be defensive at all. Second, there are doubts as to the fiduciary obligation of the trustee in voting any unallocated shares (shares not yet paid for in an ESOP loan). Department of Labor (DOL) letters of recommendation sent to Polaroid and Eastern indicate that the trustee should vote the unallocated shares in the plan participants' best interest and may not take into account employment security. The employee voters certainly would. Most companies, however, have structured their ESOPs so that the unallocated shares are voted in the same proportion as the allocated shares, despite these DOL letters of recommendation.

It should be noted that the decision in the Polaroid case frequently used the words "unique" and "particular," indicating that the court felt it imperative not to establish broad precedent upholding *any* ESOP in *any* situation. The case of *Kingsbridge Capital Group v. Dunkin' Donuts,* in which a preliminary court in Delaware upheld the ESOP established by Dunkin' Donuts, may establish further precedent or reverse the trend, depending on the action of higher courts. Neither the lack of federal-level precedent nor the ambiguity of trustee voting seems to have dampened enthusiasm for ESOPs as a takeover defense.

Study data show that of 69 companies with data available, 35 were documented takeover targets. This is not to say that the ESOP was being used as a takeover defense in those companies or that it was not a defense strategy in companies that were not listed as takeover targets, but it is safe to say that defense was probably a consideration for the financial officers in those companies that were clearly takeover targets. One issue to keep in mind is that companies could implement a small ESOP now, and it would be simpler and less suspect if the ESOP were expanded in the future. The survey results can not investigate this delayed motivation, but it is probably a factor.

What Percentage of Company Stock Is Held by ESOPs?

This brings up the issue of exactly how much stock public companies are putting into the hands of employees. The percent of the company that was channeled into the ESOP for those companies for which data were available varied widely from .72% (McDonalds Corp.) to 36% (FMC), so it is difficult to present a clear picture of the "average." Of 49 tracked companies, the arithmetic average was 15%, the median was 14%, and the mode was 15% with seven instances. Close behind, however, with six instances was 5%, so the mode is suspect. The finding of 15% is identical to the Delaware "magic number" for takeover prevention, but the 15% average found by this study should be taken with a grain of salt. There may be a reporting bias that emphasized the companies with a high percentage of ESOP ownership. Employee ownership experts believe public-company ESOPs more typically own closer to 5–7% of the total shares. For the 49 companies in this group with adequate data on the ESOP percentage, 6 put over 30% into the ESOP, and 7 were in the 20–30% range. These numbers become significant in light of congressional moves to curtail ESOPs, which are detailed in the section on Congress and ESOPs.

IMPLICATIONS OF THIS AND OTHER STUDIES

The critical aspect of this study was to determine what all these statistics about type of stock, percentage owned, and takeover defenses mean to the employees. The study was able to determine that public-company ESOPs split about 50-50 as to whether they increase or keep constant the actual financial benefit to employees. Although it was beyond the scope of this research, evidence from other studies indicates that ESOPs in public companies do indeed contribute a higher percentage of annual pay to an employee's account than other pension plans, typically 6–8% for ESOPs compared with 3–4% for other qualified plans. But this evidence may not be sufficient to convince Congress that ESOPs are an efficient use of taxpayers' money.

CONGRESS AND ESOPs

The phenomenal growth of ESOP borrowing has Congress looking very closely at the ESOP tax benefits. There is a perception, which may be accurate, that large public companies are using ESOPs for corporate purposes other than an employee benefit. Accusations of misuse center around the idea that ESOPs simply replace other, safer employee pension plans. Other contentions are that ESOPs entrench management and do not actually increase employee income. But what really has Congress examining ESOPs is that the company cash flow enhancements of ESOPs are basically funded by tax dollars.

To address these concerns in these budget cutting times, Representative Rostenkowski (D. IL) introduced a measure with an effective date of June 6, 1989, which repealed the 50% lender interest income exclusion and the Internal Revenue Service (IRS) ruling to allow qualified lenders to take the interest exclusion even though not all previous security holders were qualified lenders (a ruling that facilitates the public sale of ESOP bonds). Although Rostenkowski intended this measure to eliminate the public-company ESOPs that were "abusing" the tax benefits without providing a real employee benefit, in the next month, 20 public companies announced ESOPs borrowing over $5 billion. Clearly the interest provision and public debt market were not the motivating factors. Therefore he introduced new legislation also with an effective date of June 6, 1989, which cut the dividend deduction provision as well. This legislation appeared to have the desired effect. Public company ESOP announcements dropped dramatically.

ESOP proponents set to work on possible compromises, which under committee rules had to be revenue neutral. Congressman Anthony (D. AR) introduced a proposal to curtail the interest and dividends benefits for companies in which the ESOP holds less that 30% of the stock. This limit was consistent with the 30% holding rule for private seller rollovers and would eliminate most public companies, although our sample showed six companies that recently implemented ESOPs that would surpass this 30% threshold. Concurrently, Representative Schulze (R. PA) proposed moving the effective date of the legislation to July 10, 1989. In order to keep these proposals revenue neutral, Anthony and Schulze proposed cutting several other less frequently used ESOP provisions. The bill that finally passed the House Ways and Means Committee had an effective date of July 10, 1989, and curtailed the interest exclusion and the dividend deduction for companies in which the ESOP owns less than 30% of the company stock.

There were two bills before the Senate. One of the bills, introduced by Senator Bentsen (D. TX), also set a 30% lower limit for the lender interest exclusion but left untouched the dividend deduction. It also required full employee voting rights in any company seeking to take advantage of the lender interest income exclusion. A different version by Senator Coats (R. IN) set a 20% lower limit for the interest exclusion but with an upper limit of $100 million unless the ESOP owns 50%. This proposal was negated when the Senate Finance Committee, in action in October 1989, passed a version functionally identical to Bentsen's proposal. Ultimately, Congress required that the ESOP own 50% of the shares for lenders to receive the interest exclusion, and that employees have full voting rights on shares borrowed subject to this exclusion. Dividend deductibility was not changed. The effective date of the legislation was November 17, 1989.

CONCLUSIONS

It appears that Congress intends to limit the tax advantages for just the type of large public company that has recently exploded onto the ESOP scene.

So, to answer the question of whether public-company ESOPs abuse the tax advantages, one must decide what it is that ESOPs are supposed to do. The original intent of Congress, as expressed in the "purposes" section of the legislation, was for ESOPs to widen the ownership of capital, and they do seem to perform that function even in the large public companies, albeit usually only modestly, because ESOPs often replace existing stock contributions.

It is estimated that all employee ownership plans combined own about 2% of all corporate equity (Blasi, 1988), which means that on a macroeconomic scale, employee ownership plans do not seem to be having a tremendous impact on spreading the ownership of corporate wealth. On a micro level, however, evidence indicates that employee plans make a great deal of difference. Lowe's Companies, a home supply store, has created over 100 millionaires from line employees, and Avis employees watched their stock value triple in just two years. So, it seems that tax subsidies for ESOPs do make a difference to people. Employee ownership has the potential to increase employee wealth and spread the ownership of capital, but the process must go forward one employee ownership company at a time.

COMPLETE CHART OF RESEARCH RESULTS

The information in Table 2.1 is based primarily on reports from published sources. In some cases, NCEO contacted companies to attempt to supplement the information.

The plan start refers to the month in which, according to the best available information, the plan started. The number of employees and sales figures are from either 1988 or 1989 figures from Standard and Poor's, depending on when the plan started. The percentage owned is an estimate based on press sources. Leveraged plans are those that borrow money. The type of stock is C for common, P for preferred, and CP for convertible preferred. Whether a company is listed as a takeover target is based on a thorough search of business articles to see if in the year prior to the plan's start, the company was mentioned as a potential takeover target (including the articles announcing the ESOP). This does not mean that companies listed as yes were using their ESOPs as a defense, or that the companies listed as no were not, but it is a good indicator.

Finally, the study attempted to determine if the ESOP led to a net increase in employee benefits, replaced benefits at the same level, or decreased benefits. When possible, the table indicates what, if any, plan the ESOP affected. Only where it is specifically indicated in the table whether the plan added to or reduced benefits do we know what effect the plan had on employees. In some cases, for example, we know the plan was in addition to a 401(k) plan, but we do not know if it involved a lower contribution to the 401(k) or not.

Table 2.1
Characteristics of Public ESOP Companies

Company	Plan Start	Employees	Sales in Millions	% Owned by ESOP	Leveraged Y/N	Type of Stock	Takeover Target?	Effect
Acme Steel	11/88	2000	239		N		Y	P=
Advest	11/88	1800	206				Y	A
American Bankers	11/88	846		15	Y		N	A
Applied Power Inc	8/88	1400	166	34	N		Y	R=
Aristech Chemical	3/89	1700	919	15	Y	CP	Y	R=
Armstrong World Inc	6/89	24121	2360	12	Y	CP	Y	R=
Atlanta Gas & Light	4/89	3412	983		Y		N	N+
Brunswick	4/89	28500	3100	7	Y	C	Y	A+
Cabot Corp	10/88	5100	1420	6	Y	CP	Y	S=
Capitol Federal	4/88	460	87	9	Y		N	R=
CBI Industries	3/88	11400	1150	27	Y		N	S
Charter-Crellin	1/88	480	33	20		C	Y	N
Citizen & Southern	6/89	13244	1660	5		CP	Y	R=

Table 2.1 continued

Company	Plan Start	Employees	Sales in Millions	% Owned by ESOP	Leveraged Y/N	Type of Stock	Takeover Target?	Effect
Colgate Palmolive	6/89	37400	5640	11	Y	CP	N	E
Continental Illinois	9/88	9470	1040				Y	
Consolidated Freightway	6/89	26300	2300	19	Y	CP	N	A+
Courier	9/88	1800	123				N	
Cyprus Minerals	11/88	6740	795	5	Y	P	N	R=
DBA Systems	11/88	809	63	19	N	C	N	A=
Delta Airlines	7/89	54920	6920	14	N	CP	Y	R
Entertainment Publications	12/88	426	54	5	Y		N	R=
Figgie Internat'l	9/88	16000	920				N	R=
First Federal	7/88	360					N	R
FMC	4/89	13700	36		Y	CP	Y	R
Great Lakes Bancorp	1/88	890	305	30	N		N	
Home Depot	7/88	5400	1450	2	Y	C	N	
Hartmarx	3/86	2200	1080	15			Y	R=

J.C. Nichols	2/88	1400	50	30	Y		N	N
J.C. Penney	8/88	177000	1470	25	Y		N	R=
Jeffries Group	11/88	5000	810				N	
Kansas City Southern	11/87	174	508	13	Y		Y	A+
Key Centurion Banchares	10/88	1200	164		Y	C	N	R+
KMS	1/88	232	20	30	Y		N	
Kraft		46500	9870		Y		Y	S
Kroger Co.	10/88	170000	17700	33			Y	A+
Lockheed	4/89	92500	113200	17	Y	C	Y	R=
McDonalds Corp.	5/89	137000	4890	.72	Y	CP	Y	A+
McKesson	6/89	11100	6670	18	N	CP	N	A+
Merrill Lynch	1/89	43000	10870	25	N		N	R=
Mid-State Federal	7/88	415	80				N	
National Standard	12/87	2718	267	23	N	C	N	R=
Nibco	6/88	3150	274				N	
Nordson Corp.	6/86	1833	205		N		Y	N+
Nortek	7/88	1200	1250	10	Y		N	A+

Table 2.1 continued

Company	Plan Start	Employees	Sales in Millions	% Owned by ESOP	Leveraged Y/N	Type of Stock	Takeover Target?	Effect
Northern Trust Co.	11/88	4356	679	9	Y		N	A+
Nu Horizons	6/88	79	30				N	
Odetics	12/87	479	50	5	N		N	A+
Omnicare	7/88	1200	125		Y	C	Y	A+
OMI	2/88	700	169	15	Y	C	Y	N
Oryx	5/89	4200		13	Y	C	Y	R=
Polaroid	5/88	13622	1760	22	Y	B	Y	N
PPG Industries	1/89	36800	5180	14	Y		Y	R=
Procter & Gamble	12/88	76000	17000	20	Y	CP	Y	E+
Quaker Oats	1/89	30000	4420	10	Y	CP	Y	A+
Quantum Chemical	4/89	10343	1730		Y	C	Y	A+
Radiation Systems	6/88	470	44	10		C	Y	
Ralston Purina	2/89	63508	5870		Y	CP	Y	R=
Resdel Industries	2/89	200	17				N	

Company	Date							
Scan Optics	1/88	550	45	5	Y		N	A+
Standard Motor Products	12/88	3200	356	15	Y		Y	A-
St. Paul Companies	11/88	8354	3370	5	Y		Y	A+
Thermo Electron	12/87	3899	383		Y		N	A+
Tribune Company	4/89	14000	2160	15	Y	CP	Y	R
Tyler Corp	9/88	7500	1100				N	R=
United Technologies	7/89	62000	17170	6	Y	C	N	
Universal Foods	9/88	19000		10			Y	
Whitman Corp.	1/89			15	Y	P	Y	A+
Xerox	7/89	99032	15120	11	Y	CP	Y	R
Yellow Freight	7/88	25500	1760	6	Y		N	A+

Key: A: Addition
E: Expanding an ESOP
N: New Plan
P: Partial replacement
R: Replacement
S: Restructuring
+, −, =: Effect on employee benefits

3

Financial Issues in Public-Company ESOPs

SECTION 1: THE PUBLIC MARKET FOR ESOP NOTES *

Jenny A. Hourihan of Salomon Brothers Inc

The U.S. Congress enacted Section 133 of the Internal Revenue Code to lower the cost of funding for leveraged employee stock ownership plans by providing tax incentives to financial institutions that make ESOP loans. Under Section 133, certain qualified institutional lenders may exclude 50% of the interest on a qualifying ESOP loan from gross income, providing the ESOP owns 50% of the stock and employees have full voting rights on shares acquired subject to this provision. A sister section of the Code, 404(k), was enacted to further encourage ESOPs by allowing the deduction of dividends paid to an ESOP, if the dividends are in turn paid to employees or are used to pay down the ESOP's borrowings.

Salomon Brothers requested a private letter ruling from the Internal Revenue Service in March 1988, in order to clarify certain regulatory ambiguities concerning Section 133 that had precluded the development of a public market for ESOP notes. The lack of a public market presented a market anomaly that was probably not the intention of Congress and that impeded ESOP borrowers' access to the full range of funding sources characteristic of U.S. capital markets. Rather than issue a private ruling, the Internal Revenue Service published Revenue Ruling 89-76 in June 1989, an important step in making access to the public markets and secondary market liquidity available for ESOP issues. This development was particularly important for the ESOPs of large, public companies for which the public debt market is often the most competitive source of funding.

Revenue Ruling 89-76 did not expand the categories of institutions that are qualified ESOP lenders able to exclude 50% of ESOP loan interest income from federal taxable income. The ability to purchase publicly registered and traded securities means, however, that more investors in these categories can now participate in ESOP lending. These were the key advantages that motivated the pursuit of this ruling: the development of a diversity of funding sources, improved access to a broader universe of lenders for issuers, and access to ESOP investments for investors. This next step in the evolution of ESOP funding seems certain to enhance the ESOP market.

THE PRIVATE ESOP MARKET

As has been true of other growing market sectors, the ESOP funding market evolved over time to meet the changing needs of both issuers and investors. Commercial banks, one category of Section 133 qualified lenders, first made direct floating rate loans to ESOPs and their sponsors. As the need for funding grew, lenders expanded capacity using put bonds with floating interest rates marketed primarily to an expanded universe of banks in unregistered formats.

The desire of ESOPs and their sponsors to secure long-term, fixed-rate funding was met by banks and by the entry of leading insurance companies (the second major category of qualified lenders) into this market in recent years. The private market, while the sole source of funding, provided a variety of financing formats and a growing supply of funds as ESOPs themselves grew in size and number and financing volume expanded rapidly. By mid-1989, however, the large supply of fixed-rate ESOP debt in a market dominated by a relatively small number of sophisticated lenders caused the pricing and terms of ESOP debt increasingly to favor investors.

Despite the growth of the private market, there are constraints on the capacity of some institutions that qualify for the 50% interest exclusion to participate in this market. These constraints fall into three general categories—structural, portfolio, and liquidity.

Structural Constraints

Private placement financings are individually analyzed, negotiated, and documented, often a cumbersome process for smaller institutions. In particular, smaller institutional lenders do not necessarily have the internal expertise to evaluate the legal requirements of ESOP lending or the personnel infrastructure to respond to private market opportunities in competition with larger lenders that have personnel dedicated to this market.

Portfolio Constraints

Many financial institutions must invest in particular types of securities or market sectors either set by legal limitations or credit and investment parameters established internally. For example, many mutual funds are limited by their charters in their ability to purchase private securities, as well as the type of income they can receive and pass on to their shareholders. Banks and thrifts face higher capital reserve requirements for private securities than they do for liquid, rated, tradable securities, which makes private securities less economical investment choices. Additionally, minimum participation requirements in a private placement are often too large for smaller institutions whose ability to purchase a large block of securities is constrained by the size of their total portfolio and diversification needs. These participation minimums are often necessary in large private placements to expedite the process of negotiating directly with a group of lenders that is a manageable size.

Liquidity Concerns

While private securities are traded and Security and Exchange Commission (SEC) Rule 144 will further enhance their liquidity, such bonds are at present much less liquid than publicly traded securities. Institutions may prefer public securities in order to facilitate portfolio changes and the liquidation of holdings to meet credit or tax objectives. This is particularly important to an institutional investor whose tax position may change over the 10 or 15 years that a loan is outstanding. If an ESOP lender is not a taxpayer in the future, the economic advantage of the ESOP tax preference will not be meaningful, and it will be rational to sell ESOP securities in order to buy higher yielding taxable investments.

WHAT DOES THE PUBLIC MARKET OFFER?

A public ESOP debt market would help to expand the base of participating ESOP lenders by offering securities that would overcome these limitations. The primary benefit of public ESOP securities, for both issuers and investors, would be:

- a broader base of ESOP investors
- secondary market liquidity
- publicly available bond ratings and credit analysis

• standard documentation and financial disclosure

• access for smaller institutions through the purchase of smaller blocks of securities

In a typical public bond offering, the terms of the securities are established prior to SEC registration by the issuer. Public issues tend to use standard terms and conditions, following precedent set by the issuer's previous bond issues or similar types of bonds in the marketplace. This facilitates the evaluation and pricing of these securities by investors and the comparability of any one issue to others that form the basis for relative pricing and investment decisions.

By definition, the public market is a broad universe of investors that includes both institutions that are active in the private market and those who are limited for practical or legal reasons to public market securities. Standard documentation and SEC regulations eliminate the need to limit the number of investors in a public issue, making it possible for smaller investors to purchase a manageable block of bonds.

WHY WAS A RULING NECESSARY?

The heart of the U.S. public debt market is secondary market liquidity. The ability to buy and sell freely transferable securities and the presence of market-makers that act as principals in supplying liquidity to investors are central to the efficient pricing and distribution of securities. In launching a public ESOP debt market, it seemed central to its success that ESOP debt, like other securities, be structured to take advantage of these market characteristics. Salomon Brothers requested a ruling from the IRS that the ambiguous, temporary regulations issued pursuant to Section 133 should not be read in a manner that would penalize offerings of ESOPs, either in the initial underwriting or the secondary market.

In its current form Section 133 does not specifically address publicly traded securities. Section 133(b) defines a "securities acquisition loan" as "any loan to a corporation or to an employee stock ownership plan" used to acquire qualifying employer securities. In fact, IRS Regulation Section 1.133-IT (Q&A-1) states that a "securities acquisition loan may be evidenced by any note, bond, debenture or certificate." The expansion of Section 133 in 1986 to include mutual funds as qualified lenders indicates that Congress contemplated the availability of securities that were widely distributed and could be owned by such institutions—namely, public securities.

Temporary regulation Section 1.133 (Q&A-3) provides that a "Securities acquisition loan under Section 133 may be syndicated to other lending institutions provided that such lending institutions are described in Section 133 (a) (1), (2), or (3) and the loan was originated by a qualified holder." The regulation could be read to apply only to commercial bank loans for which the term "syndication" conforms with established precedent. However, the legal community, in general, viewed Q&A-3 as arguably subject to the interpretation that all ESOP "loans," including debt instruments such as bonds and debentures, might be subject to two restrictions in order to qualify for Section 133 interest exclusion: first, that the first lender to the ESOP must itself be a financial institution described in Section 133 and second, *that each and every* subsequent holder must also be a Section 133 institution. This second concern was usually referred to as the "chain of title" issue. If the original owner, and all subsequent owners of an ESOP note, were not qualified lenders, then the availability of the interest exclusion tax preference would be in question.

Q&A-3 could be read to imply that the ESOP interest exclusion would be lost for such an ESOP security even if subsequent owners were qualified lenders. In a market in which a security would be owned by many investors prior to its redemption, this "chain of title" question posed a major economic risk to investors who purchased securities in the secondary market, since they could not reasonably be expected to identify all of its previous owners, let alone verify those prior holders' status under Section 133. Additionally, the activity of market-makers such as broker-dealers, not all of which are qualified Section 133 lenders, would possibly "taint" the tax preference by the very activity of providing liquidity to investors by buying securities into their inventory. This type of tax risk is particularly onerous not only to investors, but also to issuers. Most ESOP issues carry tax indemnification provisions that require an increase in the interest rate in the event that the debt does not qualify for this Section 133 tax preference subsequent to its issuance. Such an interest rate increase would represent a substantial increase in costs to the ESOP. Given the uncertainty posed by the temporary regulations, issuers would not want to assume the risk that a debt issue would become taxable solely as a result of its sale to an unqualified lender, an event the ESOP could not predict or control.

REVENUE RULING 89-76

Facilitating the unimpeded transferability of ESOP debt and the participation of traditional market-makers in the secondary market is central to the development of a true public ESOP market. Revenue Ruling 89-76 clarified the position of the Internal Revenue Service. It stated two main points:

(1) [A broker-dealer's] actions as an underwriter (in either a best efforts or firm commitment basis) in the sales of notes evidencing a securities acquisition loan, will not adversely affect the status, under Section 133 of the Code, of interest received or accrued by a qualified lender with respect to the ESOP notes.

(2) A qualified lender will be entitled to the partial interest exclusion of Section 133 with respect to interest received or accrued on a note evidencing a securities acquisition loan for the period that it holds the note without regard to whether each previous holder of the note was a qualified lender.

The ruling is entirely consistent with congressional intent since the interest exclusion would still be available only to qualified lenders. Non-qualified lenders' ownership of the notes would not expand the availability of tax incentives or the loss of tax revenues to the government. At the same time, the Revenue Ruling would allow ESOP debt to be distributed and traded in accordance with market norms.

Since investors who can make use of the tax preference will be willing to accept ESOP interest rates below those of fully taxable securities, competitive market pressures will provide little economic incentive for non-qualified lenders to invest in instruments with low interest rates that are fully taxable to them. However, intermediaries who are not long-term investors are willing to purchase and inventory such securities for initial distribution and in the secondary market. An example of this kind of activity is the market activities of broker-dealers who do not typically own stock long enough to qualify for the dividends received deduction (70% of dividends received are excluded from taxation) that applies to corporations owning equity securities. Nonetheless, these broker-dealers actively buy and sell stock and these activities are important to maintaining liquid markets.

Revenue Ruling 89-76 is simple in the issues it addresses. It does not expand the universe of investors who are qualified to exclude ESOP interest income from federal income taxes. It does make it clear, however, that there is no practical or legislative reason to limit the ownership of ESOP securities. The ruling made two things clear. First, it stated that all public market participants can buy and sell ESOP securities. Broker-dealers, who are market-makers, would be able to inventory securities for their investor clients providing liquidity and enhanced pricing of secondary market sales. Second, it stated that qualified holders of ESOP debt have clear right to the ESOP tax preference based on their own legal status, without the risk of unrelated transactions affecting their own tax positions.

The private market was the first market for ESOP debt and will always be an important source of funding for ESOPs as it is for other types of debt financing. The availability of a public market for ESOP debt is an important step in broadening the financing sources for leveraged ESOPs. The diversity and depth of financing alternatives open to ESOPs will directly affect the terms in which they can finance and improve the economic benefits available to participating employees.

SECTION 2: THE ROLE OF CONVERTIBLE PREFERRED STOCK IN PUBLIC-COMPANY LEVERAGED ESOP TRANSACTIONS

Chester A. Gougis

A key issue facing today's corporate leaders is the need to develop a commonality between the goals of the corporation and those of its employees. Employee ownership is one way to create a confluence of employee and shareholder interests. Reflecting this need, over the past two years many of the largest public companies in the United States have expanded the role played by employee stock ownership plans in the overall benefit packages provided to employees.

Several other factors also make ESOPs attractive to public companies. The enhanced tax benefits provided by the 1984 and 1986 Tax Acts make ESOPS a very economical way of providing employee benefits. While these tax benefits have existed for several years, only recently have companies begun to develop the sophisticated techniques for integrating ESOPs into an overall benefit structure in a cost-effective way. Furthermore, the emergence of insurance companies as a market for ESOP loans has provided a source of long-term, fixed-rate ESOP financing that gives companies much more flexibility in designing their ESOPs. Finally, the perceived advantages of significant employee ownership in addressing certain corporate governance issues motivate public companies to include ESOPs as part of their benefit programs.

For many public companies, including J.C. Penney, Procter & Gamble, and Ralston Purina, the security sold to the ESOP was a new class of convertible preferred stock having special features designed to meet the specific needs of employee ownership. These innovative securities can help solve some of the corporate finance problems associated with public-company ESOPs while providing an excellent vehicle for employee ownership.

STRUCTURING AND VALUATION OF THE CONVERTIBLE PREFERRED SECURITY

A convertible preferred security has many different elements of structure, all of which affect the risk/return trade-off offered by the security and hence its value. The most important features of a convertible preferred security are the dividend rate and the conversion premium. In essence, a convertible preferred security gives the holder the ability to participate along with common shareholders in the growth of the company while receiving a higher dividend over a certain period of time. In exchange for this larger and more secure dividend,

Figure 3.1
Trade-Off Between Yield and Conversion Premium

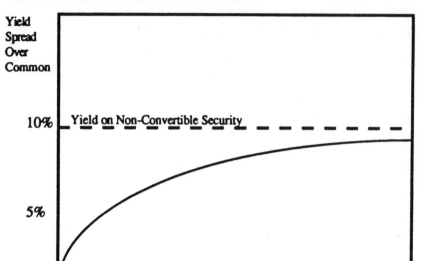

Conversion Premium

the purchaser of a convertible preferred security pays a higher price for the security. The conversion premium is a measure in percentage terms of how much higher a price is required for the superior dividend rights.

The greater the dividend on the preferred relative to the common stock and the longer the time period over which the higher dividend is available, the more the investor will have to pay for the preferred relative to the common, therefore the larger the conversion premium of the preferred. At some point, if the conversion premium is high enough, the equity value of the security is minimized and the dividend required is the same as other fixed income instruments such as straight preferred stock. Figure 3.1 illustrates the type of trade-off between conversion price and yield that a company with a strong credit rating might face in the market place today.

This trade-off will change depending on the credit quality of the issuer, the growth prospects of the underlying common stock, the expected dividend growth of the common stock, and the time period over which the investor can reasonably expect to receive the higher dividend.

Clearly, at some level of conversion premium, a convertible preferred begins to look and trade like a straight preferred security. As a result, it then becomes questionable as to whether such a security is a "convertible" security within the meaning of Section 409(1) of the Internal Revenue Code, which permits

ESOPs to purchase convertible preferred stock having a "reasonable" conversion premium. In any case, if the conversion premium is too high, the security represents less and less of an equity stake in the company and, therefore, may not have the employee incentive characteristics that most employers desire when they set up an ESOP.

Other factors that are important in valuing a convertible preferred security include the following:

• fixed versus adjustable dividend rate
• call provisions
• redemption rights
• rights in the event of a merger or acquisition
• liquidation rights
• voting rights
• anti-dilution protection against certain unusual events
• marketability
• floor put rights and other limits to downside risk
• reset provisions that change the conversion rights of the security
• fixed dollar versus share conversion

The terms associated with hybrid securities such as convertible preferred have become more complex in recent years because of the need to protect the investor from "event risk." Event risk can be defined as the possibility of a sale, restructuring, or recapitalization transaction that will hurt the rights of the convertible preferred holder either by reducing the likelihood of the dividend being paid or reducing the value of the common stock into which it is convertible. The increasing pace and complexity of corporate transactions have significantly increased event risk in recent years. As a result, the detailed terms and protections accorded to the preferred are critical elements of its value and must be weighed carefully in assessing the fairness of the transaction to the ESOP.

EMPLOYEE BENEFIT CONSIDERATIONS

The use of convertible preferred stock versus common stock in a public-company leveraged ESOP has important employee benefit considerations. One of the most serious criticisms of ESOPs is that they are a more risky type of benefit for employees because they concentrate an individual's retirement benefit in one asset: the employer's securities. This concentration is, of course, one of the attributes that create the desired motivational effects of ESOPs. Nonetheless, many employers want to mitigate this risk for their workers.

Ownership by an ESOP of convertible preferred security provides considerably less downside risk than common stock. A convertible preferred security retains more of its value even if the company's fortunes or the stock market as a whole declines. This is because of its preferred status in liquidation and, most importantly, because of its higher dividend. Therefore, this security provides employees with considerable upside as the company's common stock appreciates but will retain more of its value if the common stock does not perform well.

Of course, there is a cost to this downside protection. If the company does very well, employees will not receive as high a return with a convertible preferred security as they would have if the ESOP had purchased common stock.

Many companies have further increased the downside protection for their employees by giving them the right to sell the stock back to the company for at least face value when they are cashed out of the plan. This provision (referred to as a "floor put" or "par put") assures that employees will not be unduly harmed if the company's stock price falls significantly after benefits have been shifted into an ESOP.

A potential drawback in using a convertible preferred stock may be the difficulty of communicating the nature of the security to employees. However, most companies adopting such plans have found that, with effective communication, employees understand the key aspects of the security, namely its higher dividend and lower risk profile.

CORPORATE FINANCE CONSIDERATIONS

The key corporate attraction of using convertible preferred stock versus common stock is that there tends to be less dilution in earnings per share resulting from the convertible preferred transaction. Of course the company does not receive this advantage without a cost. The downside protection offered to the ESOP represents a higher level of risk to other shareholders. If the company's stock price grows slowly, or actually declines, the burden of repurchasing the convertible preferred stock (which will have declined less or retained its value) will be greater than if the ESOP had been common stock. A more detailed exploration of the impact of a convertible preferred transaction on a company's benefit costs and accounting earnings is presented here in a simple example.

Example of a Public Company ESOP
Using Convertible Preferred Stock

Acme Foods currently has a 401(k) plan to which it contributes 5% of yearly compensation through a company match. The company wants to enhance this benefit as well as increase employee ownership in the company. To accomplish these goals, the company decides to form a new employee ownership plan and sell it $100 million of a new issue of convertible preferred stock having terms as follows:

face value	$50/share
dividend rate	7.5%

conversion rights	to one share of common
underlying common price	$40/share
conversion premium	25%

Financing and Use of Proceeds. The ESOP raises the money to purchase the stock from the company through a 10-year bank loan. This loan is guaranteed by the company and is eligible for the tax-advantaged rates that banks and insurance companies are currently able to offer to ESOPs (based on the 50% interest exclusion granted in the Tax Reform Act of 1984, which was subsequently changed in the 1989 Budget Reconciliation Act). Lenders may still exclude 50% of the interest on a qualifying ESOP loan providing the ESOP owns 50% of the stock and employees have full voting rights on shares acquired through the loan. These voting privileges were already accorded to employees in public companies.

Acme Foods plans to use the proceeds of the sale to the ESOP to repurchase common shares in the open market. Based on the $40/share price, the company should be able to purchase 2.5 million shares using the $100 million loan proceeds. Once this is accomplished, fully diluted shares outstanding will decrease by 500,000 shares as illustrated:

Shares before transaction	20,000,000
Shares into which the stock is convertible	2,000,000
Shares repurchased from the public	− 2,500,000
Shares after the ESOP transaction	19,500,000

Impact on After-tax Benefit Costs. The company in our example plans to use the ESOP to substitute for the employer portion of the contribution to its 401(k) plan. In the most recent year, this company contribution represented a $5,750,000 expense. In the early years of the ESOP, in order to amortize the ESOP loan, the company must make a greater contribution to the ESOP than it was making to its previous benefit plan. For example, in the first year the required ESOP contribution is $8.7 million. The preferred dividend payment required is $7.5 million. Offsetting these costs is the fact that the company no longer has to pay dividends on the 2.5 million shares it repurchased from the market using the proceeds of the ESOP loan. Nonetheless, the impact of the ESOP on cash flow in the early years is significant as Table 3.1 illustrates.

In later years, however, this required ESOP contribution should stay fairly stable or decline, while the benefits provided by the ESOP will grow as the shares being allocated each year increase in value. If the existing plan had been maintained, the company would have to contribute more and more each year in order to increase benefit levels to employees. This ability to pre-fund benefit costs is one of the most attractive features of a leveraged ESOP for a public company. Of course, the company's stock price must grow on average faster

Table 3.1
Impact of ESOP on Cash Flow in 1990

	Existing Plan	ESOP
Contribution	$ -5,750,000	$ -8,700,000
Dividends	-0-	-7,500,000
Pre-tax Cost	-5,750,000	-16,200,000
Tax Savings	2,012,500	5,670,000
After-Tax Cost	-3,737,500	-10,530,000
Dividend Savings		
on Repurchased Shares	-0-	3,000,000
Net Cash Flow Impact	$ -3,737,500	$ -7,530,000

than the after-tax cost of the debt the company is using to pre-fund these benefits in order to realize these gains.

In the example, in 1996, six years after forming the ESOP, the expected contribution required to fund the ESOP is actually lower than the amount that would have been required to fund the company's existing plan (see Table 3.2). This is true despite the fact that the ESOP is providing a significantly higher

Table 3.2
Impact of ESOP on Cash Flow in 1996

	Existing Plan	ESOP
Contribution	$ -8,156,000	$ -8,154,000
Dividends	-0-	-3,520,000
Pre-Tax Cost	-8,156,000	-11,674,000
Tax Savings	2,854,600	4,085,900
After-Tax Cost	-5,301,400	-7,588,100
Dividend Savings on		
Repurchased Shares	-0-	4,400,000
Net Cash Flow Impact	$ -5,301,400	$ -3,188,100

benefit to employees at this point, assuming reasonable growth in the company's stock price.

Impact on Accounting Earnings. Since most leveraged ESOPs result in increased benefit costs in the early years, there will generally be a resulting decline in total net income. However, the impact on earnings per share (EPS), a key measure of performance for shareholders, will differ depending on the impact of the ESOP transaction on total shares outstanding. An attraction of convertible preferred stock is the fact that, if all proceeds are used to repurchase common shares, fully diluted outstanding shares may actually decline. This can offset the impact of lower total net income on primary EPS. In some transactions, the result is actually an increase in primary EPS. Fully diluted EPS, however, will usually be lower in the early years in both convertible preferred and common leveraged ESOPs. Table 3.3 illustrates the immediate impact on EPS caused by the Acme Foods convertible preferred ESOP transaction. Comparison cases show the EPS had Acme continued its existing plan converted to an ESOP using common stock.

Some accountants have proposed alternative methods of accounting for fully diluted earnings. Under one proposed method, compensation expense is also adjusted to reflect the impact of the additional ESOP contribution that might be required to service the ESOP debt if the ESOP convertible preferred were to be converted and thereby lose its higher dividend.

As Table 3.4 illustrates, assuming reasonable stock price growth, both the common stock and the preferred leveraged ESOP actually enhance primary and fully diluted EPS several years after the transaction. By 1996, the ESOP convertible preferred stock has been called, forcing conversion to common.

CORPORATE OWNERSHIP CONSIDERATIONS

While many public companies implement ESOPs for employee benefit reasons, an important secondary consideration is the impact the ESOP may have on corporate governance. A perceived benefit of the ESOP is that it moves ownership and votes into the hands of the employees, who are presumably more likely to resist a takeover attempt presenting an opportunity for short-term gains. This aspect of public-company ESOPs has grown more attractive in light of the role of Polaroid Corporation's ESOP in deterring a hostile bid by Shamrock Corporation in early 1989.

Despite the Polaroid example and the Delaware court decisions upholding the company's right to establish its ESOP, many uncertainties remain about exactly how effective a takeover deterrent ESOPs can be. Both the Employee Retirement Income Security Act and state laws leave the issues surrounding ESOP fiduciary voting responsibility unresolved.

Some important anti-takeover aspects of ESOPs will be materially affected by whether the ESOP purchases common versus convertible preferred stock. One key difference relates to the percentage of the company's votes held by

Table 3.3
Impact of ESOP on Earnings Per Share in 1990

	Existing 401K	ESOP w/ConvPref	ESOP w/Common
Earnings before expenses/taxes	$100,000,000	$100,000,000	$100,000,000
Contribution	-5,750,000	-8,700,000	-16,200,000
Pre-tax Earnings	94,250,000	91,300,000	83,800,000
Net Income	61,262,500	59,345,000	54,470,000
Pref Dividends	-0-	-4,875,000	-0-
Avail for Common	61,262,500	54,470,000	54,470,000
ESP-Primary	$3.06	$3.11	$2.72
ESP-Fully Diluted	3.06	3.04	2.72
Shares Outstanding			
--Primary	20,000,000	20,000,000	20,000,000
--Fully Diluted	20,000,000	19,500,000	20,000,000

the ESOP. Most public convertible preferred securities do possess voting rights that allow them to vote with common based on the number of common shares into which the stock is convertible. However, because of the conversion premium, for any given dollar size transaction, fewer common equivalent shares will ultimately end up in the ESOP if it buys convertible preferred instead of common stock.

Several companies have dealt with this issue by selling the ESOP convertible preferred stock, which has the same vote per dollar invested as regular common stock until converted into regular common. This allows the ESOP to have as many votes for its convertible preferred as it would have had if the plan had bought common stock.

Another impact of selling convertible preferred stock to an ESOP is that it makes the ESOP block less attractive to a corporate raider. For a given chunk of voting power, a third party seeking control would initially have to pay 20–35% more for the ESOP security because of its higher dividend. As a result, there is less likelihood that such a party would seek to buy the ESOP shares as a strategy for gaining a foothold in the company. Many companies have insured this by limiting the ability of the ESOP to sell the preferred shares without first converting them to common. The third party would have to offer a significant

Table 3.4
Impact of ESOP on Earnings Per Share in 1996

	Existing 401K	ESOP w/Conv Pref	ESOP w/Common
Earnings before expenses/taxes	$160,000,000	$160,000,000	$160,000,000
Contribution	-8,156,000	-8,154,000	-7,201,000
Pre-tax earnings	151,844,000	151,846,000	152,799,000
Net Income	98,698,600	98,699,900	99,319,350
Pref Dividends	-0-	-0-	-0-
Avail for Common	98,698,600	98,699,900	99,319,350
EPS-Primary	$4.93	$5.06	$4.97
EPS-Fully Diluted	4.93	5.06	4.97
Shares Outstanding			
--Primary	20,000,000	19,500,000	20,000,000
--Fully Diluted	20,000,000	19,500,000	20,000,000

premium to induce the ESOP to relinquish the higher convertible preferred dividend.

SUMMARY

Convertible preferred stock represents a useful instrument for public companies establishing or expanding their ESOPs. The unique attributes of this type of security can help solve some of the employee benefit and corporate finance problems posed by leveraged ESOPs and allow the company and its workers to reap the benefits of employee ownership.

SECTION 3: COMBINING ESOPS AND 401(k) PLANS

Kenneth W. Lindberg

INTRODUCTION

In 1989 there was phenomenal growth in the implementation of leveraged ESOPs by publicly held employers. A majority of these ESOPs were integrated into employer benefit structures by combining them with existing 401(k) plans. The purpose of this chapter is to present some of the key considerations in developing a combined ESOP-401(k) plan in a publicly held company. Certain rules and regulations applying to ESOPs are mentioned only in conjunction with this limited purpose.

The rapid growth in ESOPs among publicly held companies resulted in federal legislation being passed. Part of the reason for the legislative changes is that Congress is concerned that the plans are becoming a major cost to the U.S. Treasury while not benefiting employees as they should. The impact of the legislation on developing a combined ESOP-401(k) plan is noted, where appropriate.

THE ATTRACTIONS OF COMBINING ESOPS WITH 401(K) PLAN

Although ESOPs are first and foremost employee benefit plans, they must be attractive to employers if they are to be implemented at all. For most publicly held employers, the primary attraction is the potential financial savings. Four sources of potential financial savings exist for the employer:

1. Both principal and interest payments on an ESOP loan are deductible to the employer since they take the form of contributions to an employee benefit plan.

2. When the ESOP owns over 50% of the shares, and employees have full voting rights on allocated shares acquired by the loan, the employer can borrow at a lower interest rate since 50% of the interest is excluded from the taxable income of the lender.

3. Dividends on stock acquired with an ESOP loan are tax deductible if used to repay the loan or passed through to employees.

4. Future increase in stock price and dividend rates can fund a portion of future benefit obligation.

Table 3.5 shows the potential financial savings under these typical assumptions:

- Current year company match $1,000,000
- Annual increase in company match 5.0%
- Annual increase in stock price 8.0%
- Dividend (as percentage of stock price) 4.0%
- Company's tax rate 34.0%
- Company's normal borrowing rate and present discount value 10.0%
- ESOP's borrowing rate
  —prior to legislative change 8.5%
  —with legislative change 10.0%
- Term of normal and ESOP loans 15 years
- ESOP loan amount $16,500,000
- Use of dividends in allocated shares Used to repay loan
- Type of ESOP loan Level principal + interest with 2% annual "drift" (i.e., total payment increases 2%/year)

Table 3.5
Potential Financial Savings to Employer
(dollar amounts in millions)

| | Cash Flow | | After-tax Expense | |
	Actual	Present Value	Actual	Present Value
After-tax without borrowing	$15.0	$7.0	$15.0	$7.0
After-tax with normal borrowing	$29.5	$5.8	$29.5	$5.8
ESOP: Current rates	$ 0.9	$1.4	$ 0.9	$1.4
· vs. no borrowing	6%	20%	6%	20%
· vs. normal borrowing	3%	24%	3%	12%
ESOP: Without interest exclusion	$2.9	$2.4	$2.9	$2.4
· vs. no borrowing	19%	34%	19%	34%
· vs. normal borrowing	10%	41%	10%	21%
ESOP: Without interest exclusion and dividend deductibility	$9.5	$5.3	$9.5	$5.3
· vs. no borrowing	63%	76%	63%	76%
· vs. normal borrowing	32%	91%	32%	46%

As Table 3.5 indicates, there can be meaningful cash flow and expense savings to employers even with the 1989 legislative changes. Of course, different sets of assumptions and future legislation could change the results.

Two other features of ESOPs and their financial structure also may be attractive to employers. The use of convertible preferred stock is one. Depending on structure, use of this stock can result in higher earnings per share, greater dividend deductions, and/or excess cash for other employer purposes. (See Section 2 of Chapter 3 for an in-depth discussion of convertible preferred stock.)

Another feature is the employee voting status. Employees must have the right to vote shares credited to their accounts. They may also direct or at least influence the voting of shares that have not yet been allocated. The Department of Labor has issued letters of recommendation to Polaroid Corporation and Eastern Airlines indicating that the trustee should vote the unallocated shares using independent judgment. However, many plans are still structured so that the unallocated shares may be directed by the employees. Employers may find these voting rights attractive if employees are expected to vote favorably in hostile environments.

But what about employees? Does combining an ESOP and a 401(k) plan provide any attractions for them? Of course the answer depends on how the ESOP is structured. However, several potential plan features can be attractive to participants.

1. The potential financial saving to the employer means that the match can be increased for little if any cost. This often happens when the match currently is not restricted to employer stock.
2. The ESOP loan has to be repaid regardless of the employer's financial condition. Therefore, the employee gains a greater fixed commitment if the match is based on the loan agreement than on profitability.
3. Dividends are tax deductible to the employer if they are used to repay the loan or if they are passed through to the employees. Even if these dividends are currently used to repay the loan, they likely will be passed through to participants once the loan is repaid. Passed through dividends provide employees with an additional source of current taxable income.
4. Meaningful levels of employee stock ownership give employees a greater interest in their companies' well-being. They may also encourage management to focus more on employee shareholders.
5. An ESOP must provide that employees have the right to take distribution of their accounts in stock. If they do so, only the cost value of the stock is taxable to them. Any appreciation of stock price after it was acquired by the ESOP does not have to be taxable until they actually sell the shares.

BASIC STRUCTURING ISSUES

The ease with which an existing 401(k) plan can be combined with an ESOP depends in large part on the provisions of the existing plan. Some of the most important provisions to examine are the following:

The Basis for Employer Match. If the employer match is fixed (i.e., 50% of the first 6% of pay contributed by employees) it is very difficult to fund the entire match with an ESOP. (The next section has more details.) However, if some or all of the match is based on employer performance, the ESOP becomes a closer fit to the current plan.

Employer Stock as a Match. If the employer match is already being made in stock, funding the match through an ESOP usually becomes a minor issue. However, if the current employer match is in cash, with employee options on how it is invested, restriction of the match to employer stock presents a greater problem. In many cases, the match is increased to reflect the investment restrictions on the future match.

Employer Stock as an Investment Option. If employees already have the option of investing their contribution and/or employer match in employer stock, the results can be revealing. A high level of investment would suggest that employees view employer stock as an attractive investment. In this case, an ESOP is likely to be favorably received by employees. A low level of investment would suggest either that employees do not view employer stock as an attractive investment or that they do not understand stock or are unwilling to take the risk associated with investment in stock. In this case, an ESOP may require both a higher employer match and a greater commitment to employee education and communication.

Type of Stock. If the existing 401(k) plan offers investment in common stock, and common stock will be used in an ESOP, an employee communication problem usually does not exist. However, if convertible preferred stock is to be used in the ESOP, special communication needs arise. The communication material should describe how the convertible preferred stock works and why a different form of stock is now being used.

Voting of Stock. If the existing 401(k) plan permits employees to vote shares of stock in their accounts, the introduction of an ESOP usually does not present a problem. However, if employees do not currently vote shares credited to their 401(k) accounts, either some reason needs to be given about why the ESOP shares are different or voting rights should be extended to 401(k) accounts.

In-service Withdrawals and Loans. If employees currently can withdraw or borrow against the employer match, this feature needs to be addressed. Typically, if the match is in employer stock through an ESOP, withdrawals and loans are not permitted. However, the ESOP account balance is often counted in determining the funds available for withdrawal or borrowing. It should be noted that an ESOP can provide withdrawal and borrowing privileges.

SOME POTENTIAL PROBLEMS AND SOLUTIONS

Combining an existing 401(k) plan with an ESOP can present some major problems that need to be addressed early in the design process. While these problems usually do not prevent the combined plan from being established, the solutions can impact plan design, loan structure, employer cost, employee communication, and plan administration.

Desired Employer Match

In most existing 401(k) plans, some or all of the employer match is stated as a percentage of participants' contributions up to a specified percentage of pay. The employer match for the current year is relatively predictable. However, the employer match during each future year can be estimated based only on assumptions about future participants' contributions. The longer the projection period, the greater the probability that the actual employer match will be different from the projected match.

When a 401(k) plan is combined with an ESOP, two other elements are added. The first element is the ESOP loan. The loan structure determines how many shares will be released by each loan payment. Except for variations such as loan pre-payments and variable interest rates, the number of shares released each year is fixed when the loan payment schedule is established. The second element is the market value of the shares released each year. While projections can be made about future stock prices, actual stock prices are certain to vary from projected stock prices. Again, the longer the projection period, the greater the probability of differences between projected prices and actual prices. For most organizations, stock price projections are much less accurate than employer match projections.

These two additional elements result in a value of shares being released that probably will exceed or fall short of the desired match. Three potential solutions (shown in Figures 3.2, 3.3, and 3.4) are often used. First, in the "Top Up Approach," only a portion of the match is funded through the ESOP loan. Typically, the ESOP loan will fund 50% to 80% of the projected match. Any shortfall will be made up through additional employer contributions. If the ESOP loan generated more than the desired match, employees get a "super match."

This solution is sometimes unacceptable to the employer's financial staff because the employer has to contribute additional money when the stock price is depressed. If stock price is an indication of the employer's financial condition, then the additional contribution could come at a time when the employer can least afford it.

The second potential solution is the "Excess Approach." In this approach more than the projected match is funded through the ESOP loan. Typically, the ESOP loan will fund 150% or more of the projected match. This level of ESOP loan substantially reduced the potential for any shortfall. Any excess value often is allocated to all employees to broaden employee stock ownership or as a source of funds to help pay the cost of post-retirement medical benefits.

The third potential solution is the "Restated Match Approach." Instead of a

Figure 3.2
Top Up Approach

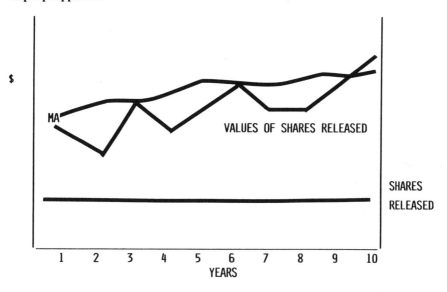

fixed percentage of participants' contributions, it becomes a variable percentage. Often, employees are told that the match is projected to be about equal to the current match but could be higher or lower depending on actual stock price and growth in employee contributions.

Figure 3.3
Excess Approach

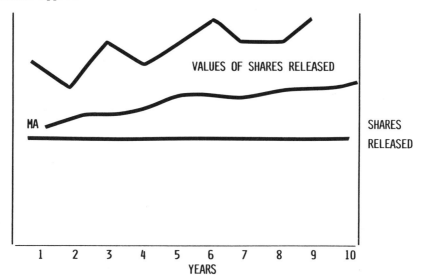

Figure 3.4
Restated Match Approach

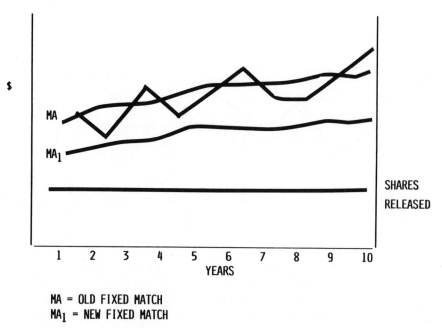

MA = OLD FIXED MATCH
MA$_1$ = NEW FIXED MATCH

Nondiscrimination Testing

Many existing 401(k) plans have three kinds of contributions:

• before-tax employee contributions (BT)
• after-tax employee contributions (AT)
• employer matching contributions (MA)

The final and proposed 401(k) and 401(m) regulations require a balance in these contributions between highly compensated employees (HC) and non-highly compensated employees (NHC). These regulations also require that the balance be determined separately for an ESOP and any other defined contribution plan.
    Two tests are required:

• a 401(k) or actual deferral percentage (ADP) test
• a 401(m) or actual contribution percentage (ACP) test

Before-tax contributions must pass the actual deferral percentage test. After-tax employee contributions and employer matching contributions must pass the actual contribution percentage test.
    In general, the ADP or the ACP for the highly compensated employees can not exceed 1.25 times the ADP or the ACP for the non-highly compensated

Table 3.6
Separation of Non-discrimination Tests

Contribution	Existing 401(k) Plan	Remaining 401(k) Plan	ESOP
BT	ADP	ADP	
AT		ACP_1	
	ACP		
MA			ACP_2

employees. A special two times/two percent rule is also available, but its use may require combining the ADP and ACP tests. Table 3.6 shows how tests must be separated when an existing 401(k) plan is combined with an ESOP. Figures 3.5 through 3.8 show sample non-discrimination tests.

In situations where the existing 401(k) plan contains all three types of contributions, separating the ACP tests under a combined 401(k)/ESOP plan often results in failure to pass these tests. Typically, after-tax contributions have to be cut back for highly compensated employees as a result (see Figures 3.6 and 3.8).

Another potential solution to the above-mentioned situation is to restrict participation by some highly compensated employees in the combined plan. Executive compensation devices that use employer stock (i.e., stock options, restricted stock, etc.) can be used to make up any loss of benefits.

Figure 3.5
Non-discrimination Testing, Before ESOP

	NONESOP				ESOP		
	HC	NHC	RATIO		HC	NHC	RATIO
BT	6.66%	4.88%	1.36				
AT	0.90	0.52	1.73				
MA	2.15	1.48	1.45				
AT & MA	3.05	2.00	1.53				
2 & 2	4.88 x 1.25		6.10%				
	2.00 x 2.00 = 4.00%						
	2.00 + 2.00 = 4.00		4.00 10.10				
	6.66 + 3.05 =		9.71 PASS				

Figure 3.6
Non-discrimination Testing, After ESOP
(2 & 2 Allocated Between ESOP and Non-ESOP)

	NONESOP				ESOP		
	HC	NHC	RATIO		HC	NHC	RATIO
BT	6.66%	4.88%	1.36				
AT	0.90	0.52	1.73				
MA					2.15%	1.48%	1.45
AT & MA							

2 & 2	4.88 x 1.25 =	6.10%
	1.48 x 2.00 = 2.96	
	1.48 + 2.00 = 3.48	2.96
		9.06
	6.66 + 2.15 =	8.81
		PASS

AT	0.65%	0.52%	1.25

Two aspects of these tests are very unclear and should be discussed with legal counsel. One aspect is how the special two times/two percent rule should be applied to a combined 401(k)/ESOP plan. While most experts believe that this rule cannot be used twice, there is disagreement as to whether the 401(k) and ESOP portions can be combined in using this rule. Figure 3.6 shows the results if these portions are combined. Figures 3.7 and 3.8 show the results if the special rule applies to only one plan.

The second unclear aspect is what amount should be used in performing the tests. Should the amount used be the value of the shares credited to the participants' accounts or a portion of the employer's contribution?

Annual Additions

Section 415 of the Internal Revenue Code (IRC) requires that the employer's contribution to a leveraged ESOP be allocated among the participants to determine each participant's "annual addition." Under current rules, if no more than one-third of these contributions are allocated to highly compensated employees, the interest payment portion of the employer's contribution and forfeitures may be excluded when determining annual addition.

Combined 401(k)/ESOP plans for many publicly held employers fail to pass the one-third test. As a result, annual additions under a combined 401(k)/ESOP plan may be higher than under the existing 401(k) plan. If dividends are used

Figure 3.7
Non-discrimination Testing, After ESOP
(2 & 2 in One Plan Only)

	NONESOP				ESOP		
	HC	NHC	RATIO		HC	NHC	RATIO
BT	6.66%	4.88%	1.36				
AT	0.90	0.52	1.73				
MA					2.15%	1.48%	1.45
AT & MA							
2 & 2	4.88 x 1.25		6.10%				
	0.52 x 2.00 = 1.04						
	0.52 + 2.00 = 2.52		1.04				
			7.14%				
	6.66 + 0.90 =		7.56				
			FAIL				

to repay the ESOP loan, the opposite result may occur. Annual additions under the combined plan may be lower than under the existing plan. Early testing is highly recommended. Figure 3.9 shows estimated annual additions under the ESOP described earlier in Table 3.5.

In situations where problems occur, three potential solutions are used:

1. Any loss of benefits to highly compensated employees can be made up through a non-qualified Employee Retirement Income Security Act (ERISA) plan.

2. The combined plan may be designed to allocate no more than one-third of the employer's contribution to highly compensated employees. This solution can result in higher amounts being credited to non-highly compensated employees.

3. Participation by some highly compensated employees in the combined plan may be restricted.

Treatment of Dividends on Allocated Shares

Dividends used to repay an ESOP loan are tax deductible to the employer. The Technical and Miscellaneous Revenue Act of 1988 (TAMRA) further clarified that dividends on allocated shares also are deductible if used to repay an ESOP loan. However, TAMRA requires that if dividends on allocated shares are used for this purpose, the participants' accounts must be credited with shares having a market value at least equal to the dividends used to repay the loan.

Figure 3.8
Non-discrimination Testing, After ESOP
(2 & 2 in One Plan Only, AT for HC Cut Back)

	NONESOP			ESOP		
	HC	NHC	RATIO	HC	NHC	RATIO
BT	6.66%	4.88%	1.36			
AT	0.90	0.52	1.73			
MA						
AT & MA				2.15%	1.48%	1.45
2 & 2	4.88 x 2.00 = 9.76					
	4.88 + 2.00 = 6.88		6.88%			
			6.66 PASS			
AT	0.65%	0.52%	1.25	1.85%	1.48%	1.25

This TAMRA requirement can be interpreted in at least two ways and should be discussed with legal counsel. One interpretation is to satisfy the requirement based on stock credited to the participants' accounts regardless of source. Another interpretation is to satisfy the requirement by making an initial allocation equal to the value of the dividends to repay the loan. A second allocation would then be required to meet the desired employer match. Possible results from these two interpretations are shown in Figure 3.10.

The second interpretation could be determined to be discriminatory because an allocation is being made based on account balance. It could also be deemed to violate Section 401(k) because the dividend allocation is not a match.

The first interpretation should result in non-discriminatory allocation. However, it eliminates dividend income on allocated shares. It also creates problems if the participant is not eligible for a regular allocation (i.e., suspended 401(k) participation).

If the size of the ESOP is the same in both cases, the first interpretation favors "fast track" employees and new hires. The second interpretation favors current employees.

The easiest solution to this potential problem is not to use dividends on allocated shares to repay the ESOP loan. However, this solution can significantly impact employee communication and the employer's costs. Therefore, this issue should be resolved early in the design process.

Figure 3.9
Annual Additions Under Section 415

TYPICAL CASE ANNUAL ADDITION

YEAR	VALUE ALLOCATED	PASS 1/3 TEST	FAIL 1/3 TEST OR NO TEST
1	100%	18%	120%
2	100	20	107
3	100	21	96
4	100	22	85
5	100	22	75
6	100	22	66
7	100	22	58
8	100	22	50
9	100	21	43
10	100	20	37
11	100	19	31
12	100	17	25
13	100	15	21
14	100	13	16
15	100	11	12

Timing

Existing 401(k) plans often credit employer match to participant accounts on a monthly or quarterly basis. ESOP loan payments are often made on a semi-annual or annual basis. This difference in timing can create a problem because ESOP shares can not be credited to participants' accounts until they have been released from the suspense account by loan payment.

Potential solutions to this problem include:

- Designing the timing of the employer match to coincide with the loan payments, or designing the timing of the loan payment to coincide with the employer match.
- Making the loan payment in advance of the employer match. Stock released by the loan payment is credited to participants' accounts during the interim period prior to the next loan payment.
- Using pseudo stock is a more complicated solution. The employer match is made in pseudo stock until the loan payment is made and actual shares of stock released. The pseudo shares in participants' accounts are then exchanged for real shares. While this solution is being used by some plans, it is not recommended because of the employee communication and record-keeping problems it creates.

Other Potential Problems

The circumstances surrounding a combined 401(k)/ESOP can result in additional potential problems. There may be a long time period between loan pay-

Figure 3.10
Treatment of Dividends on Allocated Shares

	YEAR 1		YEAR 2		YEAR 3	
	SHARES	$	SHARES	$	SHARES	$
FIRST INTERPRETATION						
DIV		$0.00		$40.00		$84.00
ALLOC	20.000	$1000.00	20.000	$1050.00	20.000	$1102.50
SECOND INTERPRETATION						
DIV		$0.00		$40.00		$84.00
ALLOC(1)	0.000	$0.00	0.762	$40.00	1.524	$84.00
ALLOC(2)	20.000	$1000.00	19.238	$1010.00	18.476	$1018.50

ment and tax deduction. Proposed SEC rules on insider trading may affect the plan. And the adding or subtracting of significant numbers of employees after the ESOP loan is in place can upset the balance created in the plan.

In addition, recent regulations on minimum coverage requirements [IRC Sections 410(b) and 401(a)(26)] could result in additional problems. Different benefit structures within a plan could be one of these problems. The average benefits test under a leveraged ESOP could be another problem.

Forthcoming regulation on general nondiscrimination [IRC Section 401(a)(4)] could result in stricter non-discrimination rules for ESOPs. The current 1.25 test under Sections 401(k) and 401(m) could be changed to a 1.00 test. This change would increase the difficulty of structuring a combined 401(k)/ESOP plan.

Finally, changes in ESOP legislation and regulation are always possible. If these changes eliminate some of the existing special ESOP features and if grandfathering is limited, another set of problems could arise.

SECTION 4: ESOPS AND CORPORATE CONTROL

Lilli Gordon and John Pound

INTRODUCTION

Employee stock ownership plans have become a focal point in the debate over takeovers, corporate governance, and corporate control. This chapter presents the results of a detailed analysis of the corporate governance implications of ESOPs adopted or expanded since the decision upholding Polaroid's ESOP in January 1989. ESOPs present troubling questions for investors involved in the corporate governance process. However, many of the problematic governance aspects of ESOPs may be dealt with by giving shareholders a more active role in the decision to create an ESOP.

This chapter provides a summary of research directed at three primary areas:

1. The likely effects of ESOPs on corporate control activity, given the structure of both company-specific charters and state laws governing takeovers.

2. The value effects associated with 60 ESOPs that have been newly created or expanded by major U.S. corporations since the Polaroid decision.

3. Measures available to investors for limiting management discretion in the establishment of ESOPs.

One purpose that ESOPs may serve is to increase employee incentives and align them with the preferences of other shareholders. If this is the dominant effect of ESOPs, then they should have a positive effect on the value of the shares of the adopting firm. However, concurrently, ESOPs may significantly alter the relative voting power of outside shareholders in the corporation. By allocating a large fraction of outstanding shares to employees, the plans may make it difficult for any outside shareholder to engage successfully in control activity. Such an effect from ESOPs could adversely affect the adopting firms' outside shareholders.

ESOPs' prominence in the corporate governance debate has been heightened since the Delaware court decisions in the Polaroid case. The Delaware law (Delaware Section 203) gives ESOPs a potentially unique role as takeover defenses. The law specifies that a hostile takeover bid must receive 85% of all non-aligned shares to be successful, and indicates that in most situations ESOP shares will be deemed non-aligned. This means that a 15% ESOP, if it votes and tenders in line with management preferences, can block all hostile bids for the company. The utility of ESOPs as takeover defenses under Section 203 was ratified by the decisions of the Delaware Chancery and Supreme Courts upholding the validity of Polaroid's ESOP-based takeover defense against Shamrock Holdings. The Delaware courts validated Polaroid's decision to allocate 14% of its stock to an ESOP, despite the clear intent of management to use the ESOP as a deterrent against Shamrock's bid. In validating the ESOP, the courts cited, among other things, the potentially positive impact of the plan on long-term corporate performance and the fact that Polaroid had clearly been considering the ESOP even before the takeover activity.

While plans established by firms incorporated in Delaware present the clearest case in which ESOPs may decrease outside shareholder control, ESOPs can also cause significant control shifts in non-Delaware corporations. The extent to which this will occur depends on the level of inside share ownership, and the corporation's voting rules for mergers and takeovers. For example, in a company with a super-majority voting rule that requires 80% approval of sales and liquidations and 10% insider ownership, the establishment of a 10% ESOP would potentially give management and management-aligned groups veto power over tender offers. Similarly, in a corporation with 35% management ownership and a simple (51%) majority voting rule, establishment of a 15% ESOP would convey veto power on insiders and inside-aligned shares.

In non-Delaware corporations, control effects of ESOPs will also depend heavily on the particular state law governing takeovers. Some state laws, such as New York's, convey to management virtually absolute veto power over unwanted takeover bids. (The New York law prevents a hostile acquirer from taking any action to alter the asset or ownership structure of the firm for five years.) This power is so great that the establishment of an ESOP is unlikely to have any direct impact on the firm's exposure to takeovers.

ESOPs in corporations governed by these restrictive state laws may also have significant control effects if they insulate the firm from unwanted proxy activity directed against management. Proxy activity is becoming an increasingly popular alternative to tender offers for bringing acquisition proposals and control challenges before shareholders. It is particularly important in states with restrictive takeover provisions in their corporate laws, such as New York and New Jersey. In these states proxy challenges represent virtually the only method for undertaking control activity against recalcitrant managements. In companies incorporated in such states, ESOPs will have substantial control effects if they make it significantly less likely that dissidents can win a proxy initiative.

Overall, ESOPs can have significant effects on the control structure of adopting corporations, by transferring control away from outside shareholders to groups likely to be aligned with management. The control effects of ESOPs may vary widely, however. ESOPs are most likely to have significant control effects on Delaware corporations, due to the provisions of the new Delaware anti-takeover statute. Elsewhere, ESOPs may alter corporate control structure depending upon the ownership structure of the firm and the majority rules governing voting. However, in the presence of stringent anti-takeover codes, such as those of New York and New Jersey, ESOPs are likely to make less difference in control

Table 3.7
Profile of 60 ESOP Adoptions/Expansions Between January 1, 1989 and July 15, 1989

	Total	Control	Partial control	Non-control	Takeover	Non-takeover
Delaware	31	10	3	18	8	23
Non-Delaware	29	2	4	23	4	25
Total number of firms	60	12	7	41	12	48

structure, unless they have a significant effect on the potential success of proxy initiatives against the adopting firm.

ESOPs AND CORPORATE VALUE

An on-line text search of the *Wall Street Journal*'s Dow Jones News Retrieval Service was used to identify corporations that had established or expanded ESOPs between January 1, 1989 and July 15, 1989. The text search isolated a sample of 60 firms. The current study reports how the ESOP decisions at these firms have affected shareholders. Overall, the evidence confirms that ESOPs present investors and the courts with a difficult challenge. The evidence shows that some, though not all, ESOPs are clearly adopted as takeover defenses and reduce shareholder wealth by transferring voting control away from outside shareholders. Those plans that are not intended as takeover defenses do not transfer control away from outside shareholders, and have no value consequences.

Table 3.7 describes some of the important characteristics of the ESOPs at the firms. As the data in the table show, the new wave of ESOP adoptions analyzed in this report by major corporations is not limited to Delaware firms. Of the 60 firms that announced the adoption or expansion of ESOPs between January and July 1989, 31 are incorporated in Delaware. Nor are the recent announcements necessarily linked to takeover activity aimed at the adopting firm. Only 12 of the firms in the sample were the subject of actual or rumored takeover activity in the period just preceding the ESOP announcement. Not surprising, however, is our finding that when ESOPs are created or significantly expanded in the face of takeover activity, they often succeed in altering the balance of voting power in the firm. This occurred in 9 of the 12 takeover-related cases. ESOPs may result in a shift in voting control where takeover activity is absent. Among the ESOPs analyzed, this occurred in 10 cases.

To assess the value effects of these ESOP adoptions or expansions, we examined the net-of-market returns for the firms in our sample on the day prior to and the day of the ESOP announcement in the *Wall Street Journal*. Table

Table 3.8
Summary Statistics for Two-Day Net-of-Market Returns for 60 ESOPs in Sample

	Delaware	Non-Delaware	Control	Partial control	Non-control	Takeover	Non-takeover
Average	0.1%	-0.6%	-4.6%	-2.2%	1.4%	-4.5%	0.8%
Standard error	0.6%	0.9%	1.3%	1.1%	0.4%	1.5%	0.4%
t-statistic	0.2	-0.7	-3.5	-2.0	3.5	-3.0	2.0
Median return	0.5%	0.3%	-4.6%	-2.1%	0.9%	-5.4%	0.5%

3.8 presents a series of statistics that summarize our findings. The results in the table show that the creation or significant expansion of ESOPs in response to takeover activity has a sizable and significant effect on stock prices. The average net-of-market return for the takeover-related ESOPs in our sample is negative 4.5% and is statistically significant. For firms that are not the subject of takeover rumors, the effects of ESOP announcements are neutral to positive.

We also analyze the net-of-market returns according to whether each firm's ESOP had a significant control effect, shifting voting rights away from outside stockholders. As Table 3.8 shows, ESOPs that shift control have a significant negative effect on stock prices. The average two-day net-of-market return for firms where the ESOP decision resulted in an unambiguous control shift is negative 4.6%. For plans that resulted in a partial control shift, the two-day net-of-market return is negative 2.2%. Those plans without a control effect do not adversely affect stock prices.

These data imply that there are at least two broad classes of ESOPs in our sample. The first class consists of ESOPs that have significant control effects and, in turn, reduce shareholder wealth. The second class consists of ESOPs that typically are not adopted in response to takeover pressure and do not have control effects. These ESOPs do not reduce stock prices.

To assess the merit of specific, non-controlling ESOPs, it is necessary to examine in more detail their provisions and apparent purpose. Plans at Delaware corporations, which involve small amounts of common stock and no takeover rumor, may be merely paving the way for broader ESOP ownership should a takeover arise. In contrast, other plans are explicitly structured so as not to constitute a control threat to outside shareholders. Plans that are structured in this manner are very different from plans that could involve a sudden change in controlling ownership. These results confirm that some ESOPs insulate corporations and reduce wealth, while others do no systematic harm to shareholders.

RECOMMENDATIONS: LIMITING MANAGEMENT DISCRETION IN THE ESTABLISHMENT OF ESOPS

ESOPs present troubling questions for investors active in the corporate governance and control process. Like poison pills, ESOP plans are typically implemented using standing authorities in the corporate charter to issue or repurchase stock. They are established at the discretion of management, without shareholder approval. The plans thus raise the question of how shareholders can take action to limit management initiatives that change corporate control without seeking shareholder assent. ESOPs probably raise this question even more vividly than poison pill plans, because the courts are unlikely to be as vigilant in policing the use of ESOP takeover defenses as they have been in policing poison pills. The Polaroid decision makes clear that the multiple purposes served by ESOPs—takeover defense, incentive alignment, performance-based compensation vehicle—make it particularly difficult for the court to overturn management's business judgment in setting up an ESOP plan.

There are several potential avenues available for limiting management discretion with respect to the establishment of ESOPs. First, shareholders could demand the right to vote on ESOPs. The primary attraction of this plan is that it would make ESOPs an unwieldy vehicle for defending against a known takeover bid. However, a simple voting requirement would not go far enough. Should shareholders be given a one-time vote to authorize the establishment of an ESOP plan? Or should shareholders also have the right to vote on ownership limitations, and on how shares are to be allocated to employees over time? A one-time vote would require shareholders to make a determination about how much discretion to give management in its use of an ESOP in the future.

Shareholders could also demand that ESOPs be structured to avoid the immediate reduction in outside shareholder control that occurs when some plans established. For example, shareholders could propose that leveraged ESOPs be vested with non-voting shares, probably preferred shares, until the stock is actually allocated to employees. Such an approach would appear to do no harm at all to the underlying incentive and compensation purposes of the ESOP, but would ensure that the ESOP creation would not transfer control away from outside shareholders. Such a structure also avoids an involved and potentially wasteful debate over how unallocated ESOP shares should be voted by a trustee, because the ESOP trustee would never have voting power.

A third possible provision that shareholders could impose would require that management immediately commence a self-tender offer upon the establishment of an ESOP, for as many shares as are to be owned by the plan. In addition, such a requirement should mandate that if the self-tender failed to receive sufficient shares, the ESOP would be canceled. These requirements would ensure that shareholders receive fair compensation for any transfer of control that the ESOP engenders. In the face of an actual outside takeover bid, a self-tender requirement would effectively force management to make a competing tender offer to establish the ESOP plan. If outside shareholders preferred the outside takeover offer to management's ESOP offer, they would simply tender to the outside bidder rather than to management. The ESOP tender offer would then fail, and the outside bidder would win control.

Finally, shareholders could take a broader approach that involved limiting management's discretion to use standing authorizations in corporate charters to protect against unwanted takeovers. Shareholders could propose charter amendments placing explicit limits on management discretion to undertake any new policies that would alter the voting rights of the corporation's outside shareholders, without securing express shareholder approval. Such a charter provision could require, for example, that any change in capital structure, including new issues of stock, options, or warrants, that dilutes existing voting power by more than 5%, must be subject to shareholder vote. This would not only limit ESOPs, but would also curtail poison pill plans, blank-check preferred stock issues, and potential new financial instruments such as Shearson Lehman Hutton's recently proposed Unbundled Stock Unit (USU) plans.

There is no doubt that charter amendments of this sort would entail costs to the corporation and its shareholders. However, the time has arrived that such restrictions in corporate charter structure may be warranted, even given the potential costs they would impose. We have entered an era in which managements frequently use standing authorizations to adopt policies that significantly affect shareholders' rights and power, without first securing shareholder consent. Sometimes these policies directly countervail shareholders' interests. This places corporate governance and corporate control on a slippery slope. De facto, it transfers power away from shareholders to the courts, which in turn become arbiters of last resort. This is not healthy for management incentives, corporate governance, or the efficiency of the legal system.

As a general matter, a charter amendment limiting management's use of standing authorities would be a useful, yet neutral, approach to limiting takeover defenses. Such a charter amendment would not preclude any particular change in capital structure; it would not preclude the use of particular financial instruments; nor would it preclude the use of certain takeover defenses. Other more ad-hoc approaches could, in contrast, preclude some potentially value-increasing financial policies. For example, the recent fire-storm of protest over USU plans effectively destroyed the potential to use these alternative financial claims, even in situations where they might have been desirable.

This approach, in contrast, would permit the use of these and other instruments, but would place explicit limits on how and to what extent they could be used without securing shareholder approval. It would, however, cast a broad net over potentially abusive shifts in corporate capital and voting structure, and mandate that any such change be approved by shareholders. Originally, corporate charters were designed to give shareholders the right to approve or disapprove corporate changes that significantly affected their rights. This proposal would merely give this right back to them, in light of the innovations in takeover defenses that have occurred in the past five years.

4

Using an ESOP as a Takeover Defense

JACK CURTIS

INTRODUCTION

Within the past several years, there has been a dramatic increase in the number of hostile takeovers of publicly traded companies that have been attempted and/or completed. An interesting by-product of this activity has been the number of employee stock ownership plans that have been established by these publicly traded companies.

Historically, ESOPs have been far more attractive to closely held companies than they have been to publicly traded companies.[1] In a large measure, this may have been because the tax incentives the U.S. Congress created to encourage companies to provide stock ownership for employees have proved more advantageous to closely held companies. Some of these tax incentives, for example, apply only to shareholders of closely held companies.[2] Other tax incentives, while available to both publicly traded and closely held companies, have nevertheless found greater applicability with respect to ESOPs established by closely held companies.[3] In fact, while the changes made by the Deficit Reduction Act of 1984 and the Tax Reform Act of 1986 made ESOPs more attractive to publicly traded corporations, prior to these two pieces of legislation, the only ESOP tax incentives were the additional investment tax credit and later the payroll-based tax credit. These credits were available (up to certain specific limits) for companies that transferred stock to ESOP-type plans, generally called TRASOPs and PAYSOPs, respectively.

What aspect of the proliferation of hostile takeovers has made ESOPs so attractive to corporations that had generally ignored the concept in the past? To best understand this phenomenon, one should look at companies incorporated in Delaware.

DELAWARE CORPORATE LAW

The General Corporation Law of the State of Delaware contains anti-take-over language that is applicable to companies incorporated in that state. Section 203 of the law prohibits an "interested stockholder" (i.e., a shareholder own-ing at least 15% of a corporation) from engaging in any business combination with that Delaware corporation for three years following the date on which he or she became an interested stockholder. A specific exception to this rule, how-ever, is the interested stockholder who acquires at least 85% of the corpora-tion's stock in a single transaction (such as a tender offer). In effect, a hostile takeover must occur as part of a single transaction in which at least 85% of the corporation's stock is acquired, or else there is a three-year "cooling off" period on the takeover. For the target company, an additional defensive mea-sure available under Delaware law is to put stock into "friendly" hands, in-cluding an ESOP or other qualified employee plan, thereby making it more difficult for the raider to achieve the minimum 85% ownership. If stock is held by one or more qualified employee benefit plans, however, it is not treated as outstanding for determining whether the minimum 85% ownership is achieved unless the participating employees "have the right to determine confidentially whether shares held subject to the plan will be tendered."[4]

From the point of view of the target company incorporated in Delaware and subject to Delaware's General Corporation Law, the pass-through to the em-ployees of the decision whether or not to tender shares is a double benefit. First, it allows the shares held by the ESOP to be treated as outstanding, in-creasing the number of shares the "interested shareholder" must acquire to achieve the minimum 85% interest. Second, because its employees may be justifiably concerned about the additional leverage that will be imposed on their company by the takeover, and may fear that their jobs will be threatened or at least wage concessions will be demanded of them, they should be less likely to tender the shares to the "raider."[5]

THE DEPARTMENT OF LABOR

Unfortunately, the U.S. Department of Labor has, on at least two occasions, taken positions that limit the ability of the target corporation, the ESOP's fi-duciaries, to allow participants to make this decision.

On April 30, 1984, DOL sent a letter to John Welch, Esquire, discussing the ability of the fiduciaries of the Profit-Sharing Retirement Plan for the Em-ployees of Carter Hawley Hale Stores, Inc. to allow participants to decide whether to tender shares in response to an outside offer and thereby relieve themselves of the potential fiduciary liability under the Employee Retirement Income Security Act of 1974. DOL's response, in pertinent part, was that for this purpose, a participant's decision whether or not to tender his or her shares had to have adequate safeguards to ensure timely dissemination of materials to participants, lack of coercion by senior management, and the opportunity for a totally independent decision by participants. Perhaps more importantly, DOL indicated that a non-response by a participant should not be viewed as a decision to sell or not, but rather the plan fiduciaries would be required to make that decision.

In a letter dated February 23, 1989, DOL advised the trustees of the Polaroid Corporation Stock Equity Plan that the decision whether to tender shares in response to a tender offer is to be treated as an act of plan asset management and, as such, is a decision that is generally required by Section 403(a) of ERISA to be made by the trustees. DOL went on to point out that one of the specific exceptions that Section 403(a) provides to this rule is when the plan expressly requires that the fiduciaries act in accordance with proper directions (defined by DOL in the letter as those directions that are in accordance with the plan and are not contrary to ERISA) from a "named fiduciary"; the DOL also confirmed that a participant may be considered a "named fiduciary" with respect to the decision whether to tender allocated shares.

However, with respect to unallocated shares (those shares acquired by the ESOP with borrowed money that has not yet been repaid), DOL clarified that a plan's fiduciaries have exclusive responsibility for the decision whether to tender them and that the trustees may follow the provisions of the plan only so long as those provisions are consistent with Title 1 of ERISA. Moreover, DOL went on to state that

in any particular tender offer triggering the applicability of these Plan provisions you, as Plan Trustee, must determine . . . whether following such provisions would result in an investment decision which would be prudent for the plan and would produce a result which would be for the exclusive purpose of providing benefits to the plan participants and beneficiaries . . . when a conflict between the prudence standard and the plan provisions occurs, section 404(a)(1)(D) [of ERISA] requires that the plan provisions give way to the statutory requirement.

In addition, DOL implied that, if the plan fiduciaries determined that the process by which participants' decisions were solicited was inadequate, or if the participants were subject to undue pressure in making their decisions, the fiduciaries may be under the responsibility to disregard participants' instructions and make an independent decision whether or not to tender shares. In effect, DOL's April 30, 1984 and February 23, 1989 letters, if universally accepted, would create a very limited vehicle by which the tender offer decision can be allocated to participants; in all other situations, the responsibility for this decision rests solely with the ESOP fiduciaries. As such, its benefit to a target company, including one incorporated in the State of Delaware, may be somewhat limited.

This does not, however, mean that the trustees must tender shares held by an ESOP merely because a third party has offered to purchase them; in fact, that someone has offered a premium over the current market value of the shares does not automatically require that they be tendered.

On January 31, 1989, at a Press Briefing on ERISA and Takeovers by the Treasury Department and DOL, David Walker (assistant secretary, Pension and Welfare Benefit Administration of DOL) specifically stated that ERISA

> does not mandate that plan fiduciaries automatically tender shares held by the plan in order to capture any premium represented by the tender offer. [He then said that] plan fiduciaries are not required to take the quick buck if they believe, based on appropriate and objective analysis, the plan can achieve higher economic value by holding the shares rather than tendering the shares and reinvesting the proceeds.

ERISA AND FIDUCIARY RESPONSIBILITIES

Section 404(a)(1) of ERISA requires plan fiduciaries to act "solely in the interest of the participants and beneficiaries. . . ." This language was reinforced by the U.S. Court of Appeals in *Donovan v Bierwirth* when it stated that the "exclusive benefit rule" mandates that the ESOP's fiduciaries make their decisions "with an eye single to the interests of the participants and beneficiaries."[6] In so acting in the face of an offer to purchase shares held by an ESOP, the fiduciaries must decide whether the proposed transaction is "prudent" and is fair to the ESOP from a financial point of view. Among the factors that DOL regulations list as being relevant to a fiduciary's decision is "the risk of loss and the opportunity for gain (or other return) associated with the . . . investment course of action. . . ."[7] This issue may be more acute if the plan fiduciaries are corporate officers or other individuals who are not "independent," rather than if an independent party is used as fiduciary. Particularly when corporate officers act as fiduciaries in a tender offer situation, they may wish to secure independent legal counsel and financial advice as part of making the decision. As the court stated in *Donovan v. Cunningham*,[8] "the focus of the inquiry [will be] how the fiduciary acted in his selection of the investment and not whether his investments succeeded or failed."

In the event that a fiduciary breaches his duty to participants in a qualified plan, he or she may be required to reimburse the plan for any losses resulting from such breach. For this reason, fiduciaries must be extremely careful in deciding whether to tender shares in response to an offer to purchase them.

Putting aside the question of who has the responsibility for deciding whether to sell shares in response to a tender offer, a second important issue related to the use of an ESOP to avoid an unwanted takeover is who should bear the cost of funding the ESOP.

As with any other qualified plan, corporate contributions to an ESOP are treated as an indirect labor cost that reduces corporate earnings. This is true for ESOP contributions to repay both principal and interest on acquisition loans. In addition, if newly issued shares of common stock are acquired by the ESOP, there will be more shares outstanding, possibly resulting in a dilution of earnings per share. In that event, the shareholders end up bearing the cost of the ESOP.

THE POLAROID CASE

A review of the court's decision in *Shamrock Holdings, Inc. v. Polaroid Corp.*[9] shows that it hinged on four key points.[10] First, the court examined the factual record and found that despite some ambiguity, the timing of the ESOP indicated that it was not established solely in response to the takeover bid.

Second, the court examined the structure of the ESOP to determine whether or not it constituted a management entrenchment. The employees have confidential and mirror voting and could just as well have chosen to accept Shamrock's offer. Therefore, the court found that the ESOP would not be a management lockup.

Third, the court examined research showing the correlation between employee ownership, participative management, and corporate performance. The decision notes: "There was a great deal of testimony that ESOPs generally promote employee morale and productivity. In corporations such as Polaroid, where there is a close identification between employees and the company, the evidence establishes that ESOPs are even more effective as employee motivation."[11] Thus the court found that management had made a sound business judgment in implementing the ESOP.

Fourth, the court considered it to be important that the ESOP be "shareholder neutral," that is, the shareholders do not have to bear the cost of the ESOP contributions. Because the ESOP represents a labor cost, the court examined Polaroid's changes to its employee compensation package and other ESOP-generated benefits[12] and found that dilution of shareholder wealth was effectively controlled because the ESOP was funded by pay cuts and benefit exchanges. The court also indicated that the likely productivity improvements would more than offset any residual cost to shareholders, thus the ESOP passed this test.

It is important to note that the court's decision in the Polaroid case was based on the fact that the ESOP was established in a company with a highly participative culture and fulfilled other criteria for being an employee benefit without hurting other shareholders' interests. This may not be true for other companies, so the effectiveness of ESOPs as a takeover defense is still unclear. In addition, the case was tried in Delaware court. There has been no precedent set at the federal level. A case pending in Delaware court, *Kingsbridge Capital Group v. Dunkin' Donuts, Inc.*,[13] may have wider implications.

OTHER CONSIDERATIONS

However, from a corporate policy point of view, it is still extremely important to keep employees' compensation and incentive packages "reasonable." Moreover, in order to continue to make its stock attractive to investors, a corporation should endeavor to minimize the cost to shareholders created by an ESOP. This may lead corporations to try to offset the cost of an ESOP by other changes to employees' compensation and benefits.

Changes to employees' compensation packages to achieve the offsetting savings for the ESOP can take several forms. Employees' wages and salaries can be reduced. Fringe benefits, such as other retirement plans, can be curtailed or eliminated. Many publicly traded companies have actually converted existing 401(k) plans into ESOPs to accomplish this objective[14] This allows employees to purchase shares of stock with their own pre-tax money. In addition, matching 401(k) contributions by the company are applied to the ESOP debt. It is important to recognize, however, that if employees are to be able to purchase shares of company stock with their 401(k) contributions, some form of registration may be required under federal or state securities laws. While for the publicly traded company this registration is not terribly expensive, there may be a time delay of several weeks before stock can be offered to employees in this manner. In a situation involving a takeover, this time delay may be critical.

To further address the problem created by the potential reduction of earnings per share by the publicly traded company that sells stock to an ESOP, corporations may sell newly issued shares of convertible preferred stock to the ESOP and use the proceeds to repurchase outstanding shares of common stock in the open market. Depending on the conversion price that is applied to the preferred stock in the ESOP, this may reduce the number of shares of corporate stock outstanding when compared with the number that would be outstanding if the ESOP purchased shares of newly issued common.[15]

In Polaroid's case, the court found the necessary offset in other labor costs and ESOP-generated benefits to determine that the ESOP was shareholder neutral. The court also found that Polaroid's history and participative culture made it likely that the company's overall performance would be enhanced by the ESOP. However, that does not mean that this will be the case in every situation, especially as courts are obliged to look at ESOP-related benefits. Corporations attempting to use ESOPs for the purposes of repelling a raider in a situation similar to Polaroid's should be careful to ensure that shareholder neutrality of cost can be demonstrated. Corporations establishing an ESOP to discourage an as-yet-unidentified third party should be comfortable that they could, if necessary, defend the reasonableness of their employee compensation costs.

A further complication for a company whose employees are represented by one or more labor unions is the requirement of the National Labor Relations Act and Railway Labor Act that changes in employees' compensation packages be collectively bargained. Put another way, a corporation that wishes to use an

ESOP for this purpose and therefore needs to adjust its employees' compensation and/or fringe benefits in order to make the ESOP shareholder cost neutral must bargain with the unions representing those employees before making those changes. In addition, corporations should recognize that some changes, such as the elimination of pension plans, are likely to be totally unacceptable to unions. On the other hand, unions, and their members, have fared so badly in companies that have been taken over by raiders that they may be more willing to find ways to make the ESOP work for everyone involved.

Finally, it is important to note that many publicly traded companies may find themselves unable to utilize some of the ESOP tax advantages in the future. The U.S. Congress, concerned about the federal budget deficit, made some changes to the ESOP rules as part of broader tax legislation in 1989. The Budget Reconciliation Act of 1989 restricts the ability of lenders to exclude 50% of the interest income from loans to ESOPs to cases in which the plan owns at least 50% of the shares, employees have full voting rights on allocated shares borrowed subject to this exclusion, and certain other requirements are met. While the legislation has deterred few public companies, future laws may have an adverse effect on public companies wishing to use an ESOP to deter a real or potential acquirer. The loss of tax benefits not only makes the ESOP less appealing, but it also makes it more difficult for the company to offset the cost of the ESOP in order to make it shareholder cost-neutral.

NOTES

1. To date, The National Center for Employee Ownership estimates that there are over 10,000 ESOPs and similar plans in the U.S. covering 11.5 million employees. NCEO calculates that approximately 90% of these ESOPs are established in closely held companies.

2. For example, under Section 1042 of the Internal Revenue Code of 1986 (the Code), individual shareholder(s) in a privately held company can sell stock to an ESOP and, provided certain statutory requirements are satisfied, may reinvest the sale proceeds in other corporate securities on a 100% tax deferred basis.

3. Company contributions to an ESOP to amortize principal on money borrowed by the ESOP to acquire stock (a leveraged ESOP) are, subject to certain requirements and limitations set forth in Section 404(a)(9) of the Code, tax deductible to the company up to 25% of covered payroll of participating employees. In addition, under Section 404 (k) of the Code, cash dividends on stock acquired by an ESOP are tax deductible to the extent that they are applied by the ESOP to amortize indebtedness incurred to acquire such stock or are passed through to participating employees, so long as such dividends do not constitute a method of tax evasion.

4. Delaware General Corporation Law 203(a).

5. A similar logic would apply to the corporation that is not incorporated in Delaware but passes through to participants voting rights on shares of employer stock held in an ESOP. Section 409(e) of the Code requires that, with respect to stock that is a "registration-type class of securities," participants must be able to direct the voting of shares of stock allocated to their ESOP accounts with respect to all corporate issues.

From a transaction point of view, this would include the ability to vote on mergers, reorganizations, and certain sales of assets. Moreover, even in the absence of a "friendly" state statute like the Delaware General Corporation Law, ESOP participants can be vested with the same decision-making authority with respect to the tendering of shares in response to a tender offer.

6. *Donovan v. Bierwirth*, 680 F. 2d 263, 271 (2d Cir.), *cert. denied*, 459 U.S. 1069 (1982).

7. DOL Regulations 2250.404a-1(b)(2).

8. *Donovan v. Cunningham*, 716 F 2d 1455, 1467 (5th Cir. 1983), *cert. denied*, 467 U.S. 1251 (1984)

9. *Shamrock Holdings, Inc. et al. v. Polaroid Corporation et al.*, Court of Chancery of the State of Delaware.

10. These points were delineated by Professor Joseph Blasi of Rutgers University, author of *Employee Ownership: Revolution or Ripoff?*, based on a thorough examination of the court record.

11. Memorandum Opinion, Carolyn Berger, Vice-Chancellor. Court of Chancery of the State of Delaware, Civil action #10, 079 *Shamrock Holdings, Inc. et al. v. Polaroid Corporation et al.*, January 6, 1989.

12. ESOP-generated benefits included the additional tax deduction generated by the ESOP contributions and increased employee motivation and productivity resulting from employee ownership.

13. *Kingsbridge Capital Group et al. v. Dunkin' Donuts*, Court of Chancery of the State of Delaware.

14. For more information on this, see Chapter 3, Section 3 by Kenneth W. Lindberg.

15. For more information on this, see Chapter 3, Section 2 by Chester Gougis.

5

Valuation Issues in Public Companies

RICHARD S. BRAUN

INTRODUCTION

The sale of stock in a publicly traded company to an ESOP involves several significant valuation issues. As with the sale of stock in a private company, the sale of publicly traded stock to an ESOP must not be at greater than fair market value. While it is frequently the case that fair market value in a publicly traded company may be defined as the freely traded market price, issues such as acquisition premiums may affect the market price and make it questionable for ESOP stock purchase purposes. It is also possible for a publicly traded company to sell a non-publicly traded security to an ESOP, such as a special issue of convertible preferred. Since such securities are not publicly traded, there is a need for a valuation. Finally, depending on the design of the securities sold to an ESOP, there may be special valuation questions that must be addressed such as the reasonableness of dividends and public-company ESOP transactions. These and other ESOP public-company valuation issues will be explored in this chapter.

ADEQUATE CONSIDERATION AND FAIR MARKET VALUE

One of the basic legal requirements for the sale of stock from certain parties in interest to an ESOP is that the transaction be for adequate consideration. A fiduciary, acting in good faith, must determine that an ESOP is receiving adequate consideration as a result of the transaction. While adequate consideration includes certain procedural matters, from an economic perspective it must include a determination that the ESOP is not paying greater than fair market value for the securities it is purchasing.

For years, adequate consideration and fair market value were somewhat undefined terms, at least when used in an ESOP context. Then, in 1988, the Department of Labor published proposed adequate consideration guidelines that included a definition of fair market value. While the proposed guidelines have not been finalized, and have been subject to significant comment by many practitioners, they are the closest thing to regulations we have at this juncture.

The proposed guidelines define fair market value as the price at which an asset would change hands between a willing buyer and a willing seller when the former is not under any compulsion to buy and the latter is not under any compulsion to sell, and both parties are able, as well as willing, to trade and are well-informed about the asset and the market for that asset. This definition of fair market value is very similar to that used in Revenue Ruling 59-60, which has served valuation experts for years. Fundamentally, it states that an ESOP should pay not more than a knowledgeable third-party investor who is entitled to all the rights and privileges, and subject to all the restrictions inherent in the securities in question.

When Is the Publicly Traded Price Fair Market Value?

In general, the publicly traded price for a security is usually recognized as its fair market value. Of course, the securities in question must be freely and actively traded on a national securities exchange, such as the New York or American Stock Exchanges. If the security is not traded on a national securities exchange, fair market value for ESOP purposes may be determined by the bid and asked prices quoted by independent sources. However, there are always exceptions to every rule, and the market price of even the most freely and actively traded public company may not constitute fair market value for ESOP purposes. Some of these exceptions are discussed later.

When Is the Publicly Traded Price Not Fair Market Value?

While the publicly traded price is generally recognized as fair market value for ESOP purposes, it is not necessarily sò. For instance, assume a company is in "play," either as the result of a tender offer or other contemplated transaction. As a result of the tender offer, the market price has risen substantially, due to the premium the suitor has offered for the stock. Can the ESOP pay a market price that includes such a premium and still not pay greater than fair market value?

According to the previously mentioned proposed adequate consideration guidelines, an ESOP is allowed to pay a control premium only if the seller would be able to obtain a control premium from an unrelated third party and that actual control, both in form and substance, is passed to the ESOP within a reasonable time and will not be dissipated within a short period of time subsequent to the acquisition. If we assume the ESOP purchase of publicly traded securities will not result in the ESOP receiving voting control and control in fact, because it is purchasing a minority albeit significant block of stock, it is questionable whether the ESOP can pay such a premium.

Another form of this dilemma is the use of an ESOP to purchase stock from a potential raider at a premium in a transaction commonly referred to as "greenmail." As a result of a greenmail purchase, the raider is usually required to abandon the attempted takeover and withdraw the offer to purchase stock. Unless another suitor steps up with an offer, it is likely that the stock price will fall as speculative pressure on its value declines. Again, it is questionable if an ESOP should pay a premium for a block of stock when, largely as a result of its purchase, the value of the block of stock declines significantly.

Suppose an ESOP decides to purchase a significant, yet minority, block of stock on the open market. As a result, demand for the stock rises and the market price is forced up. Does this constitute a premium that an ESOP is prohibited from paying because it is not receiving voting control and control in fact? Or does it merely reflect fair market value as defined as market price established by arms-length transactions in a freely and actively traded environment? The answer may lie in the unaffected fair market value of the stock in question, and the magnitude of the premium being paid. These may be valuation questions that require valuation answers.

A final example where market value may not equal fair market value for ESOP purposes is the case of a publicly traded company where large blocks of stock are held by a few individuals. Their decision to buy, hold, or sell stock may significantly affect market value by destabilizing the balance of supply and demand for the company's securities. This problem can also arise when an ESOP is offered restricted marketability securities owned by a substantial shareholder. What is the magnitude of the discount that should be taken from the market price for purposes of determining fair market value of the restricted securities? Again, these are examples of valuation issues that may arise in the sale of publicly traded securities to an ESOP.

Convertible Preferred Securities

There is a completely different set of valuation issues, however, when the securities in question are issued by a publicly traded company but are not themselves publicly traded. For instance, suppose a company with publicly traded common stock wishes to sell non-publicly traded convertible preferred to an ESOP. What is the fair market value of such securities? Are there other valuation issues that must be addressed?

The sale of convertible preferred stock to an ESOP is a common occurrence due primarily to two features. First, dividends paid on ESOP stock are generally deductible from federal taxable income as long as they are distributed to plan participants or used to amortize ESOP debt incurred to acquire the stock on which dividends are being paid. Since both contributions and dividends to an ESOP are deductible from taxable income, the company may be relatively indifferent to which is used to amortize ESOP debt. Contributions are subject to regulations that limit them to a maximum of 25 percent of payroll for the payment of principal on the ESOP note. Dividends, however, are not so directly limited, and may be used in lieu of or in addition to contributions as a means of circumventing such limitations.

The other reason convertible preferred is often the security of choice in ESOP transactions is that it results in less common stock dilution. Because of its preferred dividends, liquidation preference, option value, and other rights and privileges, investors are willing to pay more for convertible preferred than the value of the common stock into which it is convertible. As an example, if a share of convertible preferred was convertible into one share of common worth $80, an investor might pay $100 for the convertible preferred. The $20 conversion premium this example implies reflects value inherent in the convertible preferred above and beyond its right to eventually convert into one share of common.

An ESOP can pay a conversion premium for a convertible preferred stock as long as the conversion premium is reasonable. Using the numbers from above, if an ESOP purchased $1 million of common at $80 per share, it would receive 12,500 shares. On the other hand, if the ESOP purchased $1 million of convertible preferred at $100 per share, it would receive 10,000 shares of preferred, which would ultimately convert into 10,000 shares of common. Therefore, a purchase of convertible preferred rather than common results in fewer common shares eventually outstanding and, consequently, less dilution in common stock ownership.

In addition to the rights and privileges discussed above, convertible preferred sold to an ESOP may have additional features that impact value. For instance, departing plan participants may be given put rights at the greater of fair market value or a floor price. Since a floor price reduces the downside risk of a security, it has a positive valuation impact that needs to be quantified.

In addition to economic value, there are two issues that are valuation-related and often require opinions in ESOP transactions. First, as previously mentioned, dividends on ESOP securities are usually deductible from federal taxes if used to repay ESOP debt. However, in order to be allowable deductions, dividends must be reasonable and not viewed simply as a means of tax avoidance. What constitutes reasonable dividends is discussed in more detail later in this chapter.

The second economically related valuation issue involves the reasonableness of the convertible preferred's conversion premium. In our previous example, an ESOP purchased convertible preferred for $100 per share that was immediately convertible into one share of common worth $80 per share, resulting in a 25 percent conversion premium. Alternatively, the ESOP could be offered convertible preferred at $100 per share that was convertible into one share of common worth $50 per share, resulting in a 100 percent conversion premium. A framework for considering how high a conversion premium can go and still be reasonable is discussed later in this chapter.

HOW TO VALUE STOCK OF A PUBLICLY TRADED COMPANY

As we have noted, it may be possible to argue that the market price of publicly traded shares does not constitute fair market value for ESOP purposes. In addition, it is frequently the case that an ESOP is offered non-publicly traded securities, such as convertible preferred, for which no market established value exists. How can the value of such securities be determined for ESOP purposes? While it is not the purpose of this chapter to provide the reader with a comprehensive guide to public company valuation analysis, the following is an overview of some of the considerations involved in such an analysis.

The first step in such an analysis is to determine a value for the company as a whole and compare it to the market determined value. The procedure would be very similar to the valuation of a private, closely held company. An investigation should be made to determine other publicly traded companies that are as similar to the subject company as possible. The comparable companies are then compared to the subject company using numerous factors including size, liquidity, leverage, growth, profitability, and risk. The goal of such an analysis is to allow the analyst to draw certain conclusions regarding where the subject company should trade relative to the broader group of public companies.

For instance, suppose that the subject company is generally smaller, less liquid, more highly leveraged, slower growing, less profitable, and more risky than the other public companies viewed as a group. It would seem reasonable that the subject company should trade at generally lower multiples of representative earnings, cash flow, earnings before interest and taxes (EBIT), and so on, than the comparable companies taken as a whole. If this were not the case, and no reasonable explanation could be given, it is likely that the market price does not represent fair market value for ESOP purposes due to premiums or other anomalies. Through careful selection of representative levels and multiples based on a risk and return analysis, it is possible to develop valuation indications for the subject company that can be used to help determine fair market value.

In addition to a public-company comparable approach, the analyst should consider both transactions in the subject company's stock and transactions in the stock of similar publicly traded companies. For instance, if there has been a sudden, significant increase in the market value of the subject company's stock for which a good explanation is not available, it may signify speculative pressure on the market value of the stock. This would be evidence that based on prior transactions and trading history, current market value may not be suitable for ESOP purposes.

Of course, transactions may also provide evidence that the price to be paid by the ESOP for a specific block of stock is fair. For instance, suppose an ESOP is purchasing stock in a multi-investor leveraged buyout transaction involving a publicly traded company. Purchases of securities by other investors, presuming they were arms-length transactions, may provide useful valuation "pegs" for ESOP purposes. If a sophisticated investor is paying $100 per share for convertible preferred, it is strong evidence that an ESOP could pay $100 per share as well. Similarly, if an ESOP is purchasing a more risky security than a sophisticated investor, it is reasonable to assume that the ESOP should receive a higher rate of return on its investment.

In addition to an analysis of comparable companies and similar transactions, it is desirable to consider projections of the subject company's earnings and cash flow. These can be discounted to a present value using appropriately risk adjusted discount rates to provide additional indications of value. They can also be useful in determining target rates of return on the ESOP's securities. After the company's value has been determined utilizing the approaches described above, the next task is to value the company's securities. If only common stock is outstanding, and the ESOP is purchasing common stock, the problem is simplified. However, it is frequently the case that the company has more than one class of stock outstanding, or that the ESOP is purchasing convertible preferred. In such cases, the valuation issues may become very challenging.

CONVERTIBLE PREFERRED VALUATION ISSUES

As we previously discussed, convertible preferred is frequently the security offered to an ESOP largely because it results in less dilution to non-ESOP shareholders. The sale of convertible preferred stock to an ESOP virtually always requires a valuation determination even in a public company setting because it is unlikely that the ESOP securities are publicly traded. If they are not publicly traded in a free and active market, there is no basis for determining their value short of an analysis. Even if a public company has publicly traded convertible preferred outstanding, it is unlikely to be the security sold to the ESOP. The design features of an ESOP convertible preferred may be significantly different than publicly traded convertible preferred, because they are issued with different concerns in mind.

For instance, the call protection period of a convertible preferred sold to the public is generally short, because the company wants the option to call the security and eliminate the dividend if it becomes too expensive. However, in an ESOP context, having a short call protection period may not make sense. Since dividends are used to repay ESOP debt, their elimination means the company will probably have to make contributions, which have the same tax and cash flow impact as dividends. It may be desirable to have the call protection period mirror the ESOP debt repayment period, which allows the company to call the preferred and eliminate the dividend once the ESOP debt is repaid.

In addition to fair market value, there may be other questions requiring the analysis and valuation of convertible preferred stock sold to an ESOP.

• Is the dividend on the preferred reasonable?
• Is the conversion premium reasonable?
• What is the value of the underlying common stock?

These questions are all interrelated and impact the value of the convertible preferred. For instance, the larger the dividend, all other things being equal, the greater the conversion premium can be before it becomes unreasonable. But it may be useful to explore each individually before focusing on their interaction.

As previously mentioned, the dividend must be reasonable and not designed simply to avoid the payment of taxes if it is to be viewed as a deductible item. Unfortunately, the law does not specify how "reasonable" is to be determined in the context of an ESOP convertible preferred. However, it is generally acknowledged that the test for reasonableness is dual in nature. First, is the dividend reasonable as a function of the security on which it is being paid? For instance, the dividend on a preferred stock should, in general, be greater than the dividend on common stock. In addition, the dividends on securities in a highly leveraged or otherwise risky company should be greater than those on less risky companies. The test of what is reasonable should consider both the kind of security in question and the risk of the company that issued the security.

Another test of dividend reasonableness may be as a function of the compensation of the ESOP plan participants. There is general agreement that dividends on ESOP stock are not subject to strict limitations based on the size of qualifying payroll. However, there is reason to believe that a dividend that is very large relative to compensation might be interpreted as excessive and thus subject to question.

Another valuation question involving ESOP convertible preferred is whether the conversion premium is reasonable. As previously discussed, a conversion premium is defined as the amount a buyer pays for a convertible preferred that is greater than the value of the common into which it is convertible. Investors pay more for convertible preferred than its common equivalent because it has rights and attributes that make it of more value than common. For instance, convertible preferred is entitled to cumulative preferred dividends that must be paid before dividends can be paid on common. In addition, it has a liquidation preference that provides it with a certain amount of downside protection. Finally, depending on its design, it may have option value as a result of its ability to convert into common stock upon a call by the company. Thus, a convertible preferred derives its value from the combination of its rights as a preferred stock and its option on common stock value.

Convertible preferred is a security that lies between straight preferred at one end of the spectrum and straight common at the other end, gaining its value from a blend of the attributes of each. It is possible to change the blend of these features and still not change the value of the convertible preferred. For instance, a convertible preferred worth $100 would draw $50 of value from its straight preferred characteristics and $50 of value from its common stock rights. Alternatively, a convertible preferred worth $100 could realize $75 of value from straight preferred features and $25 from the underlying common.

Beyond fair market value, however, design options are limited by the requirement that the conversion premium be reasonable. A convertible preferred could be designed that derived 99% of its value from its straight preferred features and only 1% from its common attributes, but its conversion premium would be enormous and not reasonable. Thus, although it was worth $100, an ESOP could not purchase it as a qualifying employer security.

A reasonable conversion premium can be determined through a combination of empirical evidence and the application of financial theory. From an empirical point of view, it is possible to look in the public marketplace for convertible preferred securities in order to determine their conversion premiums. It would be appropriate to consider the conversion premiums of securities that had been freely and actively traded for some time as well as conversion premiums on a when-issued basis.

However, limiting the universe of observations to only publicly traded convertible preferreds is too restrictive, as it fails to consider other securities that may be more similar to ESOP convertible preferred. For instance, if ESOP convertible preferred is issued in a leveraged buyout, it may be more appropriate to look at securities issued in other leveraged buyouts as the basis for what is a reasonable conversion premium. Subordinated debt with equity "kickers" issued in leveraged buyouts is very similar to ESOP convertible preferred issued in such transactions, and the relationship between sub-debts' interim cash flows and terminal value may be very relevant when analyzing reasonableness of the ESOP securities.

Financial theory can also shed light on what is reasonable. Assume that a reasonable conversion premium means that there is a reasonable probability that the common stock will be "in the money" when the convertible preferred is called and, therefore, the holder of the preferred will convert into common rather than accept the call price. The probability of being in the money is largely a function of common stock price volatility and the length of the call protection period. All other things being equal, the common stock has a higher probability of being in the money if its price swings are volatile.

Consider a common stock worth $10 with a low volatility of 10 percent. In one year, its value is likely to be in the range of $9 to $11 per share. However, if the same $10 stock has a high volatility of 50 percent, its value after one year could be in the much broader range of $5 to $15 per share. If the call price was $12 per share, the low volatility security would have little chance of being in the money, while the high volatility security has a much more reasonable chance of being above $12 and, therefore, in the money.

A similar argument can be made regarding a long call protection period versus a short call protection period. From our previous example, assume the $10 stock with a volatility of 10% per year. At the end of one year, its value is likely to fall in the range of $9 to $11 per share. However, after two years its value is likely to fall in the broader range of $8.10 to $12.10 per share. This compounding effect means that a convertible preferred with a long call protection period has a higher probability of its common component being in the money when it is called relative to a convertible preferred with a short call protection period. Thus, a higher conversion premium may be reasonable if the call protection is long.

The final issue on convertible preferred involves the question of the value of its underlying common equity feature. Assume two convertible preferreds alike in every regard except that preferred A is convertible into one share of common worth $10 while preferred B is convertible into one share of common worth $20 per share. Clearly, preferred B is worth more than preferred A because its underlying common component is worth more.

In a similar fashion, assume preferred convertible into a minority interest versus preferred convertible into a controlling interest. A controlling interest is worth more on a pro rata basis than a minority interest because a control position gives the owner certain rights and privileges not available to minority shareholders. Similarly, the right to convert into a control position should also be worth more than the right to convert into a minority position. This is an issue that frequently arises in the context of a multi-investor leveraged buyout of a public company including an ESOP. It is important from a fair market value as well as a reasonableness viewpoint to determine the value of the common into which the preferred is ultimately convertible.

CONCLUSION

Fair market value for ESOP purposes may often be synonymous with market value for a public company freely and actively traded as a recognized national exchange. However, reasons for a valuation of public-company securities may exist due to either security design considerations or questions surrounding the market established value. In such cases, it may be prudent to secure an opinion from an independent, recognized financial advisor in support of the ESOP transaction.

6 _____

Divesting a Subsidiary Through an ESOP

MALON WILKUS

INTRODUCTION

In 1987 I became involved in an auction by a major corporation of a subsidiary with sales of $60 million. The company was heavily organized by the United Rubber Workers; labor rates were above industry averages and labor relations were poor. As little as five years ago the Rubber Workers would not have received one phone call in such a situation. However, in this case six leveraged buyout firms went calling to the union. Each of them wanted to team up with management and the union to finance a leveraged buyout of the company. They wanted the union and all the employees to support their transaction, with concessions, in return for ownership. This auction did not have a happy ending for ESOP advocates; the winning bidder was a corporate competitor. However, I believe a milestone was marked by the number of buyers prepared to consider an ESOP in their bidding strategies.

Every year hundreds of public corporations divest subsidiaries, divisions, or product lines. These divestitures are typically arranged through privately negotiated transactions or auctions conducted by investment banking firms. The entities being sold range from healthy to distressed. Buyers are typically corporations in the same line of business or companies with complementary product lines; competing firms are common bidders in corporate divestitures; and of course, leveraged buyout (LBO) firms are frequent bidders in such transactions. Divestiture to all employees through an ESOP LBO has been an alternative for many years although it has only recently become a more common event.

From 1985 through 1989, The National Center for Employee Ownership estimates that over 500 companies have been established by corporate divestitures to newly created companies having at least 25% ESOP ownership. In 1988 the Hospital Corporation of American spun off a group of its hospitals to a 100% ESOP in a $1.7 billion transaction; British Petroleum sold 100% of its Chase Brass subsidiary to its employees in a $30 million transaction; Ampco-Pittsburgh sold 80% of its Pittsburgh Forging subsidiary to employees in a $17 million transaction; and Sir James Goldsmith sold a division of his Cavenham Forest Industries, Inc. to a 60% ESOP in a $50 million transaction.

In that same year, Avis tried to be number one by becoming one of the largest employee-owned companies in the United States. Wesray, an LBO firm, divested Avis from its portfolio of companies by selling the company to a 100% ESOP in a $1.75 billion transaction. By 1989 Wesray had sold four companies to employees, using ESOPs as an effective method by which it recoups its investment. Employee buyouts are becoming an attractive alternative to the standard LBO. Why is this the case?

An ESOP can bring many benefits to the leveraged buyout of a unit of a publicly held company. First, there are the hard-to-measure, but very real, motivational effects of ownership. For the same reasons that owner-managers are motivated to improve their performance in a management buyout, the workers as a whole are motivated to strive for the success and growth of the enterprise when they are equitably included in a transaction, especially if their ownership is accompanied by real participation and communication.

Second, ESOP transactions offer significant financial benefits unavailable under any other ownership structure. The substantial tax benefits of an ESOP transaction, which will be discussed more fully later in this chapter, make an ESOP a strong bidder by increasing cash flow available for debt service.

Finally, in cases where employee concessions are needed for survival and particularly in unionized settings, employee ownership may be the only effective way of giving workers something of value in return for their sacrifices. Without such sharing of the "upside," employees may not be willing to make the sacrifices necessary for success.

This chapter outlines how ESOP leveraged buyouts of subsidiaries, divisions, and product lines can be accomplished. It is intended to show why an ESOP may be the most viable buyer—capable of paying the highest price for a corporate divestiture—and why an ESOP-structured company may result in the healthiest company. It is also intended to show the impact the ESOP can have on the value of a company and thus on the return after dilution to equity investors in ESOP LBOs.

It is hoped that more ESOP LBOs will be implemented as investors, owners, managers, unions, and employees learn that employee buyouts can be competitive bidders and that multi-investor ESOP LBOs can provide a market rate of return to all investors.

Sellers have learned that they can often maximize their return if they sell to management in an LBO transaction. Management has learned that through LBOs they too can share in the ownership of their company. It is time for sellers to learn that the advantages of selling to management are compounded when they sell to all employees. And it is time for all employees and unions alike to realize that the opportunity for ownership comes around only rarely and when it does management alone should not reach for the golden ring; instead every shop worker, clerk, engineer, secretary, supervisor, and manager alike should reach out and take a stake in their company. Only if this becomes the norm will we see a broadened ownership of wealth in this country and maintain a vigorous and dynamic free market economy.

LEVERAGED BUYOUTS OF CORPORATE DIVESTITURES

Why are buyouts of subsidiaries and divisions commonplace today? There has always been a substantial number of corporate divestitures, as companies have bought and sold operating units for strategic reasons. But the level of corporate divestitures has skyrocketed in the 1980s. There are several reasons why the number of divestitures has increased, including the emergence—and the newfound respectability—of less-than-investment grade subordinated debt.

Employees—management and non-management—are widely believed to work more efficiently when they own a piece of the action and when some of their capital is at risk in the business. There is more incentive for each employee to go the extra mile, and there is less need for the costly supervisory and monitoring systems that typify large, absentee-owned conglomerates.

As investors have focused more on cash flow and less on earnings, the rationale for corporate diversification has disappeared. If companies are judged largely on the accounting measure of earnings, then a diversified company, which pools the risk of different lines of business, seems superior to an undiversified business. Where there are no clear synergies between the elements of a corporation, the cash-flows-focused investor sees no gain from conglomeration.

Only the largest corporations in the United States can qualify for the investment-grade debt that in the past was needed to purchase a large company. In a trend initially engineered by the investment banking firm of Drexel Burnham Lambert but now widely supported by portfolio managers, financial analysts, and some economists, if not mainstream politicians, debt is now widely available to less-than-blue-chip entities. This makes it possible to finance divisional spinoffs through the public markets or through private placements to insurance companies, pension funds, or other long-term investors. Many leveraged buyouts of subsidiaries or divisions financed in this way have produced enormous financial rewards for their initiators.

In addition, there are clearly significant cultural changes in America that support the kind of corporate risk-taking and entrepreneurship that buyouts embody.

Each of these trends has contributed to the growth in divestitures of units of both public and private corporations. Some divestitures, of course, still go to strategic buyers. However, many go to senior management teamed up with LBO groups with their own equity to invest. But an increasing number are going to all the employees through the use of ESOP leveraged buyouts.

In order to fully understand the value that an ESOP can bring to a leveraged buyout, it is important first to understand how a typical management buyout is structured.

Management-Led Leveraged Buyouts

During the 1980s, it became more common for management, with the assistance of an investment group, to purchase their company, subsidiary, division, or product line. These transactions are commonly known as leveraged buyouts because the buyout group will finance the purchase price using funds attained by borrowing against the assets and projected cash flows of the unit being acquired. These transactions usually rely heavily on subordinated debt ultimately provided by insurance companies, pension funds, other institutional investors, and often the seller of the company. They rely on equity provided by management and an investor group, frequently a group that specializes in leveraged buyouts.

Leveraged buyouts are financed predominately through borrowed capital not only because these funds are readily available but because equity will reap higher returns when the transaction is financed predominately with debt. Senior lenders are not prepared to lend 100% against the collateral value of assets, whereas subordinated lenders are prepared to take second liens on assets and be paid out of the cash flows of the company in excess of requirements to service senior debt in exchange for a premium rate of return. This allows the company to be more highly leveraged and reduces the need for equity—thereby replacing equity with less costly debt. Debt is less costly than equity financing for two fundamental reasons: First, equity is at greater risk. It is subordinated to debt as to rights to cash flow, including cash flow associated with liquidation. Therefore, equity investors expect substantially higher returns on their investment than lenders. Second, interest on acquisition debt is a deductible expense whereas dividends on equity are paid with after-tax dollars. Therefore, it is more costly for a corporation to provide a return to equity than it is to provide the same level of return to debt.

Consequently, a seller can frequently receive the highest price from a buyer who relies heavily on debt financing. Today, a corporate as well as an LBO buyer will typically value a company based on the cash flowing to a capital structure composed predominately of debt. This kind of capital structure maximizes the potential return to equity, although it reduces the flexibility and increases the operating risks of the company.

The now popular belief that companies are more competitive and profitable operating independently than as part of conglomerates is precipitating the tremendous volume of corporate divestitures in the 1980s. The 1960s was a period of conglomeration, which by many accounts was a failed experiment. The 1980s has been a time of "breaking up," "spinning off," and divesting corporate "assets." The result is a de-conglomeration of corporate America. A management-led LBO will usually result in the company being operated as an independent stand-alone entity. This will frequently be the most advantageous condition for operating the company.

However, a corporation is still the most frequent buyer of corporations being sold. A corporate bidder with easy access to credit may have a powerful advantage over a management-led leveraged buyout. A prospective corporate buyer may desire to integrate the new company into the operations of other segments of its corporation and in so doing enhance the value of the entire corporation and therefore the value of the company being purchased. A corporation that believes it can attain economies of scale, greater market share, expanded product lines, additional operating capacity, or any other enhancements to its existing business as a result of the acquisition may bid far above the levels associated with the potential cash flows and earnings of the new company on a stand-alone basis. If the corporation has sufficient access to capital and believes that it can achieve important synergies between its current business and that of the new company, then it will normally be able to outbid a management-led LBO.

When competing for the purchase of a company a management-led LBO has a number of advantages over other bidders including corporate bidders, and these advantages will at times give them the edge in the bidding process. The existing management of the company usually has a better understanding of the company than any other prospective bidder. They may know of hidden values in the company that will be hard for others to discover or to realize. Management also requires less time to evaluate the company, and they generally know in advance that the company will soon be for sale. Management often will have well-thought-out plans for operating the company independently, including strategies to spur growth or reduce costs. An independent company will require less corporate reporting and will be able to eliminate overhead cost associated with its parent. Management will have personal and close ties with the company's financing sources. And their bid is often viewed sympathetically by the board of directors who must ultimately decide to whom to sell.

ESOP Leveraged Buyout

An ESOP leveraged buyout is virtually identical in structure to a non-ESOP LBO, except that the ESOP becomes one additional investor that must share in the equity of the new company. In a number of key areas an ESOP LBO has advantages over the standard LBO alternative. An ESOP LBO can expect improvements in its operations, in its level of tax payments, and in its cost of capital. These advantages will give the employees a better chance to win a bid and, if won, will result in a healthier company.

An ESOP LBO can be initiated in several ways:

Owner-Initiated. The owners of a corporation or its board of directors may realize that selling the company or divesting a division may be most effectively accomplished through an ESOP leveraged buyout. The board of directors may assist an ESOP buyout effort in either a privately negotiated sale or a semi-public auction of the company.

The board may initiate an ESOP leveraged buy out and arrange the transaction on a *private sale* basis. In this case, the board, through its management and representatives, can control virtually all aspects of the transaction. The board, to a great extent, can negotiate with itself as to the terms and conditions of the sale. The board's control of the transaction is only offset by the limits imposed by the financing sources and by the requirement that an independent, qualified valuation firm be engaged by the ESOP trustee for the purpose of opining on the fairness of the transaction to the ESOP and valuing the shares purchased by the trust. The fee earned by the valuation firm, though generally paid by the seller, cannot be contingent on the completion of the transaction so that the valuation firm can aggressively negotiate on the ESOP's behalf.

The board can also cause an *auction* to be the process by which a sale occurs and yet still support an ESOP LBO as one of the bidders in such an auction. The company can assist an ESOP buyout effort using corporate funds for the purpose of having an additional bidder with tax and other advantages. This may result in the seller gaining a higher price for the company than it might otherwise attain. In circumstances where the company is in distress, this will often assure the seller of having at least one non-liquidation bidder for the company.

Management-Initiated. A management-initiated ESOP LBO is typically initiated by senior management and can be supported by the board and owners of the corporation, even to the extent of providing corporate funds to conduct such an effort. A management-initiated ESOP LBO can be a powerful bidder because it has all the advantages of an inside management group along with the attributes of ESOP financing. If, in addition, management involves its unions, if any, and other employees in the structuring of the transaction, and gains employee sacrifices in exchange for ownership, they will be significantly more competitive in bidding for the company. If successful the transaction will result in a healthier stand-alone enterprise.

Union-Initiated. Other, non-management employees can initiate an ESOP LBO. This is typically done by one or several unions representing the employees. Such a buyout effort can also be supported by the company with corporate funds. In such a buyout attempt it is imperative for the employees to team up with qualified management to assist in the buyout effort and subsequently to operate the company.

It is common for a union-initiated employee buyout effort to invite existing management to participate with the union in buying the company. A union also has the option to seek other more qualified management with which to partici-pate or to selectively invite existing management to its side.

Non-Employee-Initiated. Any prospective bidder for a company can integrate ESOP financing into the overall financing structure of their transaction. Such an effort can reap the various tax and interest rate advantages associated with ESOP financing and therefore enhance its competitiveness. However, without the involvement and support of the overall workforce and without sharing all the rights of ownership, particularly voting rights, it is unlikely that employee sacrifices can be attained in exchange for ownership.

UNION CONSIDERATIONS

It would be nice for sellers if the employees would always be motivated to trade off concessions for ownership. However, workers typically have little discretionary income and less desire to see it taken from them. Workers gen-erally must be concerned about protecting current income as opposed to gam-bling on the future of their company. When a company undergoes a standard leveraged buyout, no one is more at risk than the employees.

Investors in such transactions typically account for 10 to 15% of the trans-action cost in the form of equity. Normally, such an investment represents only a fraction of the investor's portfolio. If the company were to fail they would experience losses, not catastrophe.

Management typically invests a portion of their net worth in LBOs in return for a sizable equity stake and continuation of their relatively high salaries. If the company were to fail, management would fall back on their accumulated resources and take their college degrees elsewhere.

In the standard LBO, the average employee invests nothing, receives noth-ing, but assumes enormous risks. For average employees, the chance of owning a home, affording a good education for their kids, and their very livelihood is tied up in the success or failure of their company. Stable income and accruing pension benefits are the bulk of their financial resources. If their company is leveraged, these resources are put at great risk. (That is not to say that there may be greater risk for the employees if the company fails to undergo a lever-aged transaction.)

If the company falters, it is the employees who are asked to sacrifice. If the company fails, it is the employees who enter the job market with limited or specialized skills and meager resources to relocate and retrain. In return for such risks, the employees normally receive no stake in the success of the com-pany.

Security of wages and benefits should be the foremost consideration of unions or employee groups. Therefore, if a fat-cat corporate buyer comes along with deep, granddaddy pockets, the employees, whether organized or not, will gen-erally opt for the role of wage earners and pass on the opportunity and risks of being owners. To outbid such corporate buyers is tough, and the concessions that may make it possible would be substantial.

However, if a corporate buyer is a union buster or is someone who is likely to move the facilities to Timbuktu, then the employees will normally consider long and hard their willingness to take concessions rather than risk losing their jobs.

If the employees on average are near retirement, and if their retirement benefits are substantial, they may view any efforts to achieve ownership as a waste of time. In situations where a distress company is for sale and employees are entitled to substantial severance or shutdown payments, they may consider it more lucrative to take such payments instead of supporting an employee buyout. In such cases, the union's interest may not be entirely aligned with existing employees and may be more aligned with job preservation through employee ownership.

If the alternative to an ESOP buyout is a leveraged buyout by a "financial buyer," then the employees should be concerned about the likelihood of workforce, wage, and benefit reductions being imposed on them so that the LBO can survive its tremendous debt load. If workers are operating under a collective bargaining agreement they will expect to face demands for give backs in the next round of negotiations. Or they will fear that their highly leveraged company will be prone to failure in any future recession or fail simply due to lack of resources to adequately invest in capital equipment, R&D, and marketing.

All of these fears are well founded. If the likely buyer is a financial buyer who intends to use leveraged buyouts techniques, the employees may as well buy the company themselves using an ESOP. If the company can be purchased on the same terms as a competing non-ESOP LBO, an ESOP's tax and other advantages will enhance the viability of the company. In this way, if the company is successful due to workers' sacrifices or for any reason, the employees will automatically reap the benefits of success through ownership of the company.

It is in the interest of a union to consider the various alternatives available to them in terms of competing bids before aligning themselves with one particular bidder. Once aligned, however, it is not in their interest to align themselves with any other bidder. If they were to do so, they would be bidding against themselves. Their objective, if they choose to buy a company, is to buy it at the lowest possible price.

A union supporting an ESOP buyout with concessions will generally demand voting pass-through and representation on the board of directors for their membership. Typically, such boards will have one-third of their directors representing the salaried employees, one-third representing the bargaining unit, and one-third composed of independent directors or directors representing cash equity investors.

In all of these cases employees are faced with very personal and significant financial considerations and, like any other buyer, will generally, but not always, make their decision based on their best judgment of the financial cost and benefits to them and their families.

LEVERAGED BUYOUT FINANCING STRUCTURE

Virtually all LBOs are financed with a combination of senior debt, subordinated debt, and equity. The amount of equity required in a transaction is determined, in part, by the amount of debt that can be borrowed. The following is a description of the various components of financing that comprise the financing structure of a typical leveraged buyout.

Senior Debt

Typically 50 to 75% of the financing of an LBO is in the form of senior financing. A senior loan is collateralized by a first lien on the current and long-term assets of the company. Senior financing is generally made available from banks, although privately placed notes to institutional investors are also possible.

Term Debt. Senior term debt is loaned to an LBO based on the appraised fair market value of the land and buildings and the orderly liquidation value of the machinery and equipment. Such loans are further limited by the predictability of cash flow to service senior debt. The term for senior term debt is typically five to eight years. Interest cost can be anywhere from prime to four over prime. But the cost to the company of this financing can typically be reduced to approximately 85% of the standard loan rate if ESOP financing is utilized.

Revolving Line of Credit. A revolving line of credit is loaned to an LBO based on the appraised orderly liquidation value of the eligible accounts receivables and inventory. Such loans are further limited by the predictability of cash flow to service senior debt. A revolving line of credit typically has a term of one year with renewal provisions. Interest cost can be anywhere from prime to four over prime. The cost to the company of this financing *cannot* be reduced due to the use of ESOP financing.

Subordinated Debt

Typically 15 to 30% of the financing of an LBO is in the form of subordinated financing. These funds are subordinated to senior debt and generally have only second claim to the collateral of the company. Subordinated financing is generally made available from insurance companies directly or is raised in the form of high-yield (''junk'') bonds from insurance companies, pension funds, other institutional investors, or through public offerings. In many LBOs, subordinated debt is given back to the seller, comprising a portion of the purchase price. The term of such financing is typically 7 to 15 years and principal payments are commonly deferred until after the senior debt is retired.

These funds are loaned based on the amount and predictability of cash flow in excess of that required to service senior debt. Interest cost can be anywhere from two to eight percentage points more than senior debt. Because subordinated debt at times has little collateral protection it may be granted an "equity kicker" with the intention of providing the lender with a 15 to 30% total return. The cost to the company of this financing may be reduced if ESOP financing is used.

Equity

Typically 10 to 20% of the financing of an LBO is in the form of equity financing. It is these funds that make up the difference in the financing requirement and the financing available in the form of debt.

Those who invest in the equity of a company typically reap six rights of ownership: (1) voting rights, (2) dividend rights, (3) trading rights, (4) appreciation rights, (5) liquidation rights, and (6) rights to information. However, dividend and liquidation rights of equity investors are typically subordinated in an LBO to the secured lenders of the company.

Management usually makes an investment in the equity of an LBO company together with an LBO fund, a corporate investor, or a group composed of institutional equity investors. The seller in some cases receives equity in the new company. An institutional investor investing in the equity of an LBO will typically seek a 35 to 45% compounded annual total return, depending on perceived risk.

In an ESOP LBO, a similar proportion of equity capital may be needed in the transaction. Equity may come from management or from outside sources such as an LBO fund or other institutional investors, or from elections by employees to roll over a portion of their pension fund assets into the new company's ESOP. Regardless of the source of the cash equity investment, equity investors must share ownership with the employees of the company via their ESOP, and the various rights of ownership must be carved up among all the equity investors. The dilution experienced by the non-ESOP equity investors is offset by the improved cash flows associated with ESOP financing and a favorable distribution of the various rights of ownership.

If the seller is prepared to take a subordinated note as part of the payment of the purchase price or if state or federal financing is available, it is possible for an ESOP buyout to occur with little or no cash equity investments. Or, if the collateral value of the assets exceeds the purchase price, it is also possible for an ESOP buyout to be achieved without a cash equity investor. However, this is rather rare and typically occurs in distress situations where the seller has no alternative buyers and substantial shutdown liabilities and when the workers are prepared to enhance the cash flow of the company by accepting concessions ("sweat equity") in return for ownership.

ESOP VERSUS NON-ESOP LEVERAGED BUYOUTS

The financing for an ESOP LBO is very similar to a non-ESOP LBO. The advantages for an ESOP LBO have to do with various improvements that can be achieved in the cash flows of the company. These improved cash flows can be used to afford a higher price for the company or can be retained by the buyer to have a positive impact on the growth in equity of the company. The example below models a typical LBO transaction and compares the growth in net worth and enterprise value of a non-ESOP LBO to an ESOP LBO with employee participation, at the same purchase price.

Non-ESOP Leveraged Buyout

A. Uses of Financing
  1. Purchase Price $ 50
  2. Transaction Expenses & Cash Reserves   5
                               TOTAL $ 55 million
B. Sources of Financing
  1. Senior and Subordinated Debt
     Straight Line Amortization Over 10 years
     Interest Rate on All Outstanding Debt: 12.5%
     a. Senior Term Debt $ 20
     b. Subordinated Term Debt   10
     c. Revolving Line of Credit   20
  2. Cash Equity Investment   5
                               TOTAL $ 55 million
C. Starting Operating Income (EBIT) $ 10 million
   (In this example EBIT will rise at a 3% an-
   nual rate over the 10-year tenure of the term
   debt.)
D. Tax Rate (federal and state combined): 40%
E. Net Worth & Enterprise Value. The net worth
   of the company will in general rise over a
   five year period as retained earnings accumulate. The enterprise value in this example
   is assumed to be five times operating income, plus cash, less outstanding debt (see
   Table 6.1).
F. Internal Rate of Return. The internal rate of
   return for the initial cash equity investment
   over a five-year period will be 33% based on
   the growth in net worth and 35% based on
   the growth in enterprise value.

Table 6.1
Non-ESOP Leveraged Buyout: Net Worth and Enterprise Value
(in millions of $)

Day					End of Year					
One	Yr 1	Yr 2	Yr 3	Yr 4	Yr 5	Yr 6	Yr 7	Yr 8	Yr 9	Yr 10
NET WORTH										
$ 5	$ 7	$10	$13	$17	$21	$25	$30	$36	$41	$48
ENTERPRISE VALUE										
	$ 2	$ 7	$11	$17	$22	$28	$35	$42	$50	$58

ESOP Leveraged Buyout

The difference between the non-ESOP described above and an ESOP LBO
is that the proceeds of the senior and subordinated term loans made to the new
company will be loaned by the company to its ESOP. It will be used by the
ESOP to purchase equity in the new corporation. The proceeds from the sale
of equity to the ESOP will be used by the company to pay the purchase price
and to cover other financing requirements.

The new company will make contributions to the ESOP over a five-year
period and these will be used by the ESOP to service its debt. The portion of
the company's contribution used by the ESOP to pay principal payments on its
debt generally must not exceed 25% of the company's payroll (see Figure 6.1).

The ESOP will enhance the cash flow of the company in a variety of ways
but it will also dilute the interest of any cash equity investor. The following
are the ways in which an ESOP as shown in Figure 6.1 can enhance the transaction, offsetting the dilutive impact of the ESOP.

Principal Deduction. Principal payments on ESOP loans can be made with
pre-tax earnings, causing a reduction in taxable income. Therefore, if the new
company is profitable, 40% of the amount used to retire principal is done with
cash flow made available from tax savings. This has a $12 million positive
impact on the net worth of the new company over a five-year period.

Lower Interest Rate. The interest rate on the senior and subordinated debt
may be lower because 50% of interest income on loans made to an ESOP or
its company by qualified lenders is deductible from taxable income of the lender
if the ESOP owns at least 50% of the company and the employees receive full
voting rights on the shares acquired by the loan. The interest rate using an
ESOP will be 10.6% or 85% of the non-ESOP rate. This increases the net
worth of the new company $2.4 million over a five-year period.

Enhancements to Earnings. The $10 million in earnings before interest and
taxes in the above example can be enhanced with an ESOP because employees
and unions are often willing to make sacrifices in wages and salaries, change

Figure 6.1
Corporate Divestitures

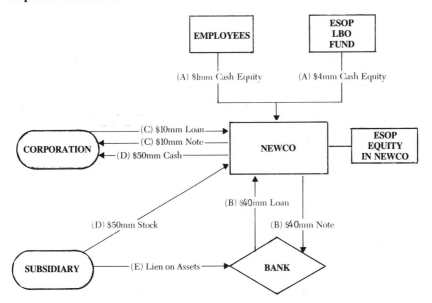

TRANSACTION ANALYSIS

	SUBSIDIARY Balance Sheet	Elements of the Transaction				ProForma NEWCO Balance Sheet
		A	B	C	D	
ASSETS						
1. Cash	0	5	40	10	(50)	5
2. Other Assets	50					50
Total Assets	50					55
LIABILITIES						
1. Senior Term Debt	0		20			20
2. Revolving Line of Credit	—		20			20
3. Subordinated Debt	—			10		10
Total Liabilities	0		40	10		50
EQUITY						
1. Existing Equity	50				(50)	0
2. Founders' Equity	—	1				1
3. ESOP LBO FUND	—	4				4
Total Equity	50	5			(50)	5
TOT. LIAB. & EQUITY	50					55

work rules, and forego certain benefits in exchange for the rights of ownership. These sacrifices are often available only if the employees are involved in the establishment of the ESOP and only if their stock is endowed with all six ownership rights described above, particularly voting rights. In addition, these sacrifices are generally more readily available if the future of the company is at stake or if the policies of the old company threaten job security. The enhancements are summarized below:

1. *Salary and Wage Reductions.* From 5 to 15% reductions in salary and wages are possible in many ESOP LBOs in exchange for substantial ownership rights. In this example, $2.1 million in annual salary and wage reductions is assumed. This enhances net worth by $10.5 million over a five-year period.

2. *Workforce Reductions.* Work conditions and the demands placed on labor in the work place are either employee benefits or negative aspects of employment. Often, the fewer the workers the more demanding and risky the job. Labor unions take a serious view of this and will often fight for strict work rules to maintain certain relations between compensation and the demands of the work place. These arrangements are contractual in collective bargaining agreements and may be difficult to alter in a non-ESOP leveraged buyout.

An ESOP structured in an LBO may create the proper environment for implementing workforce reductions that could not be implemented in a non-ESOP structured transaction. In this example, $1.2 million in annual salary, wage, and benefit reductions are assumed due to workforce reductions. These reductions increase profits and net worth by $6 million over a five-year period. Workforce reductions may be offset by increased sales, with no net loss of employment.

3. *Shift in Employee Benefits.* In most companies the employees receive significant non-wage-related employee benefits. By using ESOP financing, the company in this example is contributing over $6 million annually to an employee benefit plan, the ESOP. This is a significantly larger amount than a company this size would normally contribute to a pension plan. (However, an ESOP as a pension plan is a riskier pension vehicle for employees than a diversified pension plan. Therefore, it may be inappropriate to exchange dollar for dollar one benefit for the other.) The employees may support the reduction of certain benefits in exchange for implementing a larger benefit plan, the ESOP, and thereby reduce the operating cost of the company.

In this example, it is assumed that cash flow available for service of acquisition debt is increased $1.2 million annually due to a shift and increase in employee benefits to the ESOP. This enhances net worth by $6 million over a five-year period while increasing the pension benefits to the employees if the company is successful.

4. *Improved Productivity.* ESOP practitioners have been reticent to project cost savings in ESOP companies due to the implementation of an ESOP. However, many in the field believe that there is evidence that with high levels of

Table 6.2:
ESOP Leveraged Buyout: Net Worth and Enterprise Value
(in millions of $)

Day One	Yr 1	Yr 2	Yr 3	Yr 4	Yr 5	Yr 6	Yr 7	Yr 8	Yr 9	Yr 10

End of Year

NET WORTH

| $ 5 | $15 | $25 | $36 | $47 | $59 | $68 | $78 | $88 | $99 | $110 |

ENTERPRISE VALUE

| | $49 | $61 | $73 | $85 | $99 | $110 | $121 | $133 | $146 | $159 |

employee participation in conjunction with employee ownership, productivity can indeed be improved. In this example, costs are reduced by a modest $.15 million annually due to improved productivity. This contributes $.75 million to net worth over a five-year period.

Net Worth and Enterprise Value. The net worth of the ESOP company described in Table 6.2 rises over a five-year period as retained earnings accumulate and as the ESOP retires its debt. The enterprise value in this example is assumed to be five times operating income, plus cash, less outstanding debt.

Internal Rate of Return. The cash equity investor will receive approximately 38% of the stock of the company using the most widely used equity allocation methodology. Therefore the internal rate of return for the initial cash equity investment over a five-year period will be 34% based on the growth in net worth and 49% based on the growth in enterprise value.

Equity Allocation

A comparison between the two examples just described shows that the net worth of the company using ESOP financing rises over five years to $59 million compared to $21 million in net worth of the non-ESOP LBO (see Figure 6.2). The enterprise value of the ESOP LBO rises to $99 million over five years compared to $22 million in the non-ESOP LBO (see Figure 6.3).

The non-ESOP equity investors must share ownership with the ESOP. Using current valuation methodology for allocating equity in a multi-investor leveraged ESOP, approximately 38% of the appreciation rights will be allocated to the cash equity investors. Based on such an allocation, the Internal Rate of Return (IRR) to the investors who invest the original $5 million cash investment will be 49% or 14% better than the non-ESOP-structured LBO over the first five years. The various enhancements associated with the ESOP offset the dilutive impact of the ESOP on the cash equity investor's return.

Figure 6.2
ESOP Versus Non-ESOP LBO, Net Worth

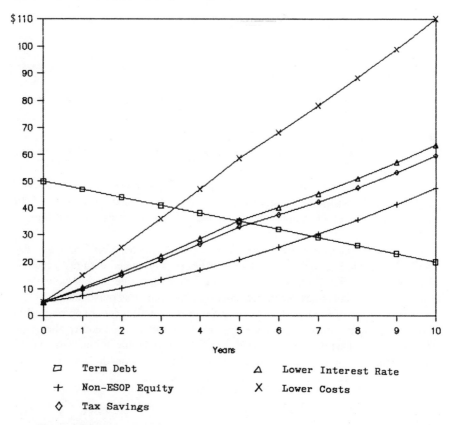

	Term Debt		△	Lower Interest Rate
+	Non-ESOP Equity		X	Lower Costs
◊	Tax Savings			

CONCLUSION

The advantages of divesting subsidiaries and divisions through ESOPs are likely to continue to make this approach attractive in years to come. Aside from the substantial tax advantages described here, a sale to an ESOP can prevent a company being on the market for several months, or longer, causing a decline in the value of the company, a loss of morale among employees, and uncertainty and concern among employees of the parent firm who may wonder if they are next.

The advantages of ESOP divestitures, however, may not be enough to outweigh other considerations that non-ESOP buyers may bring to a transaction. If a buyer can gain a market edge, or economies of scale, by purchasing a company, it may be willing to pay more than the ESOP can pay for the same division or subsidiary based solely on earnings potential. Other outside buyers may realize special tax or other financial advantages by buying divisions or subsidiaries that are not available to the ESOP, and again thus be willing to

Figure 6.3
ESOP Versus Non-ESOP LBO, Enterprise Value

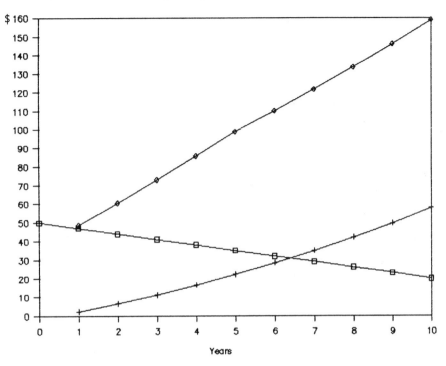

```
□    Term Debt
+    Non-ESOP Enterprise Value
◇    ESOP Enterprise Value
```

pay more. In other cases, a division's or subsidiary's management may want to buy the company, and may not want to share equity ownership with employees.

In many cases, however, an ESOP is not used simply because those involved with the sale do not know how it can be used. For the parent firm, and the employees of the divested company, this ignorance can come at the cost of a solution favorable to everyone. It is hoped that as ESOPs become better understood, they will assume their proper role as a major consideration in any divestiture.

7

ESOPs—Compensation, Performance, and Dilution: Is There a Link?

MICHAEL A. CONTE

INTRODUCTION

In the 1970s and early 1980s, Employee Stock Ownership Plans were primarily a phenomenon of the closely held company. Recently, however, public companies have expressed increasing interest in ESOPs for a variety of reasons. The powerful tax incentives associated with the 1984 and 1986 tax acts[1] and the trend away from defined benefit pension plans and toward defined contribution plans[2] have led managers of even the largest public companies to consider implementing an ESOP.[3] According to Blasi (forthcoming 1991) "approximately 250 publicly-held corporations have set up ESOPs in the last 30 months putting several tens of billions of dollars of corporate equity in the hands of employees." In 1990, total ESOP finance is expected to be five times the 1988 volume, with much of this reflecting borrowing of public companies. ESOPs may become primarily, or at least equally, a phenomenon of public companies in the future and for this reason it is important to understand how they function and what their impact is likely to be.

ESOPs in public companies are different from those in closely held firms for several reasons. First, because share values of public companies are determined on financial markets, employees' market risk is likely to be greater, although bankruptcy risk is less. This may add a premium to the average return on employee shareholdings. Second, employees are by law entitled to vote their shares in public companies that may have an effect on their attitudes and/or behavior, although several studies have provided preliminary evidence that this is not the case. Third, closely held companies typically adopt ESOPs in order to take advantage of estate-planning-related provisions that require a minimum ESOP holding of 30%. In contrast, only a small fraction of public company ESOPs hold more than 20% of their company's stock.[4] And fourth, public companies are on average much larger than closely held companies and generally have more complex organizational structures and compensation systems. Adding an ESOP to this mix may have less of an effect on things of interest like total employee compensation or measurable company performance than adding one in a closely held company.

This is the first study of ESOP firms, public or closely held, that measures all forms of employee compensation, including income from noncontributory employee benefit plans. Our income measurement, while not comprehensive, is more comprehensive than that of any previous study of employee plans. While we have not included income from bonuses, commissions, employer contributions to or returns from contributory employee pension plans, or the monetary value of insurance and health benefit plans, we have measured contributions to and returns from defined benefit pension plans, profit-sharing plans, and stock bonus plans in addition to ESOPs. Using this information, we can for the first time assess whether ESOPs increase total employee compensation (excluding the listed components). In light of the intent of the original ESOP legislation to increase employee wealth, it is important to establish whether ESOPs provide a net increase in compensation (which would allow for wealth-building), versus substituting deferred for current compensation (which would lower employees' current standard of living), or substituting a non-diversified form of deferred compensation for more highly diversified forms (which would have the effect of increasing employees' risk). There are significant possibilities for such substitution in public companies because of the complex mix of pension plans and other employee benefits that typically exists and because of the greater presence of unions in public companies. In recent years, numerous union contracts have included explicit ''stock for wages'' trade-offs.

In addition to assessing the impact of ESOPs on total employee compensation, we provide some answers to the following questions: How large are ESOP plans in public companies? To what extent do ESOPs in public companies tie the economic welfare of employees to the welfare of the company? Have ESOPs affected bottom-line performance in public companies? And, finally, do ESOPs dilute share value? These questions are all of significant policy interest.

THE DATA

Considerably more information is available about public companies than about closely held companies. We can therefore provide an in-depth view on certain issues. However, even for public companies, various types of information are not available from any public data source. For this reason, we contacted companies by mail and requested completion of a survey. (See this chapter's Appendix I for a copy of the survey.)

Table 7.1
Response Percentages

	NCEO Companies w/COMPUSTAT Data	Matching Companies
Total Surveys Sent	114	512
# of Usable Responses	18	27
Response %	16%	5%

Our primary source of information in addition to the survey was Standard and Poor's (S&P) Industrial COMPUSTAT data base. This data base provides S&P income statement and balance sheet information for many public companies. We augmented the data from these two sources with information from companies' annual reports. Finally, some checks were run, described below, using data from the 1985 Employee Plan Master File of the Department of Labor.

Survey recipients were identified as follows: a list of 180 public ESOP companies was obtained from The National Center for Employee Ownership. This list was culled from a variety of sources, but primarily from a clipping service that tracks employee stock ownership plans. It is regularly updated and is the best source of information available about ESOP incidence short of plan reports (Form 5500 and related filings) to the U.S. Department of Labor.[5] (See Appendix III for comparison of plan data from survey responses with plan data from the 1985 Employee Plan Master File.)

For each company on the NCEO list, up to five matching firms were selected on the basis of industry group and size. To measure industry group, we used the standard industrial classification (SIC) system. For each of the NCEO firms, we generated a list of all companies on COMPUSTAT's four main industrial files, which were classified in the same four-digit SIC code.[6] We then selected five firms from each of these lists (or all firms when there were fewer than five) on the basis of company size. Size was measured with two variables: number of employees and dollar value of sales. Judgment was used in cases of conflict between these two size criteria. A total of 512 matching companies was generated using this approach.

In total, therefore, our survey was sent to 792 companies. However, only 114 of the companies from the NCEO list are represented in the COMPUSTAT data base. These were the only firms from the NCEO list included in the statistical analyses. Therefore, our response percentages, presented in Table 7.1, are calculated on the basis of 114 NCEO-list companies and 512 matching companies.

Eighteen of the NCEO companies responded, for a response rate of 16%.

This is fairly high for an extensive survey of the type that was sent. This response rate resulted in part from a persistent follow-up procedure involving letters and telephone calls. The same follow-up procedure was employed for the matching companies, but it did not result in the same degree of response. Only 27, or 5%, of the matching companies ultimately provided enough information to be considered bona fide respondents to the survey. This disparity is consistent with the observation by Mitchell, Lewin, and Lawler that "firms which view themselves as innovators in the pay area are most likely to provide information."[7] This raises the issue of response bias, which is addressed in Appendix II along with the issue of selection bias (bias in selecting companies for inclusion in the study). To briefly summarize our analysis of bias, we found no evidence of selection bias but relatively convincing evidence of both absolute and differential response bias. The possible importance of these biases is discussed later in connection with our results. It is clear that future analyses (in which there are sufficient cases) should control for response bias in order to obtain definitive results.

The central purposes of the survey were to ascertain which employee plans each company had in operation, when each plan began, and how much each plan contributed to employee compensation. It was in some cases difficult to ascertain from a survey response whether the company had one or more of the types of plans about which we were inquiring, and in some cases responses about contributions, trust values, and the like were missing or ambiguous. We employed two approaches to resolve these ambiguities: we obtained copies of annual reports for the years and companies in question and also attempted to recontact respondents by both telephone and mail. If the respondent indicated a willingness to provide more data, we sent a customized data request and cover letter indicating the areas of ambiguity or missing data. Recontacting resulted in a considerable amount of additional data. However, in some cases the annual report data differed from that obtained in the first and/or second contact, and we therefore developed a credibility ranking system for determining which data items would go into the final dataset. In general, information from annual reports (which are audited) took precedence over survey responses (which are not); information from the second contact took precedence over information from the first; and information from an individual with expertise in plan management, personnel, and such took precedence over an individual with no such expertise.

The next section provides basic descriptive information about employee plans in the companies we surveyed, while later sections report our findings on the central issues of this chapter.

EMPLOYEE PLANS IN THE SURVEY COMPANIES

The first question on the survey asked companies to indicate which employee plans the company had sponsored at any point since 1980, with the following

Table 7.2
Incidence of Employee Plans Among Respondents

	NCEO	Matching	Total
#/% of Companies w/1 or more ESOPs	17/94%	4/15%	21/47%
#/% of Companies w/a TRASOP or PAYSOP	6/33%	5/19%	11/24%
#/% of Companies w/a Profit-Sharing Plan	11/61%	8/30%	19/42%
#/% of Companies w/a Pension Plan	11/61%	19/70%	31/69%

choices: Employee Stock Ownership Plan (ESOP), Profit-Sharing Plan (PSP), Stock Bonus Plan (SBP), Stock Option Plan (SOP), Stock Purchase Plan (SPP), Pension Plan (PP), or none. (Refer to Appendix I for complete survey questions.) Relatively few firms reported having a (non-ESOP) stock bonus plan, stock option plan, or stock purchase plans. The information supplied about these plans was often minimal; we therefore limited our attention in follow-ups to the other plan types and did not analyze the data on these three types of plan.

Of the 18 respondents from the NCEO list, 17 or 94% proved to have at least one tax deduction ESOP and one company had two at some point since 1980. In addition, six (33%) had TRASOPs or PAYSOPs. As expected, a much smaller proportion of the 27 respondents from the matching firms had ESOPs (4 firms, or 15%), but 5 (19%) had a TRASOP or PAYSOP. A comparison of these two groups in terms of incidence of plans of all types is provided in Table 7.2.

These numbers imply that many of the responding companies had several plans existing simultaneously, and it is interesting to ask whether patterns of plan adoption exist among this sample of public firms. The cross-tabulations reported in Tables 7.3 through 7.6 indicate that such patterns may exist; however, the patterns in our sample are somewhat surprising. Table 7.3 shows a cross-tabulation of firms with a tax deduction ESOP (TDESOP) with firms that had a tax credit ESOP (TCESOP); 21% of the companies without TDESOPs had TCESOPs, but this increased only to 29% for companies with TDESOPs, and the difference was not statistically significant. This supports the contention by Conte and Svejnar (forthcoming) that the motivating factors for adoption of TDESOPs are different from those which underlay adoption of TCESOPs.

Interestingly, there was considerably more association between TDESOPs and profit-sharing plans. Table 7.4 shows that 29% of firms without TDESOPs had PSPs, but 52% of the firms with TDESOPs had PSPs; this difference was

Table 7.3
TDESOP by TCESOP

```
        FREQUENCY
        ROW PCT   |NO TCESOP| TCESOP  |
                  |         |         |  TOTAL
        ----------+---------+---------+
        NO TDESOP |      19 |       5 |    24
                  |   79.17 |   20.83 |
        ----------+---------+---------+
        TDESOP    |      15 |       6 |    21
                  |   71.43 |   28.57 |
        ----------+---------+---------+
        TOTAL          34        11        45
```

```
CHI-SQUARE  = 0.363
PROBABILITY OF NO DIFFERENCE IN CELL MEANS = .547

TDESOP = COMPANY HAD A TAX DEDUCTION ESOP AT ANY TIME
         SINCE 1980
TCESOP = COMPANY HAD A TAX CREDIT ESOP AT ANY TIME
         SINCE 1980
```

The top number within each cell is the frequency of occurrence of the cell. The bottom number is the row percent.

nearly significant at the 10% confidence level. This is consistent with the view of Blasi (forthcoming 1991) that profit-sharing programs and ESOPs have much in common, and that adoption of these two types of employee plans is motivated by similar factors.

Table 7.5 shows that there is little correspondence between the propensity to adopt a TDESOP and the propensity to adopt a pension plan. Of the ESOP firms, 62% had pension plans, compared with 71% of the non-ESOP firms, and the difference was far from significant. This is somewhat surprising in light of (1) the general view that ESOPs have substituted for defined benefit plans, (2) the tax benefits available to companies with over-funded pensions to convert the plan to an ESOP, and (3) specific cases in our sample of companies that had done exactly that. The relationship between the incidence of defined benefit pension plans and ESOPs clearly merits further study.

The final cross-tabulation was between the incidence of ESOPs and of formal participation. Formal participation was gauged by the answer to question VII.1: "Do non-supervisory personnel participate in management decisions? If so, please indicate in what way(s)." The choices respondents were given were (1) employee board representation, (2) advisory committees with employee representation, and (3) other ways. A company was said to have formal participation if the respondent checked any of these three. Table 7.6 shows that 33% of the

Table 7.4
TDESOP by PSP

```
           FREQUENCY
            ROW PCT  |NO PSP  |PSP      |     TOTAL
           ----------+--------+--------+
            NO TDESOP |     17 |      7 |      24
                      |  70.83 |  29.17 |
           ----------+--------+--------+
            TDESOP    |     10 |     11 |      21
                      |  47.62 |  52.38 |
           ----------+--------+--------+
            TOTAL           27       18        45
```

CHI-SQUARE   = 2.515
PROBABILITY OF NO DIFFERENCE IN CELL MEANS = 0.113

TDESOP = COMPANY HAD A TAX DEDUCTION ESOP AT ANY
         TIME SINCE 1980
PSP   = COMPANY HAD A PROFIT SHARING PLAN AT ANY TIME
         SINCE 1980

The top number within each cell is the frequency of occurrence of the cell. The bottom number is the row percent.

companies without ESOPs had formal participation of some type, while only 14% of those with ESOPs did, and this difference was relatively close to being significant at the 10% confidence level. A finding that ESOP firms tend to be less participative than non-ESOP firms would be important to our understanding of how employee ownership is viewed in ESOP companies, and this relationship certainly merits additional study in a larger sample of firms.

ESOPs are the youngest of employee benefit plans, and it can therefore be expected that the ESOP plans among our respondents are also the youngest. Table 7.7 bears this out: the average age of extant TDESOP plans in our sample at the time of the survey was 6.9 years, while the average age of TCESOPs was 7.5 years. In contrast, the mean age of profit-sharing plans was 12.8 years and of pension plans was 28 years. This implies that these plans were most likely properly characterized as ESOPs, profit-sharing plans, and pension plans, although there are no corresponding population figures against which our statistics could be checked.

Table 7.8 shows the distribution of percent of employee ownership in 1986, and as expected none of the tax credit ESOPs displayed greater than 10% employee ownership, while 28 of the tax deduction ESOPs had greater than 10% of company stock in the ESOP. Two of these companies were majority employee-owned in that year.

Table 7.5
TDESOP by PP

FREQUENCY ROW PCT	NO PENSION PLAN	PENSION PLAN	TOTAL
NO TDESOP	7 29.17	17 70.83	24
TDESOP	8 38.10	13 61.90	21
TOTAL	15	30	45

```
CHI-SQUARE  = 0.402
PROBABILITY OF NO DIFFERENCE IN CELL MEANS = 0.526

TDESOP = COMPANY HAD A TAX DEDUCTION ESOP AT ANY
         TIME SINCE 1980
PP     = COMPANY HAD A DEFINED BENEFIT PENSION PLAN
         AT ANY TIME SINCE 1980
```

The top number within each cell is the frequency of occurrence of the cell. The bottom number is the row percent.

Finally, it is of significant interest to determine the extent to which public companies have contributed or sold treasury stock to the ESOP as this is the mechanism that leads to a possible dilution of pre-existing share value. The percent of companies that had either contributed or sold treasury stock to a tax deduction or tax credit ESOP at any point in the history of the plan was about the same, 36% versus 38%. This indicates that stock value dilution is a possibility, and due to this relatively high incidence of the use of treasury shares we analyze the issue further later in the chapter.

DO ESOPs AFFECT TOTAL COMPENSATION AND IF SO, HOW?

Employee plans are designed to provide alternative income to employees, but not necessarily *added* income. The principal reason for the existence of employee plans is to provide income in a different *form,* not necessarily in a different amount.

There are many reasons for which employers may wish to provide income in a different form, the principal one being to take advantage of tax incentives. The tax code permits companies to deduct deferred compensation as if it were current and simultaneously permits employees to defer taxes on this compen-

Table 7.6
TDESOP by FORMPART

```
FREQUENCY
  ROW PCT    |NO PARTI|PARTICIP|
             |CIPATION|ATION   |    TOTAL
-----------+--------+--------+
NO  TDESOP  |     16 |      8 |     24
            |  66.67 |  33.33 |
-----------+--------+--------+
TDESOP      |     18 |      3 |     21
            |  85.71 |  14.29 |
-----------+--------+--------+
TOTAL             34       11       45
```

CHI-SQUARE   = 2.200
PROBABILITY OF NO DIFFERENCE IN CELL MEANS = 0.138

TDESOP   = COMPANY HAD A TAX DEDUCTION ESOP AT ANY
            TIME SINCE 1980
FORMPART = COMPANY HAD FORMAL PARTICIPATION AT ANY
            TIME SINCE 1980

The top number within each cell is the frequency of occurrence of the cell. The bottom number is the row percent.

sation. ESOPs are subject to the same treatment as other employee plans such as defined benefit pension plans and profit-sharing plans,[8] but they have additional tax advantages resulting from provisions of the 1984 and 1986 tax acts. These provisions reflect Congress' desire to promote a specific *form* of income—namely, income tied to performance of the company's stock.

It is a common view that contributions to pension plans, profit-sharing plans, and ESOPs represent income that would not be forthcoming in the absence of the plan. While there are several good reasons for expecting this, it is not obvious why plan income should be an add-on. Economic theory suggests that if labor markets operate competitively, with both employers and employees efficiently searching the market and exercising their best opportunities, there

Table 7.7
Mean Age of Existing Plan

Plan Type	N	Mean Age
Tax Credit ESOP	12	7.5
Profit-Sharing Plan	15	12.8
Pension Plan	27	28.0

Table 7.8
Tax Deduction and Tax Credit ESOP Ownership Percent

TAX DEDUCTION ESOP OWNERSHIP PERCENT

TAX DEDUCTION ESOP OWNERSHIP PERCENT	FREQUENCY	PERCENT	CUMULATIVE FREQUENCY	CUMULATIVE PERCENT
LESS THAN 10%	39	13.9	253	90.0
10-20%	11	3.9	264	94.0
20-30%	8	2.8	272	96.8
30-40%	6	2.1	278	98.9
40-50%	1	0.4	279	99.3
50-60%	2	0.7	281	100.0

TAX CREDIT ESOP OWNERSHIP PERCENT

TAX CREDIT ESOP OWNERSHIP PERCENT	FREQUENCY	PERCENT	CUMULATIVE FREQUENCY	CUMULATIVE PERCENT
LESS THAN 10%	32	11.3	282	100.0

will arise an equilibrium wage level at which labor will trade. Labor markets are in this sense no different from the market for any other perishable good. Whether the good is purchased with cash or credit, the price is the same.

There are, however, two good reasons why plan income may partially be an add-on to basic wage and salary income. First is the fact that deferral of income diminishes its value. This is especially true in the context of defined contribution plans, for which the future benefit is not only discounted but uncertain (i.e., the amount depends in part on random events like stock market fluctuations; this is not the case for defined benefit plans). The company therefore needs to provide more income when a portion is deferred in order to achieve the same utility of compensation to employees.

Second, the tax advantages associated with all employee plan income make it less costly for firms to remunerate employees at the margin if a portion of income is deferred. This is due to the flexibility that the firm has in the timing and method of contribution.

The conclusion that one can draw from these factors is that income from employee plans may be a partial add-on to basic wage or salary compensation. This view is clearly a middle ground. For purposes of framing the question clearly, we shall also refer to two extreme views: the "gravy" view is that employee plan income is fully an add-on to basic wage and salary compensation, while the "substitution" view is that employee plan income substitutes dollar-for-dollar with wage and salary income. We test these three views in this section.

We also analyze whether ESOPs in public companies have created a dependence of individual income on company performance. Whether or not ESOP employees make more income because of the ESOP, at least one part of congressional intent is served if ESOPs create a commonality of interest between the employee and the company—that is, if employee incomes vary with stock performance. It has never been shown that this is the case for ESOP companies, and it is interesting to ask whether ESOPs create more or less of this sort of income dependence than do profit-sharing plans.

We measure income from plan participation on an accrual basis. Income from defined contribution plans is composed of two elements: company contributions to the plan and earnings on plan assets. For each of the defined contribution plans that we studied—tax deduction ESOPs, tax credit ESOPs, and profit-sharing plans—we requested sufficient information to calculate the value of total company contributions and to estimate the value of plan earnings. Contributions included cash and stock contributions, as well as contributions of other assets. The total return on plan assets included two elements: the return on investment in employer stock and the return from other investments. The return on employer stock reflected the estimated value of stock appreciation resulting from increases in adjusted stock price plus actual dividends paid.[9] We asked participating companies to provide information about the percent of the plan trust invested in employer stock. In order to maximize response, we did not inquire about the investment strategy for that portion of plan trusts not invested in employer stock. In estimating the total return on plan trusts, we therefore assumed that the balance of the trust was invested in a diversified portfolio with investment performance equal to the S&P 500 industrials. Our estimated return on plan trusts was therefore a weighted average of the return on employer stock and the return on the S&P 500, with the year-end trust principal and annual weights supplied to us by respondents.

The identical method was used to calculate employee income from participation in a profit-sharing plan. Note that profit-sharing plans are similar to ESOPs insofar as they are defined contribution plans that are permitted to invest in employer securities. We inquired about the extent to which profit-sharing plans invested in employer securities and found that several responding companies invested their profit-sharing assets heavily in their own stock. The return on profit-sharing trusts was therefore calculated in the same fashion as the return on ESOPs.

It is unnecessary to calculate the return on pension trusts in order to evaluate participant income because the benefit from participation does not depend on trust performance. The company bears all of the risk associated with portfolio decisions for defined benefit plans. We calculated the total employee income from participation in a defined benefit plan as the "normal cost," also known as "service cost," of the plan. Normal cost is the present value of future benefits resulting from participation in a defined-benefit plan. A recent Financial Accounting Standards Board rule requires that a public company's annual service cost be published in the 10K report beginning with plan year 1986; therefore, we were able to obtain this information from each of the participating companies from annual reports for the years 1986 and 1987. However, information about service cost for prior years was generally not provided, even though all first-round respondents were requested to provide this information in the second contact.

Table 7.9 presents our findings pertaining to employee compensation in the survey firms. Each firm had an average of 20,981 employees—the minimum was 100 and the maximum was about 500,000. As expected, ESOP contributions per employee for tax deduction plans were much higher than per employee contributions for tax credit plans—$549 versus $53 per employee. Contributions per participant were measured at $1,306 for TDESOPs. Fewer than 30 observations of this variable were available for tax credit ESOPs—too few to calculate a meaningful average. Contributions to cash profit-sharing plans were $277.11 per employee, just about halfway between TDESOPs and TCESOPs, while mean contributions to deferred plans were $100.45.

In a prior study, Feldman and Rosen (1985) computed the average value of employee benefits from participation in an ESOP, and found that "the average company contributed about 10.1% of payroll to its ESOP from 1980 to 1984." [10] The percent that we computed is lower than that—about 6% of participant wage and salary income. Counting only years in which contributions were made, this figure rises to about 8% (not reported in the table). However, when the return on allocated plan assets (which we calculated to be an average of 6%) [11] is added to the contribution fraction, total income from participation in a tax deduction ESOP was valued at about 12% of participants' wage and salary income, a figure that exceeds Feldman and Rosen's estimate.

Returns to employees from TCESOPs were also much smaller than for tax deduction plans—$53 versus $1,710—while returns on profit-sharing trusts per employee were $340.

Note that the variation of returns for ESOPs was much greater than that for profit-sharing plans; both had negative returns in some years, but the spread on returns per employee for TDESOPs was from a negative $4,547 to a positive $37,519 (the latter figure was highly unusual). Per employee returns for deferred-profit-sharing plans varied from a negative $1,047 to a positive $3,976. The profit-sharing plans therefore showed less downside risk but a lower overall average return per employee, consistent with normal risk/return patterns. Note that ESOPs are by nature riskier plans than profit-sharing plans because they are required to be relatively undiversified in their investment strategy.

In comparison, defined benefit pension plans in the responding companies provided considerably less income on average to plan participants. The average pension plan service cost per employee was $669, about 3% of wage and salary income.

As discussed above, it is unclear whether ESOP income should be viewed as an add-on to employee income. The fact that total TDESOP income as a fraction of wage and salary income was measured to be 12% as compared with

3% for defined benefit plans does not in and of itself imply that employees in firms with ESOPs make a higher total income. To the extent that ESOP income substitutes for basic wage and salary income, the added ESOP compensation may not really be "added," but rather may represent an alternative form of compensation.

We tested first to see whether the existence of an ESOP leads to greater income for employees. Then we tested the extent to which ESOP income adds to total income. The difference between these two tests is the following: even if ESOP income is "gravy," employees in ESOP companies may not make greater incomes than employees in non-ESOP companies if, for one of a variety of reasons, the company is operating under financial constraints (for example, because it is loss-making, because it is carrying high debt, because it is growing fast and trying to retain earnings to finance growth, etc.). However, even in such a case, the gravy theory requires that the dollar value of employee income varies with total ESOP income. This implies that two tests are necessary in order to adequately evaluate the gravy theory.

In order to conduct the first test, to see whether the existence of an ESOP leads to greater income for employees, we formulated a measure of total income (wage and salary income plus income from all employee plans, called TOTINIPE), and regressed this measure of income on three variables: ESOPEX, PSPEX and PPEX. ESOPEX took on the value "1" if there was a TDESOP in existence in the year and "0" otherwise, PSPEX took on the value "1" if there was a profit-sharing plan in existence in the year, and so on. We also regressed an alternate total income measure on these three variables: TOTIN2PE, which represented total per employee income excluding pension plan service cost. The purpose of replicating the regression with this alternative income measure was to try to gain observations, because creating this variable has fewer data requirements. However, because of the small number of observations and the nature of the independent variables (dummies taking on the values "1" or "0"), the regression suffered from multi-colinearity and could not be estimated for either dependent variable.

We therefore ran a series of three regressions for each of the two dependent variables, each with only two of the independent variables listed above. The only regressions that ran satisfactorily were those with ESOPEX and PSPEX on the right-hand side, and the results of these regressions are reported in Tables 7.10 and 7.11.

The coefficient of the variable ESOPEX was negative but insignificant in both regressions, implying that the ESOP firms in our sample did not afford greater incomes on average to their employees, while the coefficient for PSPEX was positive and significant at the 10% confidence level for both runs, indicating that profit-sharing firms did pay more.

The second step of the test was to substitute the value of income from employee plans in the regression where we previously had ESOPEX, PSPEX, and/ or PPEX. The ESOP and PSP coefficients changed sign but none of the new '

Table 7.9
Number of Employees, Number of Plan Participants, and Income from Plan Participation

VARIABLE	N	MEAN	MINIMUM	MAXIMUM
# OF EMPLOYEES IN COMPANY	429	20,981	100	500,000 *
DATA ON TAX DEDUCTION ESOPS				
NUMBER OF PARTICIPANTS IN TDESOP	58	2,519	294	14,000 *
CONTRIBUTIONS TO TAX DEDUCTION ESOP	102	$2,369,721	$0	$22,000,000 *
VALUE OF ALLOCATED SHARES IN TDESOP	91	$20,835,982	$0	$191,000,000 *
RETURN ON ALLOCATED SHARES IN TDESOP	75	$2,366,987	($68,179,002)	$64,000,000 *
TDESOP CONTRIBUTIONS PER EMPLOYEE	93	$548.75	$0.00	$3,237.07
TDESOP CONTRIBUTIONS PER PARTICIPANT	55	$1,306.01	$0.00	$17,500.00
TDESOP CONTBS/ALL W&S INCOME	55	0.047	0.00	0.16
TDESOP CONTBS/PARTICIPANT W&S INCOME	69	0.056	0.00	0.20
RETURN ON ALLOC SHRS IN TDESOP PER EMP	75	$1,710.58	($4,546.78)	$37,519.10
RETURN ON ALLOC SHRS IN TDESOP PER PART	52	$448.88	($5,238.89)	$3,003.35
TDESOP RETURN/ALL W&S INCOME	40	0.043	(0.316)	0.603
TDESOP RETURN/PARTICIPANT W&S INCOME	46	0.056	(0.440)	0.791

TOTAL TDESOP INCOME PER EMPLOYEE	68	$2,355.66	($3,061.40)	$37,519.
TOTAL TDESOP INCOME/ALL W&S INCOME	38	0.119	(0.220)	0.903
TOTAL TDESOP INCOME/PARTICIPANT W&S INC	43	0.172	0.000	1.183

DATA ON TAX CREDIT ESOPS

NUMBER OF PARTICIPANTS IN TCESOP	19	.	.	.
CONTRIBUTIONS TO TAX CREDIT ESOP	52	$4,995,562	$0	$76,000,000*
VALUE OF ALLOCATED SHARES IN TCESOP	42	$52,072,666	$0	$598,000,000*
RETURN ON ALLOCATED SHARES IN TCESOP	36	$20,605,341	($690,196)	$224,000,000*
TCESOP CONTRIBUTIONS PER EMPLOYEE	48	$52.77	$0.00	$206.98
TCESOP CONTRIBUTIONS PER PARTICIPANT	19	.	.	.
TCESOP CONTBS/ALL W&S INCOME	29	.	.	.
TCESOP CONTBS/PARTICIPANT W&S INCOME	34	0.001	0.000	0.005
RETURN ON ALLOC SHRS IN TCESOP PER EMP	36	$97.254	($46.028)	$641.205
RETURN ON ALLOC SHRS IN TCESOP PER PART	19	.	.	.
TCESOP RETURN/ALL W&S INCOME	16	.	.	.
TCESOP RETURN/PARTICIPANT W&S INCOME	13	.	.	.
TOTAL TCESOP INCOME PER EMPLOYEE	35	$133.511	($5.698)	$786.323
TOTAL TCESOP INCOME/ALL W&S INCOME	16	.	.	.

Table 7.9 continued

DATA ON PROFIT SHARING PLANS

VARIABLE	N	MEAN	MINIMUM	MAXIMUM
NUMBER OF PARTICIPANTS IN PROFSH PLAN	5	.	.	.
CONTRIBUTIONS TO CASH PROFSH PLAN	92	$19,525,307	$0	$636,000,000 *
CONTRIBUTIONS TO DEFERRED PROFSH PLAN	102	$404,882	$0	$5,800,000 *
PROFIT SHARING CONTBS	92	$20,039,668	$0	$636,000,000 *
VALUE OF ALLOCATED SHARES IN PST	79	$8,545,714	$0	$58,000,000 *
RETURN ON ALLOCATED SHARES IN PST	76	$1,458,882	($2,816,170)	$14,800,000 *
CASH PROFIT SHARING CONTBS PER EMPLOYEE	86	$277.11	$0.00	$1,984.73
CASH PROF SHARING CONTBS PER PARTICIPANT	5	.	.	.
CASH PROFSHAR CONTBS/W&S INCOME	32	0.019	0.000	0.077
CASH PROFSHAR CONTBS/PARTICIPANT W&S INC	0	.	.	.
DEFERRED PROF SHAR CONTBS PER EMPLOYEE	96	$100.45	$0.00	$1,055.21
DEFERRED PROF SHAR CONTBS PER PARTICIP	5	.	.	.
DEFERRED PROFSHAR CONTBS/W&S INCOME	32	0.001	0.000	0.029
DEFERRED PROFSHAR CONTBS/PARTICIPANT W&S	0	.	.	.
RETURN ON ALLOC SHRS IN PST PER EMP	74	$339.89	($1,046.90)	$3,975.95
RETURN ON ALLOC SHRS IN PST PER PART	5	.	.	.
PROFSH RETURN/ALL W&S INCOME	29	.	.	.
PROFSH RETURN/PARTICIPANT W&S INCOME	0	.	.	.

PROFIT SHARING INCOME PER EMPLOYEE	63	$896.89	($102.99)	$5,734.53
TOTAL INC FROM PROFSH/ALL W&S INCOME	29	.	.	.
TOTAL INC FROM PROFSH/PARTICIPANT W&S IN	0	.	.	.

DATA ON PENSION PLANS

NUMBER OF PARTICIPANTS IN PENSION PLAN	69	9,739	477	45,000*
PENSION PLAN SERVICE COST	66	$10,094,167	$153,855	$51,000,000*
PENSION PLAN SERV COST PER EMPLOYEE	58	$669.01	$64.71	$1,554.29
PENSION PLAN SERV COST PER PARTICIP	54	$939.69	$102.27	$2,656.09
NUMBER OF PARTICIPANTS IN PENSION PLAN	69	9,739.	477.	44,629.
PEN PLN SERV COST/ALL W&S INCOME	34	0.033	0.009	0.063
PEN PLN SERV COST/PARTICIPANT W&S INCOME	43	.	.	.

DATA ON NON-W&S INCOME AND ON TOTAL INCOME

TOTAL NON-WAGE & SALARY INCOME INCL PP	49	$12,869,486	$0	$50,000,000*
TOTAL NON-WAGE & SALARY INCOME EXCL PP	232	$10,895,536	($45,971,905)	$650,000,000*
TOTAL EMPLOYEE INCOME INCL PP	28	.	.	.
TOTAL EMPLOYEE INCOME EXCL PP	79	$162,140,515	$4,758,536	$2,500,000,000*

* Approximate value to retain confidentiality of respondent.
· Statistic not calculated because there were fewer than 30 available observations.

Table 7.10
Regression with Dependent Variable: Total Income Per Employee Including Income from Pension Plan

VARIABLE	PARAMETER ESTIMATE	T FOR H0: PARAMETER=0	PROB > |T|
INTERCEPT	$26,619	15.418	0.0001
ESOPEX1	-$3,282	-0.931	0.3607
PSPEX	$4,277	1.734	0.0953

variables proved to be significant. Taken at face value, this implies that profit-sharing firms pay more than other firms while ESOP firms do not; however in neither type of firm is there a demonstrable connection between individual employee compensation and firm performance. This result is not expected, and we therefore note that in larger sample sizes the coefficients might become significant. We note also that this analysis does not control for the degree of unionization in the industry, which could have a substantial impact on overall compensation. Because ESOPs have principally been instituted in non-union settings, the absence of a measured total income effect may reflect the industry distribution of ESOP firms rather than the absence of a gravy effect.

DO ESOPs IN PUBLIC COMPANIES AFFECT RETURN ON EQUITY OR SHARE PRICE?

There is an increasing body of research on the possible link between employee participation in ownership and management and company-level performance. However, there are few results for public companies. Due to difficulty in constructing a measure of value-added (which is necessary in order to estimate a production function) from the available data, we confine our attention here to assessing the impact of ESOPs on profitability; specifically, return on equity (ROE). Additionally, because of concern over the possibility that ESOPs may dilute share values, we analyze the impact of ESOPs on share price. To

Table 7.11
Regression with Dependent Variable: Total Income Per Employee Excluding Income from Pension Plan

VARIABLE	PARAMETER ESTIMATE	T FOR H0: PARAMETER=0	PROB > |T|
INTERCEPT	$25,622	15.047	0.0001
ESOPEX1	-$2,869	-0.825	0.4170
PSPEX	$4,366	1.794	0.0849

our knowledge, there has been no previous empirical evaluation of the dilution effect of ESOPs.

The variable return on equity was constructed using the annual COMPUSTAT variables Pretax Income (Data Item 122) divided by common plus preferred equity (Data Items 60 plus 56). (We also constructed an alternative version of ROE using only common equity in the denominator, and the results were virtually identical.)

A regression was estimated with the following right-hand side variables: whether the company had a tax deduction ESOP in year (TDESOPEX); whether the company had any form of formal participation in year (FORMPART); whether the company contributed or sold treasury stock to a tax deduction ESOP in the year (TDTREAS); percent of the company owned via a tax deduction ESOP trust (TDEOEQ); TDEOEQ interacted with FORMPART (TDEOEQIN); tax deduction ESOP income per employee (TDESINPE); whether the company had a tax credit ESOP in year (TCESOPEX); whether the company contributed or sold treasury stock to the TCESOP in the year (TCTREAS); percent of the company owned via a tax credit ESOP trust (TCEOEQ); TCEOEQ interacted with FORMPART (TCEOEQIN); tax credit ESOP income per employee (TCESINPE); whether the company had a profit-sharing plan in year (PSPEX); PSPEX interacted with FORMPART (PSPINT); whether the company had a pension plan in year (PPEX); and PPEX interacted with FORMPART (PPINT).

The regression results are presented in Table 7.12. Only one variable in this regression approaches significance, and that is FORMPART, which carries a negative sign and is significant at the 10% confidence level. This does not imply that formal participation lowers return on equity for two reasons: first, several other variables in the regression are interactions of formal participation with either employee ownership or the existence of employee plans. If the negative coefficient is meaningful, the appropriate conclusion would be that, *in the absence* of a plan for employee ownership, profit-sharing, or pension benefit, formal participation is associated with lower return on equity. Second, the limited number of observations makes it impossible to develop a model with causal implications. Significant coefficients should be interpreted as indicating only association, not causation.

On the basis of these results, we cannot conclude that employee ownership via ESOPs has a significant association with profitability in public companies. However, we repeat that significant results are difficult to obtain in small samples.

Our analysis of possible dilution effects was also conducted in a multiple regression framework. The dependent variable was the year-end deflated adjusted share price (ADJPRC), constructed by deflating the closing share price for the year by the Consumer Price Index (CPI) and dividing by the adjustment factor calculated by COMPUSTAT to reflect the effect of stock splits and stock dividends on share price. The independent variables used in the regression were the return on equity, the lagged value of the adjusted share price (LADJPRC),

The Expanding Role of ESOPs

Table 7.12
Regression with Dependent Variable: Return on Equity

VARIABLE	PARAMETER ESTIMATE	T FOR H0: PARAMETER=0	PROB > |T|
INTERCEP	0.35598933	4.183	0.0002
TDESOPEX	−0.143147	−0.731	0.4693
TDTREAS	0.13669619	0.593	0.5571
TDEOEQI	−0.981476	−0.238	0.8131
TDEOEQIN	2.97836090	0.532	0.5978
TDESINPE	−0.000268492	−0.649	0.5203
TCESOPEX	0.08143157	0.523	0.6040
TCTREAS	−0.0824411	−0.423	0.6749
TCEOEQ	−3.92673	−0.069	0.9453
TCEOEQIN	2.37747315	0.042	0.9665
TCESINPE	0.0003141441	0.398	0.6928
PSPEX	−0.0777353	−1.064	0.2946
PSPINT	−0.0887307	−0.206	0.8376
PPEX	−0.0281887	−0.309	0.7587
PPINT	0.15282885	1.121	0.2696
FORMPART	−0.209513	−1.724	0.0932

the lagged value of deflated contributions to a tax deduction ESOP (LTDCON), the lagged value of deflated contributions to a tax deduction ESOP effected with treasury shares (LTDTREAS), the lagged value of deflated contributions to a tax credit ESOP (LTCCON), and the lagged value of deflated contributions to a tax credit ESOP effected with treasury shares (LTCTREAS). This specification is based on the notion that movements in share price depend primarily on ROE performance, with adjustments for financial management (for example, sale or donation of stock to an ESOP).

The regression results are reported in Table 7.13. LTDCON did not exhibit any relationship with share price, implying that contributions to ESOPs do not in and of themselves dilute pre-existing shareholders' value. However, LTDTREAS was nearly significant at the 10% confidence level, implying an association between the contribution or sale of treasury shares and subsequent decline in share value. This is of course an intuitive result because a correctly specified model of share price does not predict any dilution effect when shares contributed to an ESOP are purchased from the market. As indicated above, in our sample this was the exclusive method of obtaining ESOP shares for two-thirds of the companies with ESOPs. Only one-third of the ESOP companies in our sample ever contributed or sold treasury shares to their ESOP.

Note that LTCTREAS was not close to significant, implying that contributions to tax credit ESOPs did not dilute share price even when the contribution was effected with treasury shares. This is because contributions to tax credit

Table 7.13
Dependent Variable: Adjusted Stock Price

VARIABLE	PARAMETER ESTIMATE	T FOR H0: PARAMETER=0	PROB > |T|
INTERCEP	-3.50925	-4.249	0.0001
ROE	16.91869987	4.796	0.0001
LADJPRC	1.17106114	45.324	0.0001
LTDCON	-1.88779E-09	-0.011	0.9912
LTDTREAS	-4.23975E-07	-1.600	0.1117
LTCCON	4.28870E-08	0.783	0.4350
LTCTREAS	-5.18554E-07	-0.692	0.4897

ESOPs were fully supported by tax deductions; it is actually somewhat surprising that share price was not *positively* affected by (non-treasury) contributions to tax credit ESOPs.

CONCLUSIONS

In this study an attempt is made to expand the knowledge about ESOPs in public companies, particularly with respect the issues of (1) the extent of compensation via ESOPs compared to compensation via other forms of pay in non-ESOP companies, (2) the impact of ESOPs on company earnings, and (3) whether there is a dilution effect from establishing an ESOP.

The analysis reported above provides no statistically significant findings on the second issue, although this may result from the relatively small sample size. On the other issues, however, the results are interesting and informative. ESOPs provide two to three times as much direct income to employees as other types of employee plans, although this may not reflect a net increase in the average compensation package. These findings are consistent with the notion that total employee compensation varies with a company's performance more so when the company has an ESOP than when it does not have one.

Share values are shown not to be diluted by the establishment of an ESOP when shares contributed to the trust are removed from the market. Companies that fund their ESOPs with treasury shares do appear to experience dilution effects.

NOTES

1. Joseph Blasi, *Employee Ownership: Revolution or Ripoff?* (Cambridge, MA: Ballinger, 1988).

2. Laurence J. Kotlikoff and Daniel E. Smit, *Pensions in the American Economy* (Chicago: The University of Chicago Press, 1983).

3. The increasing importance of takeover defenses has also been a factor in the growth of public ESOPs. However, it is difficult to measure the number of companies for which this was a primary motivation.

4. *The ESOP Survey, 1985, 1986* (Washington, D.C.: ESOP Association of America, 1985, 1986).

5. Putting together a time-series data base from the latter source would have gone considerably beyond the resources available to this project.

6. These are the primary, supplementary, tertiary, and over-the-counter files.

7. Daniel J. B. Mitchell, David Lewin, and Edward E. Lawler III. "Alternative Pay Systems, Firm Performance, and Productivity," in *Paying for Productivity: A Look at the Evidence,* Alan S. Blinder, ed. (Washington, DC: Brookings Institution, 1990), pp. 8–9.

8. It is often claimed that ESOPs have been afforded special tax advantages in relation to their leveraging ability. However, as discussed in Conte and Svejnar (1990), the Employee Retirement Income Security Act provided no tax incentives to ESOPs that were not previously provided to a broad variety of deferred compensation plans. The 1984 and 1986 amendments to the tax code do provide special treatment for ESOPs.

9. Adjusted stock price reflects changes in the price at which the stock trades as well as any stock splits or stock dividends that may occur. For every year, the COMPUSTAT data base provides an adjustment factor reflecting the effect of splits and dividends; the adjusted price is calculated by dividing the actual trading price at each point in time by the adjustment factor applicable to that time.

10. Jonathan Feldman and Corey Rosen, *Employee Benefits in Employee Stock Ownership Plans: How Does the Average Worker Fare?* (Oakland, CA: The National Center for Employee Ownership, 1985), p. 8.

11. While the dollar value of TDESOP returns per employee in this sample is about three times the value of per employee contributions, the fraction of wages and salaries represented by returns is measured the same as the fraction represented by contributions. This results from the pattern of nonresponse, which can cause large variations of this type in small samples.

APPENDIX I: SURVEY OF COMPENSATION PLANS

Your Name/Title   _____
Phone Number   (   ) _____
Company Name   _____
Total Employees   _____

In this survey, we wish to obtain some basic information about compensation plans in your company, over and above your normal wage and salary structure.

We are also interested in aspects of decision-making in your company which may be affected by the presence of some of these plans.

All of the information that you supply will be treated with strict confidence.

Question 1

Which of the following plans has your company sponsored at any point since 1980?

> _____   Employee Stock Ownership Plan (ESOP).
> _____   Profit Sharing Plan (PSP).
> _____   Stock Bonus Plan (SBP).
> _____   Stock Option Plan (SOP).
> _____   Stock Purchase Plan (SPP).
> _____   Pension Plan (PP).
> _____   None of the above.

For each of the above items that you checked, please complete the appropriate section which follows <u>along with Section VII</u>.

If you checked "None of the above", please complete Section VII only and return the questionnaire along with the other items requested in the cover letter to:

> Division of Business and Economic Research
> University of New Orleans
> Lakefront
> New Orleans, LA 70148
> Attn: M. Conte/K. Perra

A return envelope is provided for your convenience.

If you wish to receive a copy of our research report, please check here. _____

Thank you for your cooperation.

SECTION I

Questions about Your Employee Stock Ownership Plan (ESOP)

(I.1) When was your ESOP established? Year _____ Month _____

(I.2) When was your ESOP terminated? Year _____ Month _____
_____ Question not applicable; ESOP still exists.

(I.3) Type of ESOP: tax credit (TRASOP or PAYSOP)   _____
                           tax deduction (regular ESOP)   _____

(I.4) Has your company ever taken out a loan through your ESOP?

_____ Yes. When? _____ .   The original
                principal of the loan was $_____ .
_____ No.

(I.5) What are your company's contributions to the Employee Stock
Ownership Trust (ESOT) based on? (Please check all that apply.)

___ company profit   ___ amortization of loan
___ plan payroll   ___ there is no formula
___ other (please specify: _____)

(I.6) In what months of the year are contributions made to the ESOT?
_____ .

(I.7) Have contributions to your ESOT substituted partially or fully
for any of the following? (Please check all that apply.)

___ wages/salaries.   ___ a profit-sharing plan.
___ a pension plan.   ___ a stock bonus plan.
___ a stock purchase plan.   ___ a stock option plan.
___ no other compensation plan was diminished.

(I.8) What was the value of your company's contributions to the ESOT in
each year?

	Cash	Treasury Stock	Stock Purchased from Shareholders	Other Contributions
1980				
1981				
1982				
1983				
1984				
1985				
1986				
1987				

(I.9) What was the value of the ESOT at the end of each year? What
percent of the ESOT was invested in your company's own stock,
percent allocated to employee accounts and percent vested?

	ESOT Value	% invested in own stock	% allocated to employee accounts	% vested
1980				
1981				
1982				
1983				
1984				
1985				
1986				
1987				

SECTION II

Questions about Your Profit-Sharing Plan (PSP)

(II.1) When was your PSP established? Year _____ Month _____

(II.2) When was your PSP terminated? Year _____ Month _____
_____ Question not applicable; PSP still exists.

(II.3) Type of PSP (please check all that apply):

_____ cash   ___ for managers only
_____ deferred   ___ for nonmanagers only
_____ mixed cash and deferred ___ for managers and nonmanagers

(II.4) Since 1987, contributions to a PSP do not have to be based on your company's profits. Has your company changed the basis of its contributions to the PSP in this time?

___ No. Contributions are still on the basis of company profit.
___ Yes. Contributions are now made on the basis of _____
_____ .

(II.5) In what months of the year are contributions made to the PSP?
_____ .

(II.6) Did your Profit Sharing Plan partially or fully replace any of the following? (Please check all that apply.)

___ wages/salaries.   ___ an ESOP.
___ a pension plan.   ___ a stock option plan.
___ a stock purchase plan.   ___ a stock bonus plan.
___ no other compensation plan was diminished.

(II.7) What was the value of your company's contributions to the Profit Sharing Plan in each of the following years?

	Contributions to a Cash Plan	Contributions to a Deferred Plan
1980		
1981		
1982		
1983		
1984		
1985		
1986		
1987		

(II.8) If you have a deferred profit-sharing plan, what was the value of the Profit Sharing Trust (PST) at the end of each year? What percent of the PST was invested in your company's own stock, allocated to employee accounts and vested?

	PST Value	% invested in own stock	% allocated to employee accounts	% vested
1980				
1981				
1982				
1983				
1984				
1985				
1986				
1987				

SECTION III

Questions about Your Stock Bonus Plan (SBP)

(III.1) When was your SBP established? Year _____ Month _____

(III.2) When was your SBP terminated? Year _____ Month _____
_____ Question not applicable; SBP still exists.

(III.3) Type of SBP (please check all that apply):
_____ for managerial employees only.
_____ for nonmanagerial employees only.
_____ for both managerial & nonmanagerial employees.
_____ deferred (stock is placed in a trust for employees).
_____ nondeferred (stock is distributed directly to employees).
_____ part deferred and part nondeferred.

(III.4) What are your company's contributions to the SBP based on?
(Please check all that apply.)

___ company profit   ___ other (please specify:
___ payroll   _____)
___ there is no formula

(III.5) In what months of the year are contributions made to the SBP?
_____ .

(III.6) Did your Stock Bonus Plan partially or fully replace any of the
following? (Please check all that apply.)

___ wages/salaries.   ___ an ESOP.
___ a pension plan.   ___ a profit sharing plan.
___ a stock purchase plan. ___ a stock option plan.
___ no other compensation plan was diminished.

(III.7) What was the value of your company's contributions to the Stock
Bonus Plan in each of the following years?

	Contributions to Deferred Stock Bonus Plan	Contributions to Nondeferred Stock Bonus Plan
1980		
1981		
1982		
1983		
1984		
1985		
1986		
1987		

(III.8) If you have a deferred stock bonus plan, what was the value of
the Stock Bonus Trust (SBT) at the end of each year? What
percent of the SBT was invested in your company's own stock,
allocated to employee accounts and vested?

	SBT Value	% invested in own stock	% allocated to employee accounts	% vested
1980				
1981				
1982				
1983				
1984				
1985				
1986				
1987				

SECTION IV

Questions About Your Stock Option Plan (SOP)

(IV.1) When was your SOP established? Year _____ Month _____

(IV.2) When was your SOP terminated? Year _____ Month _____

_____ Question not applicable; SOP still exists.

(IV.3) Type of SOP (please check all that apply):

_____ for managerial employees only.

_____ for nonmanagerial employees only.

_____ for both managerial & nonmanagerial employees.

_____ deferred (when an option is exercised, stock is placed in trust for employees).

_____ nondeferred (when an option is exercised, stock is distributed directly to employees).

_____ part deferred and part nondeferred.

(IV.4) What is the availability of stock options based on? (Please check all that apply.)

____ company profit   ___ other (please specify:

____ individual performance   _____)

(IV.5) In what months of the year are options made available?

_____ .

(IV.6) Did your Stock Option Plan partially or fully replace any of the following? (Please check all that apply.)

____ wages/salaries.   ___ an ESOP.

____ a pension plan.   ___ a profit sharing plan.

____ a stock purchase plan.   ___ a stock bonus plan.

____ no other compensation plan was diminished.

(IV.7) What was the value of stock options exercised in each of the following years?

	Value of Options Exercised in a Nondeferred Plan	Value of Options Exercised in a Deferred Plan
1980		
1981		
1982		
1983		
1984		
1985		
1986		
1987		

SECTION V

Questions about Your Stock Purchase Plan (SPP)

(V.1) When was your SPP established? Year _____ Month _____

(V.2) When was your SPP terminated? Year _____ Month _____

_____ Question not applicable; SPP still exists.

(V.3) Type of SPP (please check all that apply):

_____ for managerial employees only.
_____ for nonmanagerial employees only.
_____ for both managerial & nonmanagerial employees.
_____ deferred (stock is placed in a trust for employees).
_____ nondeferred (stock is distributed directly to employees).
_____ part deferred and part nondeferred.

(V.4) Does your company provide a discounted price for its stock as part of the Stock Purchase Plan?

_____ Yes. What percent of the stock price does the company absorb? _____
_____ No.   Employees purchase stock at market or par value.

(V.5) In what months of the year are employees permitted to purchase company stock? _____ .

(V.6) Did your Stock Purchase Plan partially or fully replace any of the following? (Please check all that apply.)

_____ wages/salaries.   _____ an ESOP.
_____ a pension plan.   _____ a profit sharing plan.
_____ a stock bonus plan.   _____ a stock option plan.
_____ no other compensation plan was diminished.

(V.7) What was the market or par value of employee purchases of company stock in each of the following years?

	Value of Employee Purchases of Stock in a Nondeferred Plan	Value of Employee Purchases of Stock in a Deferred Plan
1980		
1981		
1982		
1983		
1984		
1985		
1986		
1987		

(V.8) If you have a deferred Stock Purchase Plan, what was the value of the Stock Purchase Trust (SPT) at the end of each year? What percent of the SPT was invested in your company's own stock?

	SPT Value	% invested in own stock		SPT Value	% invested in own stock
1980			1984		
1981			1985		
1982			1986		
1983			1987		

SECTION VI

Questions about Your Pension Plan (PP)

(VI.1) When was your PP established? Year _____ Month _____

(VI.2) When was your PP terminated? Year _____ Month _____

_____ Question not applicable; PP still exists.

(VI.3) Which of the following types of employees participate in your Pension Plan? (Please check all that apply.)

___ Managerial employees.
___ Nonmanagerial employees.

(VI.4) What are contributions to your PP based on? (Please check all that apply.)

___ Wages and salaries.
___ Company profits.
___ Other (please specify: _____).

(VI.5) In what months of the year are contributions made to the PP?
_____ .

(VI.6) Did your Pension Plan partially or fully replace any of the following? (Please check all that apply.)

___ wages/salaries.   ___ a profit-sharing plan.
___ an ESOP.   ___ a stock option plan.
___ a stock purchase plan.   ___ a stock bonus plan.
___ no other compensation plan was diminished.

(VI.7) What was the value of your company's contributions to the Pension Plan in each of the following years and the value of your pension fund at the end of each year. What percent of your pension fund was invested in your own company's stock at the end of each year?

	Pension Plan Contributions	Value of Pension Fund	% invested in own stock
1980	_____	_____	_____
1981	_____	_____	_____
1982	_____	_____	_____
1983	_____	_____	_____
1984	_____	_____	_____
1985	_____	_____	_____
1986	_____	_____	_____
1987	_____	_____	_____

(VI.8) What was the discounted vested and nonvested liability of your pension plan at the end of each year? Please indicate the discount rate used.

	Vested Liability	Nonvested Liability	Rate		Vested Liability	Nonvested Liability	Rate
1980	_____	_____	____	1984	_____	_____	____
1981	_____	_____	____	1985	_____	_____	____
1982	_____	_____	____	1986	_____	_____	____
1983	_____	_____	____	1987	_____	_____	____

SECTION VII

Questions about Decision-Making in Your Company

(VII.1) Do non-supervisory personnel participate in management decisions? If so, please indicate in what way(s):

_____ employee board representation. (Date begun: _____)
_____ advisory committees with employee representation. (Date begun: _____)
_____ other. (Please specify: _____) .
            (Date begun: _____).

(VII.2) If you have an Employee Stock Ownership Plan, may employees vote their ESOP shares on:

_____ all issues.
_____ only certain issues (please specify: _____).
_____ no issues.

(VII.3) In your opinion, how much say or influence do non-supervisory employees in your company have in the following areas? (Please circle appropriate letter for each area of decision-making).

A. They have no say.
B. They have no say but do receive information.
C. They are asked their opinion.
D. They make decisions together with management.
E. They make decisions alone.

Social Events..................................... A	B	C	D	E
Working Conditions.............................. A	B	C	D	E
The way workers perform their own jobs......... A	B	C	D	E
Pay and other compensation...................... A	B	C	D	E
Hiring, firing and other personnel decisions... A	B	C	D	E
Development of new products or services........ A	B	C	D	E
Strategic planning.............................. A	B	C	D	E

(VII.4) Are any of your employees covered under a union contract?

____ Yes. The approximate percentage of total employees covered by the union contract is _____ %.
____ No.

(VII.5) May union employees participate in any of the following plans? (Please answer yes or no for plans applicable to your company.)

_____ Employee Stock Ownership Plan.
_____ Profit Sharing Plan.
_____ Stock Bonus Plan.
_____ Stock Option Plan.
_____ Stock Purchase Plan.
_____ Pension Plan.

#######

Thank you for participating in this research.

APPENDIX II: ANALYSIS OF SELECTION AND RESPONSE BIAS

As discussed in the section on the data, surveys were sent to 712 companies, of which we had COMPUSTAT data for 646. These 646 companies can be divided into four groups:

Group A: Respondents from the NCEO list

Group B: Non-respondents from the NCEO list

Group C: Respondents among the matching companies

Group D: Non-respondents among the matching companies

This allowed for four comparisons:

Comparison 1: NCEO list versus matching companies (Groups A + B versus Groups C + D)

Comparison 2: Respondents versus non-respondents (Groups A + C versus Groups B + D)

Comparison 3: NCEO list respondents versus NCEO list non-respondents (Group A versus Group B)

Comparison 4: Matching company respondents versus matching company non-respondents (Group C versus Group D)

The comparison were based on all 130 data items supplied by COMPUSTAT for each of two years, 1980 and 1986. 1980 was the first year for which we requested survey data and 1986 was the last year of COMPUSTAT data for most of the companies at the time of selection. (1987 COMPUSTAT data are now available on the COMPUSTAT tapes, but a number of the originally selected companies are not represented on the new tapes. Therefore this recent data cannot be used to test for selection or response bias.)

Comparison 1 tests for selection bias, and none was found. The mean of each of the 130 data items was calculated for each of the samples (NCEO list versus matching companies) and Student's t statistic was calculated in order to test the hypothesis of no difference between the two means for each of these variables (See Table 7.AII.1). One would expect a purely random sample to result in a number of rejections of the hypothesis of similar means even if the means for the two samples were indeed similar. Therefore, it is important to count the number of rejections at a given level of confidence. There were no rejections of the hypothesis of equal means for Comparison 1 at even the .05 level of confidence, and we therefore conclude that our selection process of firms led to an unbiased *sample*. However, as shown below, response bias appears to have been a problem.

Absolute response bias is measured by Comparison 2, all respondents versus all non-respondents (see Table 7.AII.2). Of the 260 tests performed for this group, 17 reject the hypothesis of no difference in the means at the .005 level of confidence. If the means of these 260 variables were in fact the same for all respondents as they were for all non-respondents, only one to two of these rejections would have occurred. We therefore conclude that the respondents were different from the non-respondents.

The bias is observed in both subsamples, as indicated by Comparisons 3 and 4 (see Tables 7.AII.3 and 7.AII.4). In both subsamples there were in excess of 20 rejections of the null hypothesis of no difference between means for respondents and non-respondents. It is therefore difficult to know how the response bias may have affected the results.

This pattern of response indicates that future work should either seek to eliminate response bias by paring down the information request (i.e., supplementing the survey approach with more public data) or should gather enough observations to estimate a simultaneous model—one that can "explain" adoptions simultaneously while predicting its impact.

Table 7.AII.1
T Test for Difference in Means: Matching (510) Versus NCEO (114) Companies

VARIABLE	MATCHING COMPANIES' MEAN	NCEO COMPANIES' MEAN	T-VALUE	DEGREES OF FREEDOM	TEST VALUE
CASH & SHORT TERM INVESTMENTS--1980--MM$	96465	90406	0.1637	626	1
RECEIVABLES--1980--MM$	162	113	1.4167	626	1
INVEN-RIES--1980--MM$	154	95	1.8234	626	2
CURRENT ASSETS (-TAL)--1980--MM$	375	256	1.4748	626	1
CURRENT LIABILITIES (-TAL)--1980--MM$	244	181	0.9747	626	1
ASSETS/(LIABS+NET WORTH)--1980--MM$	1186	957	0.8141	626	1
PLANT (GROSS)--1980--MM$	702	539	0.7934	626	1
PLANT (NET)--1980--MM$	428	338	0.6767	626	1
LONG TERM DEBT (-TAL)--1980--MM$	156	158	-0.0358	626	1
PEFERRED S-CK @ LIQ VALUE--1980--MM$	13	16	-0.4298	626	1
COMMON EQUITY (TANGIBLE)--1980--MM$	395	257	1.4815	626	1
SALES (NET)--1980--MM$	1258181	948703	5.3785	626	4
OPER INCOME BEFORE DEPREC--1980--MM$	147	91	1.2217	626	1
DEPRECIATION & AMORTIZATION--1980--MM$	41	34	0.6386	626	1
INTEREST EXPENSE--1980--MM$	38	35	0.2033	626	1
INCOME TAXES (-TAL)--1980--MM$	47	30	1.0158	626	1
SPECIAL ITEMS--1980--MM$	-0	3	-1.1517	626	1
INC BEF EXTRA & DISC OPER--1980--MM$	58	31	1.0738	626	1
PREFERRED DIVIDENDS--1980--MM$	1	1	-0.5355	626	1
AVAIL FOR COM AFT ADJ--1980--MM$	57	30	1.0782	626	1
COMMON DIVIDENDS--1980--MM$	23	13	1.5040	626	1
PRICE (HIGH)--1980--$ & 8THS	24	27	-1.1353	626	1
PRICE (LOW)--1980--$ & 8THS	13	14	-0.9134	626	1
PRICE (CLOSE)--1980--$ & 8THS	21	23	-1.0596	626	1
COMMON SHARES OUTSTANDING--1980--M	13252	11127	0.7709	626	1
DIVIDENDS PR SHARE--1980--$ & @	726	744	-0.2203	626	1
ADJUST FAC-R (CUM)(RATIO)--1980	1909019	2156298	-9.6608	626	4
COMMON SHARES TRADED--1980--M	5474	4502	0.9676	626	1
EMPLOYEES--1980--M	11	7	2.1895	626	2
CAPITAL EXPENDITURES--1980--MM$	103	82	0.5982	626	1
INVEST & ADVANCES (EQ METH)--1980--MM$	38	27	0.8284	626	1
INVEST & ADVANCES (OTHER)--1980--MM$	22	10	1.2407	626	1
INTANGIBLES--1980--MM$	8	7	0.3726	626	1
DEBT IN CURRENT LIABILITIES--1980--MM$	85	53	1.2185	626	1
DEF TAX & INVEST CRED (B/S)--1980--MM$	56	38	0.8193	626	1
RET EARNINGS (C/S OUTSTAND)--1980--MM$	328	193	1.6710	626	2
INVESTED CAPITAL (-TAL)--1980--MM$	572739	425339	3.4541	626	4
MINORITY INTEREST (B/S)--1980--MM$	7	3	1.3859	626	1
CONVERTIBLE DEBT & PREF S-CK--1980--MM$	7	10	-0.6822	626	1
COMM SHARES RES FOR CONVER--1980--M	1	1	-0.5535	626	1
COST OF GOODS SOLD--1980--MM$	930	706	0.8103	626	1
LABOR & RELATED EXPENSE--1980--MM$	163	128	0.6533	626	1
PENSION & RETIREMENT EXPENSE--1980--MM$	16	13	0.5720	626	1
DEBT DUE IN 1 YEAR--1980--MM$	7	10	-0.6999	626	1
ADVERTISING EXPENSE--1980--MM$	9	4	1.7890	626	2
RESEARCH & DEVEL EXPENSE--1980--MM$	17	9	1.5456	626	1
RENTAL EXPENSE--1980--MM$	13	8	1.5300	626	1
EXTRAORD ITEMS & DISC OPER--1980--MM$	-0	-1	0.8175	626	1
MINORITY INTEREST (INC ACCT)--1980--MM$	1	0	1.4799	626	1
DEFERRED TAXES (INC ACCT)--1980--MM$	9	8	0.1460	626	1
INVEST TAX CREDIT (INC ACCT)--1980--MM$	4	3	0.6520	626	1
TAX LOSS CARRY FORWARD--1980--MM$	4	9	-0.5140	626	1
EARNINGS PER SHARE (PRIMARY)--1980--MM$	2	2	-0.3639	626	1
COMM SHARES USED-COMP EPS--1980--MM$	13	11	0.7220	626	1
UNCNSOL SUBSID EQ IN EARNINGS--1980--MM$	6.9	1.8	1.8388	626	2
PREF S-CK @ REDEMPTION VALUE--1980--MM$	13.3	18.1	-0.5446	626	1
EPS (FULLY DILUTED)--1980--$ & @	2.1	2.5	-1.5019	626	1
EPS (EX EXTRA/DISC)--1980--$ & @	2.1	2.3	-0.5014	626	1
INVEN-RY VALUATION METHOD--1980	36.6	45.1	-0.3700	626	1
COMMON EQUITY (AS REPORTED)--1980--MM$	407.9	268.1	1.4699	626	1

Table 7.AII.1 continued

VARIABLE	MATCHING COMPANIES' MEAN	NCEO COMPANIES' MEAN	T-VALUE	DEGREES OF FREEDOM	TEST VALUE
NONOPERATING INCOME/EXPENSE--1980--MM$	19.2	13.7	0.8572	626	1
INTEREST INCOME--1980--MM$	27.9	27.7	0.0120	626	1
INCOME TAXES (FEDERAL)--1980--MM$	13.9	12.2	0.3178	626	1
INCOME TAXES (FOREIGN)--1980--MM$	20.6	3.5	2.2320	626	2
AMORTIZATION OF INTANGIBLES--1980--MM$	0.3	0.1	1.2752	626	1
DISCONTINUED OPERATIONS--1980--MM$	-0.2	-0.1	-0.2884	626	1
RECEIVABLES (EST DOUBTFUL)--1980--MM$	2.7	2.2	0.6928	626	1
CURRENT ASSETS (OTHER)--1980--MM$	16.5	11.3	0.9237	626	1
ASSETS (OTHER)--1980--MM$	21.4	17.7	0.5487	626	1
ACCOUNTS PAYABLE--1980--MM$	102.6	79.3	0.7490	626	1
INCOME TAXES PAYABLE--1980--MM$	27.5	14.0	1.4992	626	1
CURRENT LIABILITIES (OTHER)--1980--MM$	79.3	63.3	0.6616	626	1
CONSTRUCTION IN PROGRESS--1980--MM$	15.9	9.4	1.3420	626	1
DEFERRED TAXED (B/S)--1980--MM$	54.0	37.6	0.7777	626	1
LIABILITIES (OTHER)--1980--MM$	28.5	22.1	0.5885	626	1
RAW MATERIALS--1980--MM$	26.8	11.7	2.4449	626	3
WORK IN PROGRESS--1980--MM$	20.7	11.8	0.8991	626	1
FINISHED GOODS--1980--MM$	29.6	14.2	1.8011	626	2
DEBT (CONVERTIBLE)--1980--MM$	4.7	7.2	-0.8486	626	1
DEBT (SUBORDINATED)--1980--MM$	4.0	1.4	1.6218	626	1
DEBT (NOTES)--1980--MM$	41.3	48.3	-0.4422	626	1
DEBT (DEBENTURES)--1980--MM$	52.0	38.3	0.8439	626	1
DEBT (OTHER LONG TERM)--1980--MM$	30.4	39.8	-0.5460	626	1
DEBT (CAP LEASE OBLIGATIONS)--1980--MM$	10.3	15.0	-0.7581	626	1
COMMON S-CK--1980--MM$	37.0	25.8	1.1382	626	1
TREAS S-CK (-TAL $ AMOUNT)--1980--MM$	7.9	2.3	2.0335	626	2
TREASRY S-CK (# COMMON SHARES)--1980--M	691.6	132.2	1.5516	626	1
PRES VALUE OF NONCAP LEASES--1980--MM$	0.0	-0.0	1.4142	626	1
UNFUN PENSION COSTS(VEST BEN)--1980--MM$	5.7	17.4	-1.0261	626	1
UNFUN PENSION COSTS(PAST SRV)--1980--MM$	0.7	5.7	-1.0433	626	1
DEBT MATURING IN 2ND YEAR--1980--MM$	10.3	9.0	0.4522	626	1
DEBT MATURING IN 3RD YEAR--1980--MM$	11.2	11.3	-0.0398	626	1
DEBT MATURING IN 4TH YEAR--1980--MM$	10.5	9.8	0.2309	626	1
DEBT MATURING IN 5TH YEAR--1980--MM$	15.5	10.9	1.2471	626	1
MIN RENT COMMIT 5 YRS (-TAL)--1980--MM$	21.8	15.6	1.0392	626	1
MIN RENT COMMITMENT IN 1 YEAR--1980--MM$	6.3	4.5	1.0454	626	1
RET EARNINGS (UNRESTRICTED)--1980--MM$	55.5	102.5	-0.9016	626	1
ORDER BACKLOG--1980--MM$	164.2	93.1	1.1335	626	1
RET EARNINGS (RESTATEMENT)--1980--MM$	0.5	0.1	1.1630	626	1
SHAREHOLDERS (COMMON)--1980--M	14786.8	12329.2	0.6874	626	1
INT EXPENSE ON LONG TERM DEBT--1980--MM$	2.4	5.3	-0.8977	626	1
EXCISE TAXES--1980--MM$	14.1	5.7	0.7265	626	1
DEPREC EXPENSE (SCHED V)--1980--MM$	37.1	29.4	0.7162	626	1
BORROWINGS (AVG SHORT TERM)--1980--MM$	21.4	12.1	2.0476	626	2
INT RATE (AVG ON SHORT TERM)--1980--%	6.7	8.2	-1.6612	626	2
UNREMIT EARNS OF SUBS (SCFC)--1980--MM$	-1.1	-0.5	-0.4995	626	1
SALE OF P/P/E (SCFC)--1980--MM$	4.5	4.0	0.3288	626	1
SALE OF COM/PREF S-CK (SCFC)--1980--MM$	6.3	7.9	-0.4471	626	1
SALE OF INVESTMENTS (SCFC)--1980--MM$	1	2	-0.8541	626	1
-TAL FUNDS FROM OPER (SCFC)--1980--MM$	108	68	1.0226	626	1
ISSUANCE OF L-T DEBT (SCFC)--1980--MM$	32	45	-0.6239	626	1
-TAL SOURCES OF FUNDS (SCFC)--1980--MM$	160	131	0.6114	626	1
INCR IN INVESTMENTS (SCFC)--1980--MM$	5	5	-0.0922	626	1
REDUCTION OF L-T DEBT (SCFC)--1980--MM$	18	18	-0.0470	626	1
PUR OF COMM/PREF S-CK (SCFC)--1980--MM$	3	3	0.3546	626	1
-TAL USES OF FUNDS (SCFC)--1980--MM$	161	128	0.6074	626	1
SALES (RESTATED)--1980--MM$	871841	519781	10.8583	626	4
INC BEF EXTRA/DISC OPER (RE)--1980--MM$	39	7	1.6020	626	1
EPS (PRIM) (RESTATED)--1980--MM$	1	1	-0.1473	626	1
ASSETS (-TAL) (RESTATED)--1980--MM$	642915	405333	2.5558	626	3
WORKING CAPITAL (RESTATED)--1980--MM$	76	52	1.1903	626	1

Table 7.AII.1 continued

VARIABLE	MATCHING COMPANIES' MEAN	NCEO COMPANIES' MEAN	T-VALUE	DEGREES OF FREEDOM	TEST VALUE
PRETAX INCOME (RESTATED)--1980--MM$	72	15	1.9130	626	2
INC BEF EXT/DISC OPER (SCFC)--1980--MM$	56	27	1.1495	626	1
EXTRA ITEMS/DISC OPER (SCFC)--1980--MM$	0	0	0.6532	626	1
DEPREC & AMORTIZ (SCFC)--1980--MM$	41	36	0.3840	626	1
DEFERRED TAXES (SCFC)--1980--MM$	9	8	0.2715	626	1
CASH DIVIDENDS (SCFC)--1980--MM$	23	13	1.5030	626	1
CAPITAL EXPENDITURES (SCFC)--1980--MM$	92	79	0.3503	626	1
ACQUISITIONS (SCFC)--1980--MM$	9	4	1.0014	626	1
PREF S-CK (CARRYING VALUE)--1980--MM$	8	12	-0.6368	626	1
CASH & SHORT TERM INVESTMENTS--1986--MM$	161935	152305	0.1813	626	1
RECEIVABLES--1986--MM$	186	165	0.4031	626	1
INVEN-RIES--1986--MM$	174	100	2.1385	626	2
CURRENT ASSETS (-TAL)--1986--MM$	428	342	0.8919	626	1
CURRENT LIABILITIES (-TAL)--1986--MM$	318	274	0.5133	626	1
ASSETS/(LIABS+NET WORTH)--1986--MM$	2166	1732	0.8836	626	1
PLANT (GROSS)--1986--MM$	1122	865	0.7859	626	1
PLANT (NET)--1986--MM$	664	515	0.7773	626	1
LONG TERM DEBT (-TAL)--1986--MM$	313	286	0.3371	626	1
PEFERRED S-CK @ LIQ VALUE--1986--MM$	19	15	0.5978	626	1
COMMON EQUITY (TANGIBLE)--1986--MM$	496	326	1.4612	626	1
SALES (NET)--1986--MM$	1470081	1309460	1.6230	626	1
OPER INCOME BEFORE DEPREC--1986--MM$	188	144	0.8688	626	1
DEPRECIATION & AMORTIZATION--1986--MM$	72	58	0.6663	626	1
INTEREST EXPENSE--1986--MM$	65	58	0.3548	626	1
INCOME TAXES (-TAL)--1986--MM$	40	33	0.5100	626	1
SPECIAL ITEMS--1986--MM$	-14	-8	-0.6345	626	1
INC BEF EXTRA & DISC OPER--1986--MM$	48	42	0.2214	626	1
PREFERRED DIVIDENDS--1986--MM$	2	1	0.1635	626	1
AVAIL FOR COM AFT ADJ--1986--MM$	46	41	0.2127	626	1
COMMON DIVIDENDS--1986--MM$	32	51	-0.8266	626	1
PRICE (HIGH)--1986--$ & 8THS	30	30	0.0758	626	1
PRICE (LOW)--1986--$ & 8THS	19	19	-0.3497	626	1
PRICE (CLOSE)--1986--$ & 8THS	24	24	-0.0354	626	1
COMMON SHARES OUTSTANDING--1986--M	24782	21048	0.9765	626	1
DIVIDENDS PR SHARE--1986--$ & @	586	566	0.2770	626	1
ADJUST FAC-R (CUM)(RATIO)--1986	1111734	1068362	1.3794	626	1
COMMON SHARES TRADED--1986--M	18837	17705	0.3566	626	1
EMPLOYEES--1986--M	10	9	0.8081	626	1
CAPITAL EXPENDITURES--1986--MM$	108	88	0.6734	626	1
INVEST & ADVANCES (EQ METH)--1986--MM$	70	46	0.8720	626	1
INVEST & ADVANCES (OTHER)--1986--MM$	237	70	2.2212	626	2
INTANGIBLES--1986--MM$	51	34	1.0377	626	1
DEBT IN CURRENT LIABILITIES--1986--MM$	208	159	0.5445	626	1
DEF TAX & INVEST CRED (B/S)--1986--MM$	103	77	0.6402	626	1
RET EARNINGS (C/S OUTSTAND)--1986--MM$	406	252	1.4855	626	1
INVESTED CAPITAL (-TAL)--1986--MM$	870279	617574	5.0044	626	4
MINORITY INTEREST (B/S)--1986--MM$	10	6	1.0730	626	1
CONVERTIBLE DEBT & PREF S-CK--1986--MM$	17	16	0.0397	626	1
COMM SHARES RES FOR CONVER--1986--M	3	2	1.3686	626	1
COST OF GOODS SOLD--1986--MM$	1008	895	0.4184	626	1
LABOR & RELATED EXPENSE--1986--MM$	174	148	0.3479	626	1
PENSION & RETIREMENT EXPENSE--1986--MM$	8	5	1.0276	626	1
DEBT DUE IN 1 YEAR--1986--MM$	19	28	-0.8851	626	1
ADVERTISING EXPENSE--1986--MM$	15	8	1.2780	626	1
RESEARCH & DEVEL EXPENSE--1986--MM$	28	17	1.0996	626	1
RENTAL EXPENSE--1986--MM$	19	14	1.4499	626	1
EXTRAORD ITEMS & DISC OPER--1986--MM$	1	3	-0.7225	626	1
MINORITY INTEREST (INC ACCT)--1986--MM$	1	0	1.5278	626	1
DEFERRED TAXES (INC ACCT)--1986--MM$	9	23	-1.0808	626	1
INVEST TAX CREDIT (INC ACCT)--1986--MM$	2	2	0.9815	626	1

Table 7.AII.1 continued

VARIABLE	MATCHING COMPANIES' MEAN	NCEO COMPANIES' MEAN	T-VALUE	DEGREES OF FREEDOM	TEST VALUE
TAX LOSS CARRY FORWARD--1986--MM$	23	21⁵	0.1326	626	1
EARNINGS PER SHARE (PRIMARY)--1986--MM$	1	1	0.4966	626	1
COMM SHARES USED-COMP EPS--1986--MM$	24	22	0.4927	626	1
UNCNSOL SUBSID EQ IN EARNINGS--1986--MM$	9	4	1.1913	626	1
PREF S-CK @ REDEMPTION VALUE--1986--MM$	18	14	0.6626	626	1
EPS (FULLY DILUTED)--1986--$ & @	1	1	0.5353	626	1
EPS (EX EXTRA/DISC)--1986--$ & @	1	1	0.5639	626	1
INVEN-RY VALUATION METHOD--1986	35	42	-0.3150	626	1
COMMON EQUITY (AS REPORTED)--1986--MM$	554	364	1.5869	626	1
NONOPERATING INCOME/EXPENSE--1986--MM$	23	22	0.0834	626	1
INTEREST INCOME--1986--MM$	47	45	0.0828	626	1
INCOME TAXES (FEDERAL)--1986--MM$	12	2	1.3608	626	1
INCOME TAXES (FOREIGN)--1986--MM$	13	4	1.8434	626	2
AMORTIZATION OF INTANGIBLES--1986--MM$	1	1	-0.0635	626	1
DISCONTINUED OPERATIONS--1986--MM$	0	2	-0.5963	626	1
RECEIVABLES (EST DOUBTFUL)--1986--MM$	4	3	0.9512	626	1
CURRENT ASSETS (OTHER)--1986--MM$	26	24	0.2460	626	1
ASSETS (OTHER)--1986--MM$	57	56	0.0700	626	1
ACCOUNTS PAYABLE--1986--MM$	233	167	1.0301	626	1
INCOME TAXES PAYABLE--1986--MM$	24	9	2.3527	626	3
CURRENT LIABILITIES (OTHER)--1986--MM$	125	96	0.8553	626	1
CONSTRUCTION IN PROGRESS--1986--MM$	15	15	0.0053	626	1
DEFERRED TAXED (B/S)--1986--MM$	102	76	0.6367	626	1
LIABILITIES (OTHER)--1986--MM$	102	74	0.8640	626	1
RAW MATERIALS--1986--MM$	25	13	1.7682	626	2
WORK IN PROGRESS--1986--MM$	22	10	1.6027	626	1
FINISHED GOODS--1986--MM$	35	15	2.4763	626	3
DEBT (CONVERTIBLE)--1986--MM$	10	11	-0.2964	626	1
DEBT (SUBORDINATED)--1986--MM$	21	14	0.7709	626	1
DEBT (NOTES)--1986--MM$	105	76	1.2263	626	1
DEBT (DEBENTURES)--1986--MM$	76	41	1.8946	626	2
DEBT (OTHER LONG TERM)--1986--MM$	66	55	0.5569	626	1
DEBT (CAP LEASE OBLIGATIONS)--1986--MM$	11	10	0.2593	626	1
COMMON S-CK--1986--MM$	50	35	1.4238	626	1
TREAS S-CK (-TAL $ AMOUNT)--1986--MM$	46	40	0.2383	626	1
TREASRY S-CK (# COMMON SHARES)--1986--M	1472	1344	0.2022	626	1
PRES VALUE OF NONCAP LEASES--1986--MM$	-0	-0		626	1
UNFUN PENSION COSTS(VEST BEN)--1986--MM$	2	12	-1.2969	626	1
UNFUN PENSION COSTS(PAST SRV)--1986--MM$	0	-0	1.1314	626	1
DEBT MATURING IN 2ND YEAR--1986--MM$	20	19	0.2385	626	1
DEBT MATURING IN 3RD YEAR--1986--MM$	18	23	-0.6674	626	1
DEBT MATURING IN 4TH YEAR--1986--MM$	19	18	0.1943	626	1
DEBT MATURING IN 5TH YEAR--1986--MM$	20	18	0.3984	626	1
MIN RENT COMMIT 5 YRS (-TAL)--1986--MM$	39	39	-0.0268	626	1
MIN RENT COMMITMENT IN 1 YEAR--1986--MM$	11	12	-0.4873	626	1
RET EARNINGS (UNRESTRICTED)--1986--MM$	45	111	-1.1319	626	1
ORDER BACKLOG--1986--MM$	184	168	0.1391	626	1
RET EARNINGS (RESTATEMENT)--1986--MM$	-1	-1	0.2891	626	1
SHAREHOLDERS (COMMON)--1986--M	13108	10533	0.8742	626	1
INT EXPENSE ON LONG TERM DEBT--1986--MM$	3	9	-0.8466	626	1
EXCISE TAXES--1986--MM$	16	7	0.8042	626	1
DEPREC EXPENSE (SCHED V)--1986--MM$	64	51	0.6637	626	1
BORROWINGS (AVG SHORT TERM)--1986--MM$	36	48	-0.4678	626	1
INT RATE (AVG ON SHORT TERM)--1986--%	4	4	-0.0691	626	1
UNREMIT EARNS OF SUBS (SCFC)--1986--MM$	-2	-3	0.3031	626	1
SALE OF P/P/E (SCFC)--1986--MM$	8	8	0.1209	626	1
SALE OF COM/PREF S-CK (SCFC)--1986--MM$	12	20	-1.2103	626	1
SALE OF INVESTMENTS (SCFC)--1986--MM$	75	41	1.0732	626	1
-TAL FUNDS FROM OPER (SCFC)--1986--MM$	156	121	0.7426	626	1
ISSUANCE OF L-T DEBT (SCFC)--1986--MM$	110	80	1.0132	626	1

134

Table 7.AII.1 continued

VARIABLE	MATCHING COMPANIES' MEAN	NCEO COMPANIES' MEAN	T-VALUE	DEGREES OF FREEDOM	TEST VALUE ·
-TAL SOURCES OF FUNDS (SCFC)--1986--MM$	427	314	1.2793	626	1
INCR IN INVESTMENTS (SCFC)--1986--MM$	116	46	1.7197	626	2
REDUCTION OF L-T DEBT (SCFC)--1986--MM$	63	39	1.3932	626	1
PUR OF COMM/PREF S-CK (SCFC)--1986--MM$	22	17	0.5800	626	1
-TAL USES OF FUNDS (SCFC)--1986--MM$	418	303	1.3766	626	1
SALES (RESTATED)--1986--MM$	1420158	1216057	2.1809	626	2
INC BEF EXTRA/DISC OPER (RE)--1986--MM$	45	35	0.4208	626	1
EPS (PRIM) (RESTATED)--1986--MM$	1	1	0.4774	626	1
ASSETS (-TAL) (RESTATED)--1986--MM$	1977613	1474695	5.6621	626	4
WORKING CAPITAL (RESTATED)--1986--MM$	100	57	2.1683	626	2
PRETAX INCOME (RESTATED)--1986--MM$	88	70	0.5226	626	1
INC BEF EXT/DISC OPER (SCFC)--1986--MM$	46	35	0.4536	626	1
EXTRA ITEMS/DISC OPER (SCFC)--1986--MM$	9	3	1.0266	626	1
DEPREC & AMORTIZ (SCFC)--1986--MM$	73	58	0.7188	626	1
DEFERRED TAXES (SCFC)--1986--MM$	3	18	-1.2703	626	1
CASH DIVIDENDS (SCFC)--1986--MM$	33	50	-0.7989	626	1
CAPITAL EXPENDITURES (SCFC)--1986--MM$	95	81	0.4718	626	1
ACQUISITIONS (SCFC)--1986--MM$	34	14	2.2456	626	2
PREF S-CK (CARRYING VALUE)--1986--MM$	14	11	0.4142	626	1

Table 7.AII.2
T Test for Difference in Means: Respondents Versus Non-respondents, in
Matching (510) and NCEO (114) Companies

VARIABLE	RESPONDENTS' MEAN	NON RESPONDENTS' MEAN	T-VALUE	DEGREES OF FREEDOM	TEST VALUE
CASH & SHORT TERM INVESTMENTS--1980--MM$	84312	96259	-0.2096	626	1
RECEIVABLES--1980--MM$	193	150	0.4940	626	1
INVEN-RIES--1980--MM$	284	131	1.1179	626	1
CURRENT ASSETS (-TAL)--1980--MM$	580	334	0.8607	626	1
CURRENT LIABILITIES (-TAL)--1980--MM$	456	214	0.9502	626	1
ASSETS/(LIABS+NET WORTH)--1980--MM$	1287	1132	0.2512	626	1
PLANT (GROSS)--1980--MM$	719	668	0.1212	626	1
PLANT (NET)--1980--MM$	418	411	0.0286	626	1
LONG TERM DEBT (-TAL)--1980--MM$	165	156	0.1190	626	1
PEFERRED S-CK @ LIQ VALUE--1980--MM$	40	11	0.9489	626	1
COMMON EQUITY (TANGIBLE)--1980--MM$	424	365	0.2776	626	1
SALES (NET)--1980--MM$	1766308	1154233	4.4457	626	4
OPER INCOME BEFORE DEPREC--1980--MM$	64	142	-1.6029	626	1
DEPRECIATION & AMORTIZATION--1980--MM$	63	38	0.5926	626	1
INTEREST EXPENSE--1980--MM$	42	37	0.2236	626	1
INCOME TAXES (-TAL)--1980--MM$	-1	48	-2.6341	626	4
SPECIAL ITEMS--1980--MM$	0	0	0.0163	626	1
INC BEF EXTRA & DISC OPER--1980--MM$	-4	58	-1.5268	626	1
PREFERRED DIVIDENDS--1980--MM$	2	1	0.8410	626	1
AVAIL FOR COM AFT ADJ--1980--MM$	-5	57	-1.5250	626	1
COMMON DIVIDENDS--1980--MM$	19	21	-0.1888	626	1
PRICE (HIGH)--1980--$ & 8THS	23	25	-0.6020	626	1
PRICE (LOW)--1980--$ & 8THS	13	13	-0.3036	626	1
PRICE (CLOSE)--1980--$ & 8THS	19	21	-0.9510	626	1
COMMON SHARES OUTSTANDING--1980--M	11015	13012	-0.5314	626	1
DIVIDENDS PR SHARE--1980--$ & @	804	723	0.6381	626	1
ADJUST FAC-R (CUM)(RATIO)--1980	2248894	1930347	41.4530	626	4
COMMON SHARES TRADED--1980--M	5736	5258	0.2923	626	1
EMPLOYEES--1980--M	21	10	1.0223	626	1
CAPITAL EXPENDITURES--1980--MM$	108	99	0.1482	626	1
INVEST & ADVANCES (EQ METH)--1980--MM$	133	28	1.4095	626	1
INVEST & ADVANCES (OTHER)--1980--MM$	10	21	-1.0886	626	1
INTANGIBLES--1980--MM$	8	8	-0.1163	626	1
DEBT IN CURRENT LIABILITIES--1980--MM$	107	77	0.4990	626	1
DEF TAX & INVEST CRED (B/S)--1980--MM$	45	53	-0.2846	626	1
RET EARNINGS (C/S OUTSTAND)--1980--MM$	371	297	0.3792	626	1
INVESTED CAPITAL (-TAL)--1980--MM$	643495	537403	3.2843	626	4
MINORITY INTEREST (B/S)--1980--MM$	7	7	0.1404	626	1
CONVERTIBLE DEBT & PREF S-CK--1980--MM$	13	7	0.8237	626	1
COMM SHARES RES FOR CONVER--1980--M	2	1	0.6762	626	1
COST OF GOODS SOLD--1980--MM$	1495	839	0.8169	626	1
LABOR & RELATED EXPENSE--1980--MM$	382	138	0.8649	626	1
PENSION & RETIREMENT EXPENSE--1980--MM$	30	14	0.9296	626	1
DEBT DUE IN 1 YEAR--1980--MM$	9	8	0.3576	626	1
ADVERTISING EXPENSE--1980--MM$	19	8	0.8840	626	1
RESEARCH & DEVEL EXPENSE--1980--MM$	54	12	1.1678	626	1
RENTAL EXPENSE--1980--MM$	11	12	-0.1305	626	1
EXTRAORD ITEMS & DISC OPER--1980--MM$	-1	-0	-0.4614	626	1
MINORITY INTEREST (INC ACCT)--1980--MM$	1	1	0.1869	626	1
DEFERRED TAXES (INC ACCT)--1980--MM$	3	9	-2.5696	626	3
INVEST TAX CREDIT (INC ACCT)--1980--MM$	2	4	-2.3728	626	3
TAX LOSS CARRY FORWARD--1980--MM$	4	5	-0.2985	626	1
EARNINGS PER SHARE (PRIMARY)--1980--MM$	2	2	-1.1495	626	1
COMM SHARES USED-COMP EPS--1980--MM$	11.5	13.0	-0.3564	626	1
UNCNSOL SUBSID EQ IN EARNINGS--1980--MM$	14.9	5.2	1.1107	626	1
PREF S-CK @ REDEMPTION VALUE--1980--MM$	42.8	11.9	0.9429	626	1
EPS (FULLY DILUTED)--1980--$ & @	1.9	2.2	-0.7341	626	1

Table 7.AII.2 continued

VARIABLE	RESPONDENTS' MEAN	NON RESPONDENTS' MEAN	T-VALUE	DEGREES OF FREEDOM	TEST VALUE
EPS (EX EXTRA/DISC)--1980--$ & @	1.7	2.2	-0.9492	626	1
INVEN-RY VALUATION METHOD--1980	81.4	34.6	0.9087	626	1
COMMON EQUITY (AS REPORTED)--1980--MM$	450.0	376.5	0.3368	626	1
NONOPERATING INCOME/EXPENSE--1980--MM$	30.9	17.1	0.7783	626	1
INTEREST INCOME--1980--MM$	16.0	28.9	-0.9274	626	1
INCOME TAXES (FEDERAL)--1980--MM$	-6.6	15.2	-1.5506	626	1
INCOME TAXES (FOREIGN)--1980--MM$	10.2	18.0	-0.8773	626	1
AMORTIZATION OF INTANGIBLES--1980--MM$	0.2	0.3	-0.5716	626	1
DISCONTINUED OPERATIONS--1980--MM$	-0.2	-0.2	0.0074	626	1
RECEIVABLES (EST DOUBTFUL)--1980--MM$	3.8	2.6	0.5564	626	1
CURRENT ASSETS (OTHER)--1980--MM$	30.6	14.3	0.8622	626	1
ASSETS (OTHER)--1980--MM$	26.8	20.3	0.4609	626	1
ACCOUNTS PAYABLE--1980--MM$	145.8	94.4	0.6546	626	1
INCOME TAXES PAYABLE--1980--MM$	18.5	25.5	-0.6194	626	1
CURRENT LIABILITIES (OTHER)--1980--MM$	189.3	67.0	1.0845	626	1
CONSTRUCTION IN PROGRESS--1980--MM$	13.6	14.8	-0.1061	626	1
DEFERRED TAXED (B/S)--1980--MM$	44.8	51.5	-0.2467	626	1
LIABILITIES (OTHER)--1980--MM$	56.6	24.9	0.8797	626	1
RAW MATERIALS--1980--MM$	39.2	22.7	0.5517	626	1
WORK IN PROGRESS--1980--MM$	28.7	18.2	0.5633	626	1
FINISHED GOODS--1980--MM$	95.8	21.1	1.2905	626	1
DEBT (CONVERTIBLE)--1980--MM$	7.4	5.0	0.3838	626	1
DEBT (SUBORDINATED)--1980--MM$	4.0	3.4	0.1677	626	1
DEBT (NOTES)--1980--MM$	41.3	42.7	-0.0684	626	1
DEBT (DEBENTURES)--1980--MM$	25.8	51.4	-1.3662	626	1
DEBT (OTHER LONG TERM)--1980--MM$	22.9	32.9	-0.5155	626	1
DEBT (CAP LEASE OBLIGATIONS)--1980--MM$	6.3	11.5	-2.0215	626	2
COMMON S-CK--1980--MM$	30.8	35.3	-0.2907	626	1
TREAS S-CK (-TAL $ AMOUNT)--1980--MM$	2.8	7.2	-1.5020	626	1
TREASURY S-CK (# COMMON SHARES)--1980--M	217.8	618.9	-1.1747	626	1
PRES VALUE OF NONCAP LEASES--1980--MM$	-0.0	0.0	-1.4450	626	1
UNFUN PENSION COSTS(VEST BEN)--1980--MM$	0.6	8.5	-3.1165	626	4
UNFUN PENSION COSTS(PAST SRV)--1980--MM$	0.4	1.7	-1.3293	626	1
DEBT MATURING IN 2ND YEAR--1980--MM$	21.7	9.1	1.0173	626	1
DEBT MATURING IN 3RD YEAR--1980--MM$	15.9	10.8	0.6608	626	1
DEBT MATURING IN 4TH YEAR--1980--MM$	10.5	10.4	0.0370	626	1
DEBT MATURING IN 5TH YEAR--1980--MM$	35.3	12.9	1.1654	626	1
MIN RENT COMMIT 5 YRS (-TAL)--1980--MM$	27.7	20.1	0.5838	626	1
MIN RENT COMMITMENT IN 1 YEAR--1980--MM$	8.5	5.8	0.6782	626	1
RET EARNINGS (UNRESTRICTED)--1980--MM$	68.7	63.8	0.1186	626	1
ORDER BACKLOG--1980--MM$	280.5	140.4	0.7903	626	1
RET EARNINGS (RESTATEMENT)--1980--MM$	0.2	0.4	-0.3964	626	1
SHAREHOLDERS (COMMON)--1980--M	17590.2	14063.3	0.4250	626	1
INT EXPENSE ON LONG TERM DEBT--1980--MM$	2.9	2.9	0.0051	626	1
EXCISE TAXES--1980--MM$	0.1	13.5	-1.4169	626	1
DEPREC EXPENSE (SCHED V)--1980--MM$	42.8	35.0	0.3155	626	1
BORROWINGS (AVG SHORT TERM)--1980--MM$	22.7	19.5	0.1658	626	1
INT RATE (AVG ON SHORT TERM)--1980--%	9.0	6.8	1.4876	626	1
UNREMIT EARNS OF SUBS (SCFC)--1980--MM$	-6.6	-0.5	-1.3151	626	1
SALE OF P/P/E (SCFC)--1980--MM$	10	4	0.7454	626	1
SALE OF COM/PREF S-CK (SCFC)--1980--MM$	6	7	-0.0739	626	1
SALE OF INVESTMENTS (SCFC)--1980--MM$	0	1	-0.9842	626	1
-TAL FUNDS FROM OPER (SCFC)--1980--MM$	51	105	-1.4574	626	1
ISSUANCE OF L-T DEBT (SCFC)--1980--MM$	51	33	0.6577	626	1
-TAL SOURCES OF FUNDS (SCFC)--1980--MM$	123	157	-0.5205	626	1
INCR IN INVESTMENTS (SCFC)--1980--MM$	3	5	-1.0043	626	1
REDUCTION OF L-T DEBT (SCFC)--1980--MM$	32	16	0.7766	626	1
PUR OF COMM/PREF S-CK (SCFC)--1980--MM$	0	4	-2.6951	626	4

137

Table 7.AII.2 continued

VARIABLE	RESPONDENTS' MEAN	NON RESPONDENTS' MEAN	T-VALUE	DEGREES OF FREEDOM	TEST VALUE
-TAL USES OF FUNDS (SCFC)--1980--MM$	169	154	0.1719	626	1
SALES (RESTATED)--1980--MM$	1138225	779383	6.4185	626	4
INC BEF EXTRA/DISC OPER (RE)--1980--MM$	-21	38	-1.7231	626	2
EPS (PRIM) (RESTATED)--1980--MM$	1	1	-0.2549	626	1
ASSETS (-TAL) (RESTATED)--1980--MM$	634194	596120	0.4725	626	1
WORKING CAPITAL (RESTATED)--1980--MM$	28	75	-2.6744	626	4
PRETAX INCOME (RESTATED)--1980--MM$	-25	68	-2.0001	626	2
INC BEF EXT/DISC OPER (SCFC)--1980--MM$	-8	56	-1.5715	626	1
EXTRA ITEMS/DISC OPER (SCFC)--1980--MM$	-0	0	-0.2880	626	1
DEPREC & AMORTIZ (SCFC)--1980--MM$	64	38	0.5978	626	1
DEFERRED TAXES (SCFC)--1980--MM$	0	10	-2.5243	626	3
CASH DIVIDENDS (SCFC)--1980--MM$	20	21	-0.0956	626	1
CAPITAL EXPENDITURES (SCFC)--1980--MM$	106	88	0.2765	626	1
ACQUISITIONS (SCFC)--1980--MM$	2	8	-1.2617	626	1
PREF S-CK (CARRYING VALUE)--1980--MM$	21	8	0.8702	626	1
CASH & SHORT TERM INVESTMENTS--1986--MM$	241254	153445	2.1601	626	2
RECEIVABLES--1986--MM$	191	182	0.1155	626	1
INVEN-RIES--1986--MM$	222	155	0.5393	626	1
CURRENT ASSETS (-TAL)--1986--MM$	650	392	0.6605	626	1
CURRENT LIABILITIES (-TAL)--1986--MM$	503	294	0.6340	626	1
ASSETS/(LIABS+NET WORTH)--1986--MM$	1746	2114	-0.4254	626	1
PLANT (GROSS)--1986--MM$	893	1089	-0.3365	626	1
PLANT (NET)--1986--MM$	469	650	-0.6044	626	1
LONG TERM DEBT (-TAL)--1986--MM$	197	318	-1.6080	626	1
PEFERRED S-CK @ LIQ VALUE--1986--MM$	30	17	0.7048	626	1
COMMON EQUITY (TANGIBLE)--1986--MM$	581	455	0.3698	626	1
SALES (NET)--1986--MM$	2211631	1376587	22.0984	626	4
OPER INCOME BEFORE DEPREC--1986--MM$	210	177	0.2234	626	1
DEPRECIATION & AMORTIZATION--1986--MM$	85	68	0.2683	626	1
INTEREST EXPENSE--1986--MM$	37	66	-1.8651	626	2
INCOME TAXES (-TAL)--1986--MM$	62	37	0.6413	626	1
SPECIAL ITEMS--1986--MM$	4	-15	2.0732	626	2
INC BEF EXTRA & DISC OPER--1986--MM$	99	42	0.8138	626	1
PREFERRED DIVIDENDS--1986--MM$	1	2	-0.4057	626	1
AVAIL FOR COM AFT ADJ--1986--MM$	99	41	0.8262	626	1
COMMON DIVIDENDS--1986--MM$	23	37	-0.9686	626	1
PRICE (HIGH)--1986--$ & 8THS	32	30	0.4810	626	1
PRICE (LOW)--1986--$ & 8THS	20	19	0.3420	626	1
PRICE (CLOSE)--1986--$ & 8THS	25	24	0.4383	626	1
COMMON SHARES OUTSTANDING--1986--M	22808	24198	-0.2071	626	1
DIVIDENDS PR SHARE--1986--$ & @	493	590	-1.1459	626	1
ADJUST FAC-R (CUM)(RATIO)--1986	1073541	1106220	-0.7836	626	1
COMMON SHARES TRADED--1986--M	20096	18506	0.2486	626	1
EMPLOYEES--1986--M	15	10	0.6266	626	1
CAPITAL EXPENDITURES--1986--MM$	110	103	0.0942	626	1
INVEST & ADVANCES (EQ METH)--1986--MM$	245	51	1.2574	626	1
INVEST & ADVANCES (OTHER)--1986--MM$	42	219	-2.8454	626	4
INTANGIBLES--1986--MM$	36	49	-0.6712	626	1
DEBT IN CURRENT LIABILITIES--1986--MM$	66	210	-2.6272	626	4
DEF TAX & INVEST CRED (B/S)--1986--MM$	40	103	-1.7546	626	2
RET EARNINGS (C/S OUTSTAND)--1986--MM$	488	368	0.3827	626	1
INVESTED CAPITAL (-TAL)--1986--MM$	818371	824034	-0.0501	626	1
MINORITY INTEREST (B/S)--1986--MM$	9	10	-0.1977	626	1
CONVERTIBLE DEBT & PREF S-CK--1986--MM$	18	16	0.1597	626	1
COMM SHARES RES FOR CONVER--1986--M	3	3	-0.4149	626	1
COST OF GOODS SOLD--1986--MM$	1739	925	0.7395	626	1
LABOR & RELATED EXPENSE--1986--MM$	328	156	0.5401	626	1

Table 7.AII.2 continued

VARIABLE	RESPONDENTS' MEAN	NON RESPONDENTS' MEAN	T-VALUE	DEGREES OF FREEDOM	TEST VALUE
PENSION & RETIREMENT EXPENSE--1986--MM$	19	7	0.7989	626	1
DEBT DUE IN 1 YEAR--1986--MM$	10	21	-2.1292	626	2
ADVERTISING EXPENSE--1986--MM$	28	12	0.7623	626	1
RESEARCH & DEVEL EXPENSE--1986--MM$	69	22	0.9582	626	1
RENTAL EXPENSE--1986--MM$	12	19	-1.2161	626	1
EXTRAORD ITEMS & DISC OPER--1986--MM$	1	2	-0.5760	626	1
MINORITY INTEREST (INC ACCT)--1986--MM$	2	1	0.8156	626	1
DEFERRED TAXES (INC ACCT)--1986--MM$	8	12	-0.5895	626	1
INVEST TAX CREDIT (INC ACCT)--1986--MM$	0	2	-4.3707	626	4
TAX LOSS CARRY FORWARD--1986--MM$	31	22	0.3241	626	1
EARNINGS PER SHARE (PRIMARY)--1986--MM$	1	1	1.3304	626	1
COMM SHARES USED-COMP EPS--1986--MM$	23	24	-0.2081	626	1
UNCNSOL SUBSID EQ IN EARNINGS--1986--MM$	38	5	1.3123	626	1
PREF S-CK @ REDEMPTION VALUE--1986--MM$	27	16	0.6629	626	1
EPS (FULLY DILUTED)--1986--$ & @	1	1	1.3947	626	1
EPS (EX EXTRA/DISC)--1986--$ & @	1	1	1.3921	626	1
INVEN-RY VALUATION METHOD--1986	81	33	0.9449	626	1
COMMON EQUITY (AS REPORTED)--1986--MM$	629	510	0.3464	626	1
NONOPERATING INCOME/EXPENSE--1986--MM$	58	20	1.0260	626	1
INTEREST INCOME--1986--MM$	25	48	-1.1612	626	1
INCOME TAXES (FEDERAL)--1986--MM$	24	9	0.8980	626	1
INCOME TAXES (FOREIGN)--1986--MM$	16	11	0.3878	626	1
AMORTIZATION OF INTANGIBLES--1986--MM$	1	1	-1.2927	626	1
DISCONTINUED OPERATIONS--1986--MM$	-0	1	-0.8741	626	1
RECEIVABLES (EST DOUBTFUL)--1986--MM$	4	4	0.0751	626	1
CURRENT ASSETS (OTHER)--1986--MM$	28	25	0.1642	626	1
ASSETS (OTHER)--1986--MM$	59	57	0.0829	626	1
ACCOUNTS PAYABLE--1986--MM$	205	222	-0.1299	626	1
INCOME TAXES PAYABLE--1986--MM$	21	21	0.0073	626	1
CURRENT LIABILITIES (OTHER)--1986--MM$	249	109	0.8412	626	1
CONSTRUCTION IN PROGRESS--1986--MM$	25	14	0.6057	626	1
DEFERRED TAXED (B/S)--1986--MM$	40	102	-1.7191	626	2
LIABILITIES (OTHER)--1986--MM$	129	94	0.4153	626	1
RAW MATERIALS--1986--MM$	21	23	-0.2890	626	1
WORK IN PROGRESS--1986--MM$	21	20	0.1565	626	1
FINISHED GOODS--1986--MM$	75	27	0.9008	626	1
DEBT (CONVERTIBLE)--1986--MM$	7	11	-0.8068	626	1
DEBT (SUBORDINATED)--1986--MM$	12	21	-1.2558	626	1
DEBT (NOTES)--1986--MM$	33	105	-4.5059	626	4
DEBT (DEBENTURES)--1986--MM$	16	74	-4.4372	626	4
DEBT (OTHER LONG TERM)--1986--MM$	65	64	0.0090	626	1
DEBT (CAP LEASE OBLIGATIONS)--1986--MM$	4	11	-3.1405	626	4
COMMON S-CK--1986--MM$	79	45	0.9751	626	1
TREAS S-CK (-TAL $ AMOUNT)--1986--MM$	14	48	-2.0200	626	2
TREASRY S-CK (# COMMON SHARES)--1986--M	800	1502	-1.4583	626	1
PRES VALUE OF NONCAP LEASES--1986--MM$	-0	-0	.	626	1
UNFUN PENSION COSTS(VEST BEN)--1986--MM$	7	3	0.5627	626	1
UNFUN PENSION COSTS(PAST SRV)--1986--MM$	-0	0	-1.2042	626	1
DEBT MATURING IN 2ND YEAR--1986--MM$	22	20	0.2078	626	1
DEBT MATURING IN 3RD YEAR--1986--MM$	13	20	-0.9352	626	1
DEBT MATURING IN 4TH YEAR--1986--MM$	17	19	-0.2753	626	1
DEBT MATURING IN 5TH YEAR--1986--MM$	12	21	-1.5831	626	1
MIN RENT COMMIT 5 YRS (-TAL)--1986--MM$	39	39	0.0052	626	1
MIN RENT COMMITMENT IN 1 YEAR--1986--MM$	11	11	-0.0368	626	1
RET EARNINGS (UNRESTRICTED)--1986--MM$	90	55	0.6123	626	1
ORDER BACKLOG--1986--MM$	177	181	-0.0373	626	1
RET EARNINGS (RESTATEMENT)--1986--MM$	0	-1	2.0146	626	2

Table 7.AII.2 continued

VARIABLE	RESPONDENTS' MEAN	NON RESPONDENTS' MEAN	T-VALUE	DEGREES OF FREEDOM	TEST VALUE
SHAREHOLDERS (COMMON)--1986--M	13602	12552	0.1679	626	1
INT EXPENSE ON LONG TERM DEBT--1986--MM$	1	4	-2.0133	626	2
EXCISE TAXES--1986--MM$	0	16	-1.6725	626	2
DEPREC EXPENSE (SCHED V)--1986--MM$	57	62	-0.1483	626	1
BORROWINGS (AVG SHORT TERM)--1986--MM$	35	39	-0.1474	626	1
INT RATE (AVG ON SHORT TERM)--1986--%	4	4	0.3915	626	1
UNREMIT EARNS OF SUBS (SCFC)--1986--MM$	-8	-2	-0.4205	626	1
SALE OF P/P/E (SCFC)--1986--MM$	7	8	-0.2568	626	1
SALE OF COM/PREF S-CK (SCFC)--1986--MM$	6	14	-2.1537	626	2
SALE OF INVESTMENTS (SCFC)--1986--MM$	13	74	-2.5534	626	3
-TAL FUNDS FROM OPER (SCFC)--1986--MM$	214	144	0.4936	626	1
ISSUANCE OF L-T DEBT (SCFC)--1986--MM$	73	107	-1.1662	626	1
-TAL SOURCES OF FUNDS (SCFC)--1986--MM$	381	408	-0.1386	626	1
INCR IN INVESTMENTS (SCFC)--1986--MM$	21	110	-2.7566	626	4
REDUCTION OF L-T DEBT (SCFC)--1986--MM$	62	58	0.1235	626	1
PUR OF COMM/PREF S-CK (SCFC)--1986--MM$	19	22	-0.1963	626	1
-TAL USES OF FUNDS (SCFC)--1986--MM$	311	404	-0.6456	626	1
SALES (RESTATED)--1986--MM$	2119319	1321476	21.3682	626	4
INC BEF EXTRA/DISC OPER (RE)--1986--MM$	94	39	0.7784	626	1
EPS (PRIM) (RESTATED)--1986--MM$	1	1	1.1760	626	1
ASSETS (-TAL) (RESTATED)--1986--MM$	1265645	1935951	-9.8866	626	4
WORKING CAPITAL (RESTATED)--1986--MM$	45	96	-2.7632	626	4
PRETAX INCOME (RESTATED)--1986--MM$	155	79	0.6931	626	1
INC BEF EXT/DISC OPER (SCFC)--1986--MM$	95	39	0.7945	626	1
EXTRA ITEMS/DISC OPER (SCFC)--1986--MM$	8	8	0.0359	626	1
DEPREC & AMORTIZ (SCFC)--1986--MM$	88	68	0.3188	626	1
DEFERRED TAXES (SCFC)--1986--MM$	2	6	-1.1287	626	1
CASH DIVIDENDS (SCFC)--1986--MM$	22	37	-1.0318	626	1
CAPITAL EXPENDITURES (SCFC)--1986--MM$	104	92	0.1801	626	1
ACQUISITIONS (SCFC)--1986--MM$	32	30	0.0769	626	1
PREF S-CK (CARRYING VALUE)--1986--MM$	18	13	0.5310	626	1

Table 7.AII.3
T Test for Difference in Means: Respondents Versus Non-respondents, NCEO (114) Companies

VARIABLE	RESPONDENTS' MEAN	NON RESPONDENTS' MEAN	T-VALUE	DEGREES OF FREEDOM	TEST VALUE
CASH & SHORT TERM INVESTMENTS--1980--MM$	11696	106803	-2.4938	114	3
RECEIVABLES--1980--MM$	35	129	-3.0538	114	4
INVEN-RIES--1980--MM$	49	104	-1.6731	114	2
CURRENT ASSETS (-TAL)--1980--MM$	100	288	-2.6091	114	3
CURRENT LIABILITIES (-TAL)--1980--MM$	45	210	-2.9706	114	4
ASSETS/(LIABS+NET WORTH)--1980--MM$	170	1122	-3.4634	114	4
PLANT (GROSS)--1980--MM$	124	626	-2.4479	114	3
PLANT (NET)--1980--MM$	63	395	-2.4836	114	3
LONG TERM DEBT (-TAL)--1980--MM$	31	184	-2.8507	114	4
PEFERRED S-CK @ LIQ VALUE--1980--MM$	2	18	-2.1504	114	2
COMMON EQUITY (TANGIBLE)--1980--MM$	85	293	-2.3607	114	3
SALES (NET)--1980--MM$	358247	1071714	-5.1760	114	4
OPER INCOME BEFORE DEPREC--1980--MM$	30	104	-1.7266	114	2
DEPRECIATION & AMORTIZATION--1980--MM$	8	39	-2.5117	114	3
INTEREST EXPENSE--1980--MM$	4	42	-2.7476	114	4
INCOME TAXES (-TAL)--1980--MM$	8	34	-1.9189	114	2
SPECIAL ITEMS--1980--MM$	0	3	-0.9777	114	1
INC BEF EXTRA & DISC OPER--1980--MM$	12	35	-0.8983	114	1
PREFERRED DIVIDENDS--1980--MM$	0	1	-2.6509	114	4
AVAIL FOR COM AFT ADJ--1980--MM$	12	34	-0.8573	114	1
COMMON DIVIDENDS--1980--MM$	4	15	-2.3276	114	2
PRICE (HIGH)--1980--$ & 8THS	22	28	-1.3614	114	1
PRICE (LOW)--1980--$ & 8THS	12	14	-1.0472	114	1
PRICE (CLOSE)--1980--$ & 8THS	19	24	-1.3023	114	1
COMMON SHARES OUTSTANDING--1980--M	4059	12600	-2.8956	114	4
DIVIDENDS PR SHARE--1980--$ & @	729	747	-0.1087	114	1
ADJUST FAC-R (CUM)(RATIO)--1980	2203516	2146461	0.3798	114	1
COMMON SHARES TRADED--1980--M	1166	5197	-3.6762	114	4
EMPLOYEES--1980--M	3	8	-2.7001	114	4
CAPITAL EXPENDITURES--1980--MM$	14	96	-2.3073	114	2
INVEST & ADVANCES (EQ METH)--1980--MM$	2	32	-2.2475	114	2
INVEST & ADVANCES (OTHER)--1980--MM$	1	12	-2.1631	114	2
INTANGIBLES--1980--MM$	1	8	-1.7190	114	2
DEBT IN CURRENT LIABILITIES--1980--MM$	8	63	-2.1633	114	2
DEF TAX & INVEST CRED (B/S)--1980--MM$	3	46	-2.1927	114	2
RET EARNINGS (C/S OUTSTAND)--1980--MM$	57	221	-2.2902	114	2
INVESTED CAPITAL (-TAL)--1980--MM$	120001	488951	-6.8720	114	4
MINORITY INTEREST (B/S)--1980--MM$	0	3	-1.5370	114	1
CONVERTIBLE DEBT & PREF S-CK--1980--MM$	2	11	-2.2537	114	2
COMM SHARES RES FOR CONVER--1980--M	0	2	-2.4015	114	3
COST OF GOODS SOLD--1980--MM$	283	794	-2.0042	114	2
LABOR & RELATED EXPENSE--1980--MM$	16	151	-2.5412	114	3
PENSION & RETIREMENT EXPENSE--1980--MM$	4	15	-2.3104	114	2
DEBT DUE IN 1 YEAR--1980--MM$	2	11	-2.3160	114	2
ADVERTISING EXPENSE--1980--MM$	2	5	-1.2158	114	1
RESEARCH & DEVEL EXPENSE--1980--MM$	5	10	-0.9745	114	1
RENTAL EXPENSE--1980--MM$	2	9	-2.5141	114	3
EXTRAORD ITEMS & DISC OPER--1980--MM$	-1	-1	-0.0967	114	1

Table 7.AII.3 continued

VARIABLE	RESPONDENTS' MEAN	NON RESPONDENTS' MEAN	T-VALUE	DEGREES OF FREEDOM	TEST VALUE
MINORITY INTEREST (INC ACCT)--1980--MM$	0	0	-1.5589	114	1
DEFERRED TAXES (INC ACCT)--1980--MM$	0	10	-1.8154	114	2
INVEST TAX CREDIT (INC ACCT)--1980--MM$	1	4	-2.3496	114	2
TAX LOSS CARRY FORWARD--1980--MM$	0	11	-1.0058	114	1
EARNINGS PER SHARE (PRIMARY)--1980--MM$	2	2	-0.2370	114	1
COMM SHARES USED-COMP EPS--1980--MM$	4.15	12.7	-2.8171	114	4
UNCNSOL SUBSID EQ IN EARNINGS--1980--MM$	0.30	2.1	-1.3178	114	1
PREF S-CK @ REDEMPTION VALUE--1980--MM$	2.35	21.4	-1.9370	114	2
EPS (FULLY DILUTED)--1980--$ & @	2.47	2.5	-0.0445	114	1
EPS (EX EXTRA/DISC)--1980--$ & @	2.46	2.3	0.2607	114	1
INVEN-RY VALUATION METHOD--1980	140.30	25.2	0.9507	114	1
COMMON EQUITY (AS REPORTED)--1980--MM$	87.05	305.8	-2.4087	114	3
NONOPERATING INCOME/EXPENSE--1980--MM$	2.73	16.0	-2.5324	114	3
INTEREST INCOME--1980--MM$	1.12	33.3	-1.9455	114	2
INCOME TAXES (FEDERAL)--1980--MM$	4.65	13.8	-1.8140	114	2
INCOME TAXES (FOREIGN)--1980--MM$	2.03	3.8	-0.8445	114	1
AMORTIZATION OF INTANGIBLES--1980--MM$	0.02	0.1	-1.2724	114	1
DISCONTINUED OPERATIONS--1980--MM$	-0.56	-0.0	-0.8329	114	1
RECEIVABLES (EST DOUBTFUL)--1980--MM$	1.03	2.5	-1.8467	114	2
CURRENT ASSETS (OTHER)--1980--MM$	4.30	12.8	-2.0719	114	2
ASSETS (OTHER)--1980--MM$	3.02	20.8	-2.7263	114	4
ACCOUNTS PAYABLE--1980--MM$	21.70	91.3	-2.6184	114	3
INCOME TAXES PAYABLE--1980--MM$	2.57	16.3	-2.1230	114	2
CURRENT LIABILITIES (OTHER)--1980--MM$	12.03	74.0	-2.5523	114	3
CONSTRUCTION IN PROGRESS--1980--MM$	1.03	11.2	-2.3325	114	2
DEFERRED TAXED (B/S)--1980--MM$	2.60	44.9	-2.1577	114	2
LIABILITIES (OTHER)--1980--MM$	2.58	26.2	-2.1944	114	2
RAW MATERIALS--1980--MM$	8.16	12.4	-0.6698	114	1
WORK IN PROGRESS--1980--MM$	4.49	13.3	-1.0920	114	1
FINISHED GOODS--1980--MM$	6.82	15.7	-1.3620	114	1
DEBT (CONVERTIBLE)--1980--MM$	0.10	8.7	-2.5630	114	3
DEBT (SUBORDINATED)--1980--MM$	0.28	1.6	-1.9750	114	2
DEBT (NOTES)--1980--MM$	19.70	54.3	-1.8197	114	2
DEBT (DEBENTURES)--1980--MM$	4.67	45.4	-2.4605	114	3
DEBT (OTHER LONG TERM)--1980--MM$	2.49	47.6	-2.3845	114	3
DEBT (CAP LEASE OBLIGATIONS)--1980--MM$	5.05	17.0	-1.5974	114	1
COMMON S-CK--1980--MM$	7.91	29.5	-2.3369	114	2
TREAS S-CK (-TAL $ AMOUNT)--1980--MM$	1.37	2.5	-1.0690	114	1
TREASRY S-CK (# COMMON SHARES)--1980--M	85.55	141.9	-1.0934	114	1
PRES VALUE OF NONCAP LEASES--1980--MM$	-0.00	-0.0	.	114	1
UNFUN PENSION COSTS(VEST BEN)--1980--MM$	-0.00	21.1	-1.5421	114	1
UNFUN PENSION COSTS(PAST SRV)--1980--MM$	0.30	6.8	-1.1273	114	1
DEBT MATURING IN 2ND YEAR--1980--MM$	3.39	10.1	-2.0740	114	2
DEBT MATURING IN 3RD YEAR--1980--MM$	2.73	13.1	-2.4914	114	3
DEBT MATURING IN 4TH YEAR--1980--MM$	2.32	11.4	-2.8325	114	4
DEBT MATURING IN 5TH YEAR--1980--MM$	4.17	12.3	-2.0084	114	2
MIN RENT COMMIT 5 YRS (-TAL)--1980--MM$	6.47	17.5	-1.8199	114	2

Table 7.AII.3 continued

VARIABLE	RESPONDENTS' MEAN	NON RESPONDENTS' MEAN	T-VALUE	DEGREES OF FREEDOM	TEST VALUE
MIN RENT COMMITMENT IN 1 YEAR--1980--MM$	1.86	5.0	-1.8915	114	2
RET EARNINGS (UNRESTRICTED)--1980--MM$	27.26	118.1	-1.4496	114	1
ORDER BACKLOG--1980--MM$	10.52	110.3	-2.0342	114	2
RET EARNINGS (RESTATEMENT)--1980--MM$	0.00	0.1	-0.9496	114	1
SHAREHOLDERS (COMMON)--1980--M	2606.80	14354.7	-3.2385	114	4
INT EXPENSE ON LONG TERM DEBT--1980--MM$	0.48	6.3	-1.4998	114	1
EXCISE TAXES--1980--MM$	0.00	6.9	-1.3889	114	1
DEPREC EXPENSE (SCHED V)--1980--MM$	7.89	33.8	-2.3788	114	3
BORROWINGS (AVG SHORT TERM)--1980--MM$	4.93	13.6	-2.3167	114	2
INT RATE (AVG ON SHORT TERM)--1980--%	12.19	7.3	1.7566	114	2
UNREMIT EARNS OF SUBS (SCFC)--1980--MM$	-0.05	-0.6	0.4877	114	1
SALE OF P/P/E (SCFC)--1980--MM$	2	4	-1.7216	114	2
SALE OF COM/PREF S-CK (SCFC)--1980--MM$	0	9	-2.1978	114	2
SALE OF INVESTMENTS (SCFC)--1980--MM$	0	2	-1.5041	114	1
-TAL FUNDS FROM OPER (SCFC)--1980--MM$	21	78	-1.5026	114	1
ISSUANCE OF L-T DEBT (SCFC)--1980--MM$	3	54	-2.1631	114	2
-TAL SOURCES OF FUNDS (SCFC)--1980--MM$	26	153	-2.5760	114	3
INCR IN INVESTMENTS (SCFC)--1980--MM$	0	7	-1.3724	114	1
REDUCTION OF L-T DEBT (SCFC)--1980--MM$	3	21	-2.2727	114	2
PUR OF COMM/PREF S-CK (SCFC)--1980--MM$	0	3	-1.4363	114	1
-TAL USES OF FUNDS (SCFC)--1980--MM$	22	151	-2.2972	114	2
SALES (RESTATED)--1980--MM$	358244	553434	-1.6567	114	1
INC BEF EXTRA/DISC OPER (RE)--1980--MM$	12	6	0.2771	114	1
EPS (PRIM) (RESTATED)--1980--MM$	1	1	1.3401	114	1
ASSETS (-TAL) (RESTATED)--1980--MM$	169626	454438	-4.6941	114	4
uWORKING CAPITAL (RESTATED)--1980--MM$	49	52	-0.1132	114	1
PRETAX INCOME (RESTATED)--1980--MM$	20	14	0.2443	114	1
INC BEF EXT/DISC OPER (SCFC)--1980--MM$	12	31	-0.7405	114	1
EXTRA ITEMS/DISC OPER (SCFC)--1980--MM$	0	0	0.2816	114	1
DEPREC & AMORTIZ (SCFC)--1980--MM$	9	42	-2.3029	114	2
DEFERRED TAXES (SCFC)--1980--MM$	1	9	-1.5735	114	1
CASH DIVIDENDS (SCFC)--1980--MM$	4	15	-2.2336	114	2
CAPITAL EXPENDITURES (SCFC)--1980--MM$	13	93	-2.1415	114	2
ACQUISITIONS (SCFC)--1980--MM$	1	4	-1.4697	114	1
PREF S-CK (CARRYING VALUE)--1980--MM$	2	14	-1.9074	114	2
CASH & SHORT TERM INVESTMENTS--1986--MM$	36172	176499	-2.5215	114	3
RECEIVABLES--1986--MM$	46	190	-2.4496	114	3
INVEN-RIES--1986--MM$	79	105	-0.7576	114	1
CURRENT ASSETS (-TAL)--1986--MM$	159	381	-2.1669	114	2
CURRENT LIABILITIES (-TAL)--1986--MM$	77	315	-2.7843	114	4
ASSETS/(LIABS+NET WORTH)--1986--MM$	374	2015	-3.2205	114	4
PLANT (GROSS)--1986--MM$	215	1000	-2.4641	114	3
PLANT (NET)--1986--MM$	115	598	-2.6391	114	4
LONG TERM DEBT (-TAL)--1986--MM$	68	332	-2.9206	114	4
PEFERRED S-CK @ LIQ VALUE--1986--MM$	0	19	-2.9947	114	4
COMMON EQUITY (TANGIBLE)--1986--MM$	139	365	-2.0757	114	2
SALES (NET)--1986--MM$	647407	1447388	-3.5874	114	4
OPER INCOME BEFORE DEPREC--1986--MM$	47	164	-2.4149	114	3

Table 7.AII.3 continued

VARIABLE	RESPONDENTS' MEAN	NON RESPONDENTS' MEAN	T-VALUE	DEGREES OF FREEDOM	TEST VALUE
DEPRECIATION & AMORTIZATION--1986--MM$	14	67	-2.6704	114	4
INTEREST EXPENSE--1986--MM$	8	69	-2.7578	114	4
INCOME TAXES (-TAL)--1986--MM$	12	37	-1.8236	114	2
SPECIAL ITEMS--1986--MM$	0	-10	1.5883	114	1
INC BEF EXTRA & DISC OPER--1986--MM$	17	48	-1.4077	114	1
PREFERRED DIVIDENDS--1986--MM$	0	2	-2.8379	114	4
AVAIL FOR COM AFT ADJ--1986--MM$	17	46	-1.3367	114	1
COMMON DIVIDENDS--1986--MM$	6	60	-2.0968	114	2
PRICE (HIGH)--1986--$ & 8THS	29	30	-0.1661	114	1
PRICE (LOW)--1986--$ & 8THS	20	19	0.1602	114	1
PRICE (CLOSE)--1986--$ & 8THS	24	24	0.0110	114	1
COMMON SHARES OUTSTANDING--1986--M	11696	22996	-2.1198	114	2
DIVIDENDS PR SHARE--1986--$ & @	458	589	-1.1460	114	1
ADJUST FAC-R (CUM)(RATIO)--1986	1076500	1066666	0.1651	114	1
COMMON SHARES TRADED--1986--M	9542	19405	-2.2168	114	2
EMPLOYEES--1986--M	4	10	-2.3681	114	3
CAPITAL EXPENDITURES--1986--MM$	32	99	-2.1133	114	2
INVEST & ADVANCES (EQ METH)--1986--MM$	6	55	-1.8182	114	2
INVEST & ADVANCES (OTHER)--1986--MM$	63	72	-0.1100	114	1
INTANGIBLES--1986--MM$	10	39	-1.6871	114	2
DEBT IN CURRENT LIABILITIES--1986--MM$	15	190	-1.9560	114	2
DEF TAX & INVEST CRED (B/S)--1986--MM$	6	92	-2.1852	114	2
RET EARNINGS (C/S OUTSTAND)--1986--MM$	100	284	-1.9376	114	2
INVESTED CAPITAL (-TAL)--1986--MM$	218957	700620	-5.2133	114	4
MINORITY INTEREST (B/S)--1986--MM$	2	7	-1.3365	114	1
CONVERTIBLE DEBT & PREF S-CK--1986--MM$	4	19	-2.6068	114	3
COMM SHARES RES FOR CONVER--1986--M	1	3	-3.6202	114	4
COST OF GOODS SOLD--1986--MM$	506	976	-1.4675	114	1
LABOR & RELATED EXPENSE--1986--MM$	20	175	-1.9869	114	2
PENSION & RETIREMENT EXPENSE--1986--MM$	0	6	-2.0192	114	2
DEBT DUE IN 1 YEAR--1986--MM$	6	32	-2.1005	114	2
ADVERTISING EXPENSE--1986--MM$	4	9	-1.0198	114	1
RESEARCH & DEVEL EXPENSE--1986--MM$	9	18	-0.8573	114	1
RENTAL EXPENSE--1986--MM$	4	16	-3.3924	114	4
EXTRAORD ITEMS & DISC OPER--1986--MM$	1	3	-1.3534	114	1
MINORITY INTEREST (INC ACCT)--1986--MM$	0	0	-1.1571	114	1
DEFERRED TAXES (INC ACCT)--1986--MM$	1	28	-1.7228	114	2
INVEST TAX CREDIT (INC ACCT)--1986--MM$	0	2	-2.7732	114	4
TAX LOSS CARRY FORWARD--1986--MM$	3	25	-1.7593	114	2
EARNINGS PER SHARE (PRIMARY)--1986--MM$	1	0	1.4605	114	1
COMM SHARES USED-COMP EPS--1986--MM$	12	25	-2.3494	114	2
UNCNSOL SUBSID EQ IN EARNINGS--1986--MM$	1	4	-1.1184	114	1
PREF S-CK @ REDEMPTION VALUE--1986--MM$	0	16	-2.6445	114	4
EPS (FULLY DILUTED)--1986--$ & @	1	0	1.3713	114	1
EPS (EX EXTRA/DISC)--1986--$ & @	1	0	1.3937	114	1
INVEN-RY VALUATION METHOD--1986	135	23	0.9360	114	1
COMMON EQUITY (AS REPORTED)--1986--MM$	149	409	-2.2796	114	2
NONOPERATING INCOME/EXPENSE--1986--MM$	3	26	-1.8414	114	2

Table 7.AII.3 continued

VARIABLE	RESPONDENTS' MEAN	NON RESPONDENTS' MEAN	T-VALUE	DEGREES OF FREEDOM	TEST VALUE
INTEREST INCOME--1986--MM$	1	54	-1.9481	114	2
INCOME TAXES (FEDERAL)--1986--MM$	5	1	0.4012	114	1
INCOME TAXES (FOREIGN)--1986--MM$	5	4	0.0633	114	1
AMORTIZATION OF INTANGIBLES--1986--MM$	0	1	-1.0908	114	1
DISCONTINUED OPERATIONS--1986--MM$	0	2	-1.2305	114	1
RECEIVABLES (EST DOUBTFUL)--1986--MM$	2	3	-0.6074	114	1
CURRENT ASSETS (OTHER)--1986--MM$	8	27	-2.2880	114	2
ASSETS (OTHER)--1986--MM$	11	65	-2.9357	114	4
ACCOUNTS PAYABLE--1986--MM$	96	181	-1.0597	114	1
INCOME TAXES PAYABLE--1986--MM$	2	11	-2.7875	114	4
CURRENT LIABILITIES (OTHER)--1986--MM$	26	111	-2.4637	114	3
CONSTRUCTION IN PROGRESS--1986--MM$	5	17	-1.0330	114	1
DEFERRED TAXED (B/S)--1986--MM$	6	90	-2.1568	114	2
LIABILITIES (OTHER)--1986--MM$	11	87	-2.5201	114	3
RAW MATERIALS--1986--MM$	6	14	-1.0835	114	1
WORK IN PROGRESS--1986--MM$	5	11	-1.1546	114	1
FINISHED GOODS--1986--MM$	8	16	-1.3631	114	1
DEBT (CONVERTIBLE)--1986--MM$	4	13	-1.8714	114	2
DEBT (SUBORDINATED)--1986--MM$	0	17	-1.9313	114	2
DEBT (NOTES)--1986--MM$	39	84	-1.6985	114	2
DEBT (DEBENTURES)--1986--MM$	11	47	-2.0154	114	2
DEBT (OTHER LONG TERM)--1986--MM$	12	64	-2.681	114	4
DEBT (CAP LEASE OBLIGATIONS)--1986--MM$	4	11	-1.569	114	1
COMMON S-CK--1986--MM$	26	37	-0.779	114	1
TREAS S-CK (-TAL $ AMOUNT)--1986--MM$	16	45	-1.010	114	1
TREASRY S-CK (# COMMON SHARES)--1986--M	826	1451	-0.841	114	1
PRES VALUE OF NONCAP LEASES--1986--MM$	-0	-0	.	114	1
UNFUN PENSION COSTS(VEST BEN)--1986--MM$	-0	14	-1.518	114	1
UNFUN PENSION COSTS(PAST SRV)--1986--MM$	-0	-0	.	114	1
DEBT MATURING IN 2ND YEAR--1986--MM$	4	22	-2.867	114	4
DEBT MATURING IN 3RD YEAR--1986--MM$	6	27	-2.393	114	3
DEBT MATURING IN 4TH YEAR--1986--MM$	4	21	-3.398	114	4
DEBT MATURING IN 5TH YEAR--1986--MM$	3	21	-3.000	114	4
MIN RENT COMMIT 5 YRS (-TAL)--1986--MM$	14	45	-2.785	114	4
MIN RENT COMMITMENT IN 1 YEAR--1986--MM$	4	14	-2.751	114	4
RET EARNINGS (UNRESTRICTED)--1986--MM$	31	127	-1.346	114	1
ORDER BACKLOG--1986--MM$	12	200	-1.521	114	1
RET EARNINGS (RESTATEMENT)--1986--MM$	0	-2	0.958	114	1
SHAREHOLDERS (COMMON)--1986--M	2856	12132	-3.273	114	4
INT EXPENSE ON LONG TERM DEBT--1986--MM$	1	11	-1.092	114	1
EXCISE TAXES--1986--MM$	0	8	-1.372	114	1
DEPREC EXPENSE (SCHED V)--1986--MM$	13	59	-2.394	114	3
BORROWINGS (AVG SHORT TERM)--1986--MM$	9	56	-1.667	114	2
INT RATE (AVG ON SHORT TERM)--1986--%	5	4	0.422	114	1
UNREMIT EARNS OF SUBS (SCFC)--1986--MM$	-0	-3	1.079	114	1
SALE OF P/P/E (SCFC)--1986--MM$	5	8	-0.577	114	1
SALE OF COM/PREF S-CK (SCFC)--1986--MM$	8	22	-1.542	114	1
SALE OF INVESTMENTS (SCFC)--1986--MM$	29	43	-0.357	114	1

145

Table 7.AII.3 continued

VARIABLE	RESPONDENTS' MEAN	NON RESPONDENTS' MEAN	T-VALUE	DEGREES OF FREEDOM	TEST VALUE
-TAL FUNDS FROM OPER (SCFC)--1986--MM$	35	139	-2.187	114	2
ISSUANCE OF L-T DEBT (SCFC)--1986--MM$	24	92	-2.197	114	2
-TAL SOURCES OF FUNDS (SCFC)--1986--MM$	108	356	-2.706	114	4
INCR IN INVESTMENTS (SCFC)--1986--MM$	30	49	-0.472	114	1
REDUCTION OF L-T DEBT (SCFC)--1986--MM$	18	44	-1.530	114	1
PUR OF COMM/PREF S-CK (SCFC)--1986--MM$	7	19	-1.608	114	1
-TAL USES OF FUNDS (SCFC)--1986--MM$	101	345	-2.818	114	4
SALES (RESTATED)--1986--MM$	647717	1334461	-3.089	114	4
INC BEF EXTRA/DISC OPER (RE)--1986--MM$	17	39	-1.072	114	1
EPS (PRIM) (RESTATED)--1986--MM$	1	0	1.507	114	1
ASSETS (-TAL) (RESTATED)--1986--MM$	374128	1703980	-11.343	114	4
WORKING CAPITAL (RESTATED)--1986--MM$	74	54	0.615	114	1
PRETAX INCOME (RESTATED)--1986--MM$	29	78	-1.444	114	1
INC BEF EXT/DISC OPER (SCFC)--1986--MM$	17	39	-1.072	114	1
EXTRA ITEMS/DISC OPER (SCFC)--1986--MM$	1	4	-1.177	114	1
DEPREC & AMORTIZ (SCFC)--1986--MM$	15	66	-2.514	114	3
DEFERRED TAXES (SCFC)--1986--MM$	1	21	-1.510	114	1
CASH DIVIDENDS (SCFC)--1986--MM$	6	60	-2.081	114	2
CAPITAL EXPENDITURES (SCFC)--1986--MM$	30	92	-1.954	114	2
ACQUISITIONS (SCFC)--1986--MM$	3	16	-1.819	114	2
PREF S-CK (CARRYING VALUE)--1986--MM$	0	14	-2.395	114	3

Table 7.AII.4
T Test for Difference in Means: Respondents Versus Non-respondents, Matching Companies (510)

VARIABLE	RESPONDENTS' MEAN	NON RESPONDENTS' MEAN	T-VALUE	DEGREES OF FREEDOM	TEST VALUE
CASH & SHORT TERM INVESTMENTS--1980--MM$	136181	94168	0.4453	510	1
RECEIVABLES--1980--MM$	306	154	1.0568	510	1
INVEN-RIES--1980--MM$	452	137	1.3733	510	1
CURRENT ASSETS (-TAL)--1980--MM$	924	343	1.2115	510	1
CURRENT LIABILITIES (-TAL)--1980--MM$	749	214	1.2476	510	1
ASSETS/(LIABS+NET WORTH)--1980--MM$	2085	1134	0.9295	510	1
PLANT (GROSS)--1980--MM$	1144	676	0.6672	510	1
PLANT (NET)--1980--MM$	671	414	0.6396	510	1
LONG TERM DEBT (-TAL)--1980--MM$	261	150	0.8544	510	1
PEFERRED S-CK @ LIQ VALUE--1980--MM$	67	9	1.1079	510	1
COMMON EQUITY (TANGIBLE)--1980--MM$	665	380	0.8225	510	1
SALES (NET)--1980--MM$	2772066	1170601	1.1091	510	1
OPER INCOME BEFORE DEPREC--1980--MM$	89	150	-0.8045	510	1
DEPRECIATION & AMORTIZATION--1980--MM$	102	38	0.8969	510	1
INTEREST EXPENSE--1980--MM$	68	36	0.9364	510	1
INCOME TAXES (-TAL)--1980--MM$	-7	51	-2.0547	510	2
SPECIAL ITEMS--1980--MM$	0	-0	0.1017	510	1
INC BEF EXTRA & DISC OPER--1980--MM$	-16	62	-1.1411	510	1
PREFERRED DIVIDENDS--1980--MM$	3	1	1.0722	510	1
AVAIL FOR COM AFT ADJ--1980--MM$	-16	62	-1.1462	510	1
COMMON DIVIDENDS--1980--MM$	31	23	0.5121	510	1
PRICE (HIGH)--1980--$ & 8THS	24	24	0.0454	510	1
PRICE (LOW)--1980--$ & 8THS	13	13	0.1619	510	1
PRICE (CLOSE)--1980--$ & 8THS	19	21	-0.4207	510	1
COMMON SHARES OUTSTANDING--1980--M	15984	13094	0.4776	510	1
DIVIDENDS PR SHARE--1980--$ & @	858	718	0.7472	510	1
ADJUST FAC-R (CUM)(RATIO)--1980	2281307	1887482	0.9053	510	1
COMMON SHARES TRADED--1980--M	9001	5270	1.4462	510	1
EMPLOYEES--1980--M	34	10	1.2754	510	1
CAPITAL EXPENDITURES--1980--MM$	175	99	0.7165	510	1
INVEST & ADVANCES (EQ METH)--1980--MM$	226	27	1.5860	510	1
INVEST & ADVANCES (OTHER)--1980--MM$	16	23	-0.4310	510	1
INTANGIBLES--1980--MM$	13	8	0.7165	510	1
DEBT IN CURRENT LIABILITIES--1980--MM$	177	79	0.9704	510	1
DEF TAX & INVEST CRED (B/S)--1980--MM$	76	54	0.4986	510	1
RET EARNINGS (C/S OUTSTAND)--1980--MM$	595	312	0.8804	510	1
INVESTED CAPITAL (-TAL)--1980--MM$	1017418	547013	0.9423	510	1
MINORITY INTEREST (B/S)--1980--MM$	13	7	0.5715	510	1
CONVERTIBLE DEBT & PREF S-CK--1980--MM$	21	7	1.2247	510	1
COMM SHARES RES FOR CONVER--1980--M	3	1	1.2209	510	1
COST OF GOODS SOLD--1980--MM$	2361	847	1.1235	510	1
LABOR & RELATED EXPENSE--1980--MM$	643	135	1.0577	510	1
PENSION & RETIREMENT EXPENSE--1980--MM$	49	14	1.1958	510	1
DEBT DUE IN 1 YEAR--1980--MM$	15	7	0.9191	510	1
ADVERTISING EXPENSE--1980--MM$	32	8	1.0490	510	1
RESEARCH & DEVEL EXPENSE--1980--MM$	90	12	1.2527	510	1
RENTAL EXPENSE--1980--MM$	18	13	0.4243	510	1
EXTRAORD ITEMS & DISC OPER--1980--MM$	-1	-0	-0.3433	510	1
MINORITY INTEREST (INC ACCT)--1980--MM$	2	1	0.4463	510	1
DEFERRED TAXES (INC ACCT)--1980--MM$	4	9	-1.5810	510	1
INVEST TAX CREDIT (INC ACCT)--1980--MM$	2	4	-1.1716	510	1
TAX LOSS CARRY FORWARD--1980--MM$	6	4	0.3789	510	1
EARNINGS PER SHARE (PRIMARY)--1980--MM$	1	2	-1.1596	510	1
COMM SHARES USED-COMP EPS--1980--MM$	16.8	13.1	0.5698	510	1
UNCNSOL SUBSID EQ IN EARNINGS--1980--MM$	25.3	5.8	1.3438	510	1
PREF S-CK @ REDEMPTION VALUE--1980--MM$	71.7	10.0	1.1039	510	1
EPS (FULLY DILUTED)--1980--$ & @	1.4	2.2	-1.0812	510	1
EPS (EX EXTRA/DISC)--1980--$ & @	1.1	2.2	-1.2698	510	1
INVEN-RY VALUATION METHOD--1980	39.4	36.5	0.1514	510	1
COMMON EQUITY (AS REPORTED)--1980--MM$	709.2	390.5	0.8826	510	1

147

Table 7.AII.4 continued

VARIABLE	RESPONDENTS' MEAN	NON RESPONDENTS' MEAN	T-VALUE	DEGREES OF FREEDOM	TEST VALUE
NONOPERATING INCOME/EXPENSE--1980--MM$	51.1	17.3	1.1369	510	1
INTEREST INCOME--1980--MM$	26.5	28.0	-0.0672	510	1
INCOME TAXES (FEDERAL)--1980--MM$	-14.5	15.5	-1.2618	510	1
INCOME TAXES (FOREIGN)--1980--MM$	16.1	20.8	-0.3717	510	1
AMORTIZATION OF INTANGIBLES--1980--MM$	0.3	0.3	-0.0695	510	1
DISCONTINUED OPERATIONS--1980--MM$	0.1	-0.2	0.2076	510	1
RECEIVABLES (EST DOUBTFUL)--1980--MM$	5.8	2.6	0.8455	510	1
CURRENT ASSETS (OTHER)--1980--MM$	49.5	14.6	1.0948	510	1
ASSETS (OTHER)--1980--MM$	43.8	20.1	1.0031	510	1
ACCOUNTS PAYABLE--1980--MM$	234.4	95.0	1.0674	510	1
INCOME TAXES PAYABLE--1980--MM$	29.8	27.4	0.1399	510	1
CURRENT LIABILITIES (OTHER)--1980--MM$	316.0	65.6	1.3121	510	1
CONSTRUCTION IN PROGRESS--1980--MM$	22.6	15.6	0.3699	510	1
DEFERRED TAXED (B/S)--1980--MM$	75.0	52.8	0.5204	510	1
LIABILITIES (OTHER)--1980--MM$	95.2	24.6	1.1592	510	1
RAW MATERIALS--1980--MM$	61.5	24.7	0.7187	510	1
WORK IN PROGRESS--1980--MM$	45.9	19.2	0.8770	510	1
FINISHED GOODS--1980--MM$	159.3	22.1	1.3993	510	1
DEBT (CONVERTIBLE)--1980--MM$	12.7	4.3	0.7769	510	1
DEBT (SUBORDINATED)--1980--MM$	6.6	3.8	0.5386	510	1
DEBT (NOTES)--1980--MM$	56.7	40.4	0.4816	510	1
DEBT (DEBENTURES)--1980--MM$	40.9	52.6	-0.3905	510	1
DEBT (OTHER LONG TERM)--1980--MM$	37.4	30.0	0.2316	510	1
DEBT (CAP LEASE OBLIGATIONS)--1980--MM$	7.2	10.4	-0.9989	510	1
COMMON S-CK--1980--MM$	47.2	36.4	0.4364	510	1
TREAS S-CK (-TAL $ AMOUNT)--1980--MM$	3.9	8.2	-1.0623	510	1
TREASRY S-CK (# COMMON SHARES)--1980--M	312.2	713.5	-0.9193	510	1
PRES VALUE OF NONCAP LEASES--1980--MM$	-0.0	0.0	-1.4080	510	1
UNFUN PENSION COSTS(VEST BEN)--1980--MM$	1.1	6.0	-3.4784	510	4
UNFUN PENSION COSTS(PAST SRV)--1980--MM$	0.4	0.7	-0.6442	510	1
DEBT MATURING IN 2ND YEAR--1980--MM$	34.8	8.9	1.2362	510	1
DEBT MATURING IN 3RD YEAR--1980--MM$	25.4	10.3	1.1577	510	1
DEBT MATURING IN 4TH YEAR--1980--MM$	16.4	10.2	0.7663	510	1
DEBT MATURING IN 5TH YEAR--1980--MM$	57.6	13.1	1.3746	510	1
MIN RENT COMMIT 5 YRS (-TAL)--1980--MM$	42.8	20.6	1.0333	510	1
MIN RENT COMMITMENT IN 1 YEAR--1980--MM$	13.3	5.9	1.1005	510	1
RET EARNINGS (UNRESTRICTED)--1980--MM$	98.3	53.0	0.6720	510	1
ORDER BACKLOG--1980--MM$	473.3	146.3	1.1032	510	1
RET EARNINGS (RESTATEMENT)--1980--MM$	0.4	0.5	-0.0900	510	1
SHAREHOLDERS (COMMON)--1980--M	28292.6	14005.4	1.0359	510	1
INT EXPENSE ON LONG TERM DEBT--1980--MM$	4.6	2.2	0.5828	510	1
EXCISE TAXES--1980--MM$	0.2	14.9	-1.2969	510	1
DEPREC EXPENSE (SCHED V)--1980--MM$	67.7	35.3	0.7900	510	1
BORROWINGS (AVG SHORT TERM)--1980--MM$	35.4	20.6	0.4456	510	1
INT RATE (AVG ON SHORT TERM)--1980--%	6.7	6.7	0.0277	510	1
UNREMIT EARNS OF SUBS (SCFC)--1980--MM$	-11.2	-0.5	-1.3743	510	1
SALE OF P/P/E (SCFC)--1980--MM$	17	4	0.8600	510	1
SALE OF COM/PREF S-CK (SCFC)--1980--MM$	11	6	0.6567	510	1
SALE OF INVESTMENTS (SCFC)--1980--MM$	0	1	-0.7247	510	1
-TAL FUNDS FROM OPER (SCFC)--1980--MM$	73	110	-0.6653	510	1
ISSUANCE OF L-T DEBT (SCFC)--1980--MM$	86	29	1.2394	510	1
-TAL SOURCES OF FUNDS (SCFC)--1980--MM$	192	158	0.3101	510	1
INCR IN INVESTMENTS (SCFC)--1980--MM$	5	5	-0.0073	510	1
REDUCTION OF L-T DEBT (SCFC)--1980--MM$	53	16	1.0929	510	1
PUR OF COMM/PREF S-CK (SCFC)--1980--MM$	0	4	-2.3191	510	2
-TAL USES OF FUNDS (SCFC)--1980--MM$	274	154	0.8139	510	1

Table 7.AII.4 continued

VARIABLE	RESPONDENTS' MEAN	NON RESPONDENTS' MEAN	T-VALUE	DEGREES OF FREEDOM	TEST VALUE
SALES (RESTATED)--1980--MM$	1695354	824200	0.6603	510	1
INC BEF EXTRA/DISC OPER (RE)--1980--MM$	-45	44	-1.5574	510	1
EPS (PRIM) (RESTATED)--1980--MM$	0	1	-1.0544	510	1
ASSETS (-TAL) (RESTATED)--1980--MM$	966029	624222	0.3944	510	1
WORKING CAPITAL (RESTATED)--1980--MM$	13	80	-3.7078	510	4
PRETAX INCOME (RESTATED)--1980--MM$	-58	79	-1.8066	510	2
INC BEF EXT/DISC OPER (SCFC)--1980--MM$	-22	61	-1.2133	510	1
EXTRA ITEMS/DISC OPER (SCFC)--1980--MM$	-0	0	-0.2386	510	1
DEPREC & AMORTIZ (SCFC)--1980--MM$	103	37	0.9090	510	1
DEFERRED TAXES (SCFC)--1980--MM$	-0	10	-2.1336	510	2
CASH DIVIDENDS (SCFC)--1980--MM$	32	22	0.5438	510	1
CAPITAL EXPENDITURES (SCFC)--1980--MM$	172	87	0.8003	510	1
ACQUISITIONS (SCFC)--1980--MM$	3	9	-0.9604	510	1
PREF S-CK (CARRYING VALUE)--1980--MM$	35	7	1.1089	510	1
CASH & SHORT TERM INVESTMENTS--1986--MM$	387741	148872	0.7819	510	1
RECEIVABLES--1986--MM$	295	180	0.8341	510	1
INVEN-RIES--1986--MM$	324	165	0.7625	510	1
CURRENT ASSETS (-TAL)--1986--MM$	1001	394	0.9149	510	1
CURRENT LIABILITIES (-TAL)--1986--MM$	807	290	0.9250	510	1
ASSETS/(LIABS+NET WORTH)--1986--MM$	2727	2134	0.4145	510	1
PLANT (GROSS)--1986--MM$	1377	1107	0.2792	510	1
PLANT (NET)--1986--MM$	721	660	0.1237	510	1
LONG TERM DEBT (-TAL)--1986--MM$	288	315	-0.2222	510	1
PEFERRED S-CK @ LIQ VALUE--1986--MM$	51	17	1.1395	510	1
COMMON EQUITY (TANGIBLE)--1986--MM$	897	473	0.7395	510	1
SALES (NET)--1986--MM$	3328935	1362544	5.9391	510	4
OPER INCOME BEFORE DEPREC--1986--MM$	326	179	0.5856	510	1
DEPRECIATION & AMORTIZATION--1986--MM$	135	68	0.6324	510	1
INTEREST EXPENSE--1986--MM$	57	66	-0.3628	510	1
INCOME TAXES (-TAL)--1986--MM$	98	37	0.9224	510	1
SPECIAL ITEMS--1986--MM$	7	-16	1.7105	510	2
INC BEF EXTRA & DISC OPER--1986--MM$	158	41	0.9889	510	1
PREFERRED DIVIDENDS--1986--MM$	2	1	0.5605	510	1
AVAIL FOR COM AFT ADJ--1986--MM$	157	40	0.9928	510	1
COMMON DIVIDENDS--1986--MM$	35	32	0.1164	510	1
PRICE (HIGH)--1986--$ & 8THS	34	30	0.6096	510	1
PRICE (LOW)--1986--$ & 8THS	20	19	0.2449	510	1
PRICE (CLOSE)--1986--$ & 8THS	26	24	0.4772	510	1
COMMON SHARES OUTSTANDING--1986--M	30746	24437	0.5886	510	1
DIVIDENDS PR SHARE--1986--$ & @	518	590	-0.5768	510	1
ADJUST FAC-R (CUM)(RATIO)--1986	1071428	1114066	-0.7749	510	1
COMMON SHARES TRADED--1986--M	27635	18328	0.8912	510	1
EMPLOYEES--1986--M	23	10	0.9312	510	1
CAPITAL EXPENDITURES--1986--MM$	166	104	0.5137	510	1
INVEST & ADVANCES (EQ METH)--1986--MM$	415	51	1.3995	510	1
INVEST & ADVANCES (OTHER)--1986--MM$	27	249	-3.2579	510	4
INTANGIBLES--1986--MM$	54	51	0.1283	510	1
DEBT IN CURRENT LIABILITIES--1986--MM$	102	214	-1.5445	510	1
DEF TAX & INVEST CRED (B/S)--1986--MM$	64	106	-0.7596	510	1
RET EARNINGS (C/S OUTSTAND)--1986--MM$	765	385	0.7198	510	1
INVESTED CAPITAL (-TAL)--1986--MM$	1246523	848513	0.5857	510	1
MINORITY INTEREST (B/S)--1986--MM$	13	10	0.3635	510	1
CONVERTIBLE DEBT & PREF S-CK--1986--MM$	28	16	0.8576	510	1
COMM SHARES RES FOR CONVER--1986--M	4	3	0.4336	510	1
COST OF GOODS SOLD--1986--MM$	2620	915	0.9107	510	1
LABOR & RELATED EXPENSE--1986--MM$	548	152	0.7254	510	1
PENSION & RETIREMENT EXPENSE--1986--MM$	32	7	0.9867	510	1

Table 7.AII.4 continued

VARIABLE	RESPONDENTS' MEAN	NON RESPONDENTS' MEAN	T-VALUE	DEGREES OF FREEDOM	TEST VALUE
DEBT DUE IN 1 YEAR--1986--MM$	14	19	-0.7595	510	1
ADVERTISING EXPENSE--1986--MM$	45	13	0.9314	510	1
RESEARCH & DEVEL EXPENSE--1986--MM$	112	23	1.0680	510	1
RENTAL EXPENSE--1986--MM$	17	19	-0.2432	510	1
EXTRAORD ITEMS & DISC OPER--1986--MM$	1	1	-0.2640	510	1
MINORITY INTEREST (INC ACCT)--1986--MM$	3	1	1.1038	510	1
DEFERRED TAXES (INC ACCT)--1986--MM$	13	9	0.3931	510	1
INVEST TAX CREDIT (INC ACCT)--1986--MM$	0	2	-3.9811	510	4
TAX LOSS CARRY FORWARD--1986--MM$	51	21	0.6150	510	1
EARNINGS PER SHARE (PRIMARY)--1986--MM$	1	1	0.7103	510	1
COMM SHARES USED-COMP EPS--1986--MM$	31	24	0.6047	510	1
UNCNSOL SUBSID EQ IN EARNINGS--1986--MM$	65	5	1.3990	510	1
PREF S-CK @ REDEMPTION VALUE--1986--MM$	46	16	1.0792	510	1
EPS (FULLY DILUTED)--1986--$ & @	1	1	0.8222	510	1
EPS (EX EXTRA/DISC)--1986--$ & @	1	1	0.8008	510	1
INVEN-RY VALUATION METHOD--1986	42	35	0.4014	510	1
COMMON EQUITY (AS REPORTED)--1986--MM$	972	530	0.7675	510	1
NONOPERATING INCOME/EXPENSE--1986--MM$	97	19	1.2546	510	1
INTEREST INCOME--1986--MM$	42	47	-0.1657	510	1
INCOME TAXES (FEDERAL)--1986--MM$	38	10	0.9518	510	1
INCOME TAXES (FOREIGN)--1986--MM$	25	12	0.5316	510	1
AMORTIZATION OF INTANGIBLES--1986--MM$	1	1	-0.5550	510	1
DISCONTINUED OPERATIONS--1986--MM$	-1	1	-0.7292	510	1
RECEIVABLES (EST DOUBTFUL)--1986--MM$	5	4	0.4435	510	1
CURRENT ASSETS (OTHER)--1986--MM$	42	25	0.7207	510	1
ASSETS (OTHER)--1986--MM$	93	55	0.8089	510	1
ACCOUNTS PAYABLE--1986--MM$	283	230	0.2552	510	1
INCOME TAXES PAYABLE--1986--MM$	35	23	0.4309	510	1
CURRENT LIABILITIES (OTHER)--1986--MM$	408	109	1.0618	510	1
CONSTRUCTION IN PROGRESS--1986--MM$	38	14	0.8452	510	1
DEFERRED TAXED (B/S)--1986--MM$	64	104	-0.7354	510	1
LIABILITIES (OTHER)--1986--MM$	214	96	0.8345	510	1
RAW MATERIALS--1986--MM$	31	25	0.3513	510	1
WORK IN PROGRESS--1986--MM$	33	21	0.6538	510	1
FINISHED GOODS--1986--MM$	123	30	1.0347	510	1
DEBT (CONVERTIBLE)--1986--MM$	10	10	0.0056	510	1
DEBT (SUBORDINATED)--1986--MM$	20	21	-0.1285	510	1
DEBT (NOTES)--1986--MM$	28	110	-4.0187	510	4
DEBT (DEBENTURES)--1986--MM$	19	79	-3.4217	510	4
DEBT (OTHER LONG TERM)--1986--MM$	102	64	0.4892	510	1
DEBT (CAP LEASE OBLIGATIONS)--1986--MM$	4	11	-2.6301	510	4
COMMON S-CK--1986--MM$	117	46	1.2088	510	1
TREAS S-CK (-TAL $ AMOUNT)--1986--MM$	12	48	-1.8502	510	2
TREASRY S-CK (# COMMON SHARES)--1986--M	782	1512	-1.2578	510	1
PRES VALUE OF NONCAP LEASES--1986--MM$	-0	-0	.	510	1
UNFUN PENSION COSTS(VEST BEN)--1986--MM$	13	1	0.9350	510	1
UNFUN PENSION COSTS(PAST SRV)--1986--MM$	-0	0	-1.1000	510	1
DEBT MATURING IN 2ND YEAR--1986--MM$	35	19	0.7413	510	1
DEBT MATURING IN 3RD YEAR--1986--MM$	19	18	0.0551	510	1
DEBT MATURING IN 4TH YEAR--1986--MM$	26	18	0.5242	510	1
DEBT MATURING IN 5TH YEAR--1986--MM$	18	21	-0.3205	510	1
MIN RENT COMMIT 5 YRS (-TAL)--1986--MM$	57	38	0.7743	510	1
MIN RENT COMMITMENT IN 1 YEAR--1986--MM$	16	10	0.7730	510	1
RET EARNINGS (UNRESTRICTED)--1986--MM$	133	40	0.9495	510	1
ORDER BACKLOG--1986--MM$	294	177	0.6820	510	1
RET EARNINGS (RESTATEMENT)--1986--MM$	0	-1	1.7728	510	2
SHAREHOLDERS (COMMON)--1986--M	21277	12635	0.8357	510	1

150

Table 7.AII.4 continued

VARIABLE	RESPONDENTS' MEAN	NON RESPONDENTS' MEAN	T-VALUE	DEGREES OF FREEDOM	TEST VALUE
INT EXPENSE ON LONG TERM DEBT--1986--MM$	1	3	-2.1629	510	2
EXCISE TAXES--1986--MM$	0	17	-1.5355	510	1
DEPREC EXPENSE (SCHED V)--1986--MM$	88	63	0.4089	510	1
BORROWINGS (AVG SHORT TERM)--1986--MM$	54	35	0.4371	510	1
INT RATE (AVG ON SHORT TERM)--1986--%	4	4	0.1297	510	1
UNREMIT EARNS OF SUBS (SCFC)--1986--MM$	-13	-1	-0.4810	510	1
SALE OF P/P/E (SCFC)--1986--MM$	9	8	0.1306	510	1
SALE OF COM/PREF S-CK (SCFC)--1986--MM$	5	12	-2.0659	510	2
SALE OF INVESTMENTS (SCFC)--1986--MM$	1	80	-3.2584	510	4
-TAL FUNDS FROM OPER (SCFC)--1986--MM$	341	145	0.8234	510	1
ISSUANCE OF L-T DEBT (SCFC)--1986--MM$	107	110	-0.0548	510	1
-TAL SOURCES OF FUNDS (SCFC)--1986--MM$	577	419	0.4829	510	1
INCR IN INVESTMENTS (SCFC)--1986--MM$	14	122	-2.9200	510	4
REDUCTION OF L-T DEBT (SCFC)--1986--MM$	93	61	0.6904	510	1
PUR OF COMM/PREF S-CK (SCFC)--1986--MM$	27	22	0.1886	510	1
-TAL USES OF FUNDS (SCFC)--1986--MM$	462	416	0.1937	510	1
SALES (RESTATED)--1986--MM$	3170463	1318901	5.5043	510	4
INC BEF EXTRA/DISC OPER (RE)--1986--MM$	148	39	0.9228	510	1
EPS (PRIM) (RESTATED)--1986--MM$	1	1	0.4807	510	1
ASSETS (-TAL) (RESTATED)--1986--MM$	1902444	1981962	-0.0591	510	1
WORKING CAPITAL (RESTATED)--1986--MM$	25	104	-4.2029	510	4
PRETAX INCOME (RESTATED)--1986--MM$	245	79	0.8957	510	1
INC BEF EXT/DISC OPER (SCFC)--1986--MM$	151	39	0.9417	510	1
EXTRA ITEMS/DISC OPER (SCFC)--1986--MM$	14	9	0.4034	510	1
DEPREC & AMORTIZ (SCFC)--1986--MM$	141	69	0.6787	510	1
DEFERRED TAXES (SCFC)--1986--MM$	3	3	-0.1185	510	1
CASH DIVIDENDS (SCFC)--1986--MM$	34	33	0.0430	510	1
CAPITAL EXPENDITURES (SCFC)--1986--MM$	157	92	0.5466	510	1
ACQUISITIONS (SCFC)--1986--MM$	52	33	0.6675	510	1
PREF S-CK (CARRYING VALUE)--1986--MM$	31	13	1.0934	510	1

APPENDIX III: COMPARISON OF PLAN DATA FROM SURVEY RESPONSES WITH PLAN DATA FROM THE 1985 EMPLOYEE PLAN MASTER FILE

In order to assess the validity of our data about plans sponsored by respondent firms, we obtained a copy of the 1985 Form 5500 Employee Plan Master File (EPMF) produced by the U.S. Department of Labor. This file contains all of the computerized response information from Form 5500 filings for plans with plan years ending in the calendar year 1985. All employee benefit plans with 100 or more participants are required to file Form 5500 each plan year.

The data in the EPMF are organized by plan rather than by company. Therefore a given company should have as many records in the dataset as it has plans for which it filed Form 5500 in 1985. Using Employer Identification Numbers, we identified all plans from the EPMF associated with each survey respondent and attempted to characterize the plan using three items of information: Type of Pension Benefit Plan (TPBP), Type Benefit (TB) and Does Plan Have ESOP Features (ESOP features). TPBP is coded "1" for defined benefit plans and "2" for defined contribution plans. For defined contribution plans, TB is coded "A" for profit-sharing, "B" for stock bonus, "C" for target benefit, "D" for other money purchase, and "E" for other. We characterized a plan as an ESOP if TPBP was coded "2," TB was coded "B," and the plan was said to have ESOP features. We further broke ESOPs into two groups: an ESOP was characterized as a tax credit ESOP if the plan name contained the words "Tax Reduction" or "Payroll." If an ESOP name did not contain either of these phrases, it was classified as a tax deduction ESOP (listed in Table 7.AIII.1 simply as "ESOP").

A plan was classified as a defined benefit pension plan if TPBP was coded "1." It was coded as a profit-sharing plan if TPBP was coded "2" and TB was coded "A," and a stock bonus plan if TB was coded "B." No attention was paid to the name of the plan, which in some cases implied a different type than that indicated by the codes described above.

We then developed two lists of plans for each company; the first list was derived from the survey responses, and the second from the EPMF data. Table 7.AIII.1 shows the firm-by-firm mixture of plans from the survey responses on the left, while to the right is shown the mixture derived from the EPMF data. (Because the data were gathered with a promise of confidentiality, firms are listed by number only.) Of the 45 study companies, the EPMF had Form 5500 data for 38. For these 38, there were 13 "perfect matches"—that is, in 13 cases the characterization of a company's plans on the basis of survey information coincided exactly with that compiled from the EPMF data. This may appear to be a low score, but there are numerous factors that cannot be controlled for and that may intervene in this comparison process. One such factor is that some plans may have had fewer than 100 participants, and therefore may not have been reported on Form 5500 in that year. Another factor is that only plans with plan years ending in 1985 were included in the EPMF, whereas the survey requested information by calendar year. Some additional slippage resulted from the fact that respondents most probably mischaracterized several plans, just as we would have had we employed the plan name in characterizing a plan type rather than using the three variables described above.

For this reason, the number of perfect matches is probably too exacting a standard on which to judge the accuracy of our plan characterizations. Rather, we used the fraction of plans on which the two information sources agreed. Of the 190 plans identified from survey responses, 155 or 81.5% were similarly characterized using the EPMF data. Given the various potential sources of slippage in correspondence between the two sources, we regard this as a relatively high correspondence.

Table 7.AIII.1
Comparison of Information from Survey Responses Versus 1985 Employee Plan Master File for the 45 Study Companies

	INFORMATION FROM SURVEY RESPONSE					INFORMATION FROM 1985 EPMF TAPE				
IN 1985, COMPANY HAD AT LEAST ONE:	ESOP	TRASOP OR PAYSOP	PSP	SBP	PP	ESOP	TRASOP OR PAYSOP	PSP	SBP	PP
COMPANY 1	Y	N	N	N	Y	Y	N	Y	N	N
COMPANY 2	N	N	N	N	Y	--	--	--	--	--
COMPANY 3	N	N	Y	N	Y	N	N	Y	N	Y
COMPANY 4	Y	Y	N	N	N	Y	N	N	N	N
COMPANY 5	Y	Y	Y	N	Y	Y	Y	N	N	Y
COMPANY 6	N	N	N	N	N	--	--	--	--	--
COMPANY 7	N	N	N	N	Y	N	N	N	N	N
COMPANY 8	N	Y	N	N	Y	Y	N	N	N	Y
COMPANY 9	Y	N	N	N	N	Y	Y	N	N	Y
COMPANY 10	N	N	N	N	Y	N	N	N	N	N
COMPANY 11	Y	N	N	N	Y	N	Y	Y	N	Y
COMPANY 12	N	N	Y	N	Y	N	Y	Y	N	Y
COMPANY 13	N	N	N	N	Y	--	--	--	--	--
COMPANY 14	N	Y	Y	N	Y	N	Y	N	N	Y
COMPANY 15	N	Y	N	N	Y	Y	N	Y	N	Y
COMPANY 16	N	N	Y	N	N	Y	N	Y	N	N
COMPANY 17	Y	N	N	N	Y	N	Y	N	N	Y
COMPANY 18	N	N	N	N	N	N	N	N	N	N
COMPANY 19	Y	N	Y	N	N	Y	Y	Y	N	N
COMPANY 20	N	N	N	N	Y	N	N	N	N	Y
COMPANY 21	Y	N	N	N	Y	N	N	N	N	Y
COMPANY 22	Y	Y	N	N	N	Y	N	Y	N	N
COMPANY 23	N	N	Y	N	N	N	N	Y	N	N
COMPANY 24	Y	N	Y	N	N	Y	N	Y	N	N
COMPANY 25	Y	Y	N	N	Y	--	--	--	--	--
COMPANY 26	N	N	Y	N	Y	Y	N	Y	N	Y
COMPANY 27	N	N	N	N	Y	N	N	N	N	Y
COMPANY 28	N	N	N	N	N	N	N	N	N	N
COMPANY 29	Y	N	Y	N	Y	Y	N	N	N	Y
COMPANY 30	N	Y	N	N	Y	N	N	N	N	Y
COMPANY 31	Y	Y	Y	N	N	Y	N	Y	N	N
COMPANY 32	Y	N	Y	N	Y	Y	N	N	N	N
COMPANY 33	N	N	Y	N	Y	N	N	Y	N	Y
COMPANY 34	Y	N	Y	N	Y	Y	N	Y	N	Y
COMPANY 35	N	N	N	Y	N	--	--	--	--	--

COMPANY 36	Y	N	Y	N	Y	Y	N	N	N	Y
COMPANY 37	N	N	N	N	N	--	--	--	--	--
COMPANY 38	Y	N	N	N	N	Y	N	N	N	N
COMPANY 39	N	N	N	N	Y	N	N	N	N	Y
COMPANY 40	Y	N	N	Y	Y	Y	N	N	N	Y
COMPANY 41	N	N	N	Y	Y	--	--	--	--	--
COMPANY 42	N	N	N	N	Y	N	N	Y	N	Y
COMPANY 43	N	N	N	N	Y	Y	N	N	N	Y
COMPANY 44	N	N	Y	N	N	N	N	Y	N	N
COMPANY 45	N	Y	Y	N	Y	N	Y	Y	N	Y

C

155

8

Managing an Employee Ownership Company

KAREN M. YOUNG

People often comment that it is only reasonable that workers who are also owners or part owners of a business would, of course, work harder and more economically. Some companies' management people also credit employee ownership with improved productivity, attracting quality employees, lower turnover, and other activities that better company performance. Intuitively, we might all agree with these pronouncements. However, research on the subject does not support these beliefs that employee ownership alone improves profits, productivity, or employee behaviors. What the research to date does indicate is that corporate performance is enhanced in employee ownership companies when employees are involved in company affairs, when information about the company is shared on a regular basis, and input is allowed and encouraged. Then the company is likely to see results to the good. Neither employee ownership nor participation by themselves can bring about the motivation that the combination of the two does. In other words, a synergy is created when employee ownership and employee participation are brought together.

Think about it. The more informed people are about any subject, the better able they are to draw reasonable conclusions and make intelligent decisions about the matter. And, seeing that people are kept informed also makes them feel involved, which is a powerful motivational construct itself. Also asking and expecting people to be engaged in providing information or making a decision about an issue creates a larger pool of ideas and information on which to base determinations about a subject. This contributes to the probability of a better decision being made. And, again, involving people in this way makes the decision or action taken theirs. People are much more likely to carry through when this is the case. This is true in a work environment as well as other life areas. Communication and participation are the terms we use to identify these activities of sharing information and involving employees in a company setting.

As stated earlier, empirical work indicates that employee ownership and participatory management are a powerful combination toward increasing motivation and improving productivity. But aside from the corporate performance aspect, both employee ownership and participatory management make good sense, for our economic/social structure as a whole (the macro perspective) and for the individuals involved (the micro perspective). Wealth is extremely concentrated in the United States.[1] Best-selling economist Ravi Batra believes that this condition of wealth being held by such a few hands has led to the deterioration of our competitive position in the world market and will lead to the downfall of our economic system.[2] Broadening the ownership of wealth through employee stock ownership is one way to alleviate this extreme concentration and possibly avoid the economic ills such a skewed holding of wealth ordains. From the micro or individual perspective there is research work that strongly supports the notion that employees with a commitment to their organizations are also more satisfied with other areas of their lives.[3] Employee ownership is a significant correlate of organizational commitment,[4] and participation is an avenue through which this commitment can be activated. This work indicates that employee ownership and participatory management have the potential to help create a healthier economy and a healthier society.

Much of the research for this chapter was done in 1986 and 1987 before the wave of ESOPs in public companies described in the rest of this book. What few significant ESOPs there were in public firms were often supplemental benefits, and only rarely were they part of the company's core philosophy. The recent boom in public-company ESOPs is too new to provide us with enough data about management practices in these companies to make general statements as to how these practices might correlate with employee attitudes or corporate performance in public companies *per se*.

Nonetheless, the approaches cited in this chapter are just as applicable in public as well as private companies. Size is not a determinant of positive employee attitudes or improved corporate performance. Research has already tested that factor. The eloquent examples of participative firms such as Weirton Steel, Avis, Herman Miller, Science Applications, and other firms with thousands of employees address this point persuasively. Nor is the percentage of the company owned by the ESOP a consideration. Again, the research is decisive on this issue. Employees report that they would prefer to work for a 20% ESOP-owned company that makes a large contribution to the plan each year and treats them like owners than a 100% ESOP-owned company that does neither. And last, having public shareholders does not preclude employee involvement as a motivator.

Public companies have embraced ESOPs of late for a number of reasons primarily having to do with tax savings or spurning an unwanted suitor. But a company's bottom line is much more influenced by the ideas and information all its people can bring to bear on serving its competitive needs than by tax manipulations. And there is no better "poison rose" than a company already maximizing shareholder value through effective management.

How some of the most successful employee ownership companies have communicated their plans and have gotten the employees involved in their companies will be presented in the rest of this chapter.

COMMUNICATIONS IN EMPLOYEE OWNERSHIP COMPANIES

The ESOP as a vehicle for employee stock ownership has been on the law books for a decade and a half now. Early discussions of ESOPs concentrated almost solely on the financial and technical considerations of establishing and administering a plan. Business people who were introduced to the idea were, of course, interested in how the ESOP would fit in with the company's overall business situation. How would high-salaried employees be affected by initiation of the plan? What configuration of tax incentives would give the company the greatest tax benefit? Would the employees want to run the company if they owned stock? How could ESOPs be used to purchase shares of existing owners? How would the ESOP fit with other benefit plans? These were all prime considerations when contemplating an ESOP. And they are legitimate questions with which a prudent business person should be concerned. Early on, it seems, not a lot of thought was given to communicating with the employees about the plan. It was just another vehicle in the tax code.

As more companies implemented ESOPs it became clearer that ESOPs were not just another item at the salad counter. ESOPs are special. People who would probably not otherwise have access to stock ownership can become stock owners—at no cost to themselves! Wait. Let's back up a little here. There is a cost to the workers. The employees, as stock owners, need to take some responsibility to see that their stock does well. As owners, employees have responsibilities as well as rights. The old adage "You don't get something for nothing" is applicable here as in many of life's situations. However, what you get can will be worth the effort. Look at this scenario. You, as an employee, are given stock. Wouldn't it be foolish to do things that would or could make that stock less valuable? Wouldn't it be wise to do things that would or could make that stock more valuable? Granted, the person giving you the stock is also benefiting. She or he may be getting a market for that stock; the company is getting a tax deduction; the company may be borrowing money at lower rates. However, you, as the employee, are also benefiting from this action by the company. The company could have been sold to someone else with perhaps perilous consequences for you. And if the company is getting a deduction or using borrowed funds for expansion, you as a stockholder profit from that.

Making sure employees understand these benefits and their attendant responsibilities is the first step toward making an employee ownership plan work better for the good of all concerned. But just telling employees what a great deal the ESOP is is not enough. Both the law and common sense require that you explain to the employees the benefits and the risks as well. By making sure employees know what the nature of these plans is, you help create an atmosphere of trust and fair play crucial to the ESOP's potential being exploited.

As it became more apparent that employee ownership inherently had the potential to inspire workers, it became the manager's job to inform workers about how the plan could work for the employee and the company. Having an employee ownership plan can be very advantageous for the company and for the employees. Having employee ownership combined with efforts to inform the employees about the benefits and how they can contribute to increasing those benefits can be even more advantageous. How to do this has become an area of growing interest in employee ownership companies in recent years.

Communicating is not as easy as simply handing out a brochure or holding an occasional meeting. Many employees have never owned stock and have little or no understanding of what stock is. Many will be suspicious, especially about ESOPs, believing there "must be a catch" or that the company must be in trouble. Even if these problems can be solved, ESOPs are complicated legal instruments, not easy even for sophisticated people to grasp. Imagine how employees will react.

Even if you can explain how ESOPs work, you still have a long way to go before you have an effective communications program. Communications means information-sharing. You need to find ways to have employees tell you things and then listen and respond to what employees tell you, not just hurl booklets, memos, t-shirts, and pens through the wind and hope they hit their mark. The effort involved can be substantial, but so is the reward.

What Others Have Found About Information-Sharing

Why is it important to have open communications? According to a survey of nearly 3,000 workers in employee ownership companies, communications was one of the four key correlates with satisfaction and commitment. You may say, "Well, that's obvious." But look at the variables for which there was no correlation: percent of the company owned, reason the plan was established, the age of the plan, company size, line of business, and employee demographics. So communication is a very important factor in guiding employee attitudes toward "ownership." Moreover, open communication means better information flows within the company; more people know more about what is going on, and can act accordingly. Four major factors affect communications. Each is discussed below.

Different Perspectives. Both the senders and the receivers of a message bring with them a set of expectations and values through which they filter information. The more that can be done to reduce impediments between communicators, the more likely it is that the intended messages will be conveyed. Different status positions, for example, can decrease compatibility and trust between parties. When communications are reinforced by actions, the distrust and incompatibility can be reduced. For instance, management cannot tell workers one thing and do another and expect to establish open communication channels.

The following example illustrates how far apart perceptions can be about the same issues. Managers in 24 industrial plants were asked to rank 10 factors in order of importance to employees. The items they placed in the last three places were:

8. full appreciation of work

9. feeling "in" on things

10. sympathetic help on personal problems

Employees were asked to do the same thing. The employees ranked those same three factors as 1, 2, and 3 in order of importance to them.[5] These two groups, managers and employees, were like "ships passing in the night." Management was probably issuing directives to employees, and employees were probably talking among themselves, but neither side was really communicating, really *sharing* information with the other. Mutual and reciprocal communications are necessary to set the stage for behavioral and attitudinal changes to take place.

So the very first consideration before entering into an interchange is for both parties to realize that they are approaching the situation with different ways of looking at things. Knowing this, parties must try to put themselves in the other's place. This practice will lead to a better understanding of the other's actions and methods. In the vernacular, "where the other person is coming from" will be more clear.

Many Messages and Mediums. The second major point made in the research literature about communications is that many messages and mediums should be used. Do not depend on one message or one avenue to get the idea across. A continuous flow of information is necessary to reach and hold the receiver's attention. Some common types of communication media used by companies are:

Written	*Oral*
Bulletin Boards	Face-to-Face
Handbooks	Speeches
Magazines	Meetings
Newspapers	Television
Letters	PA Systems
Posters	Telephones
Suggestions Box	

A combination of oral and written communications methods is most effective in providing information about a concept like employee ownership. Generally, face-to-face communications is the most effective and computer printouts of numbers with no or little explanation are the least effective methods of communicating. Of course, it is impossible and inefficient to continually carry on face-to-face communications. However, a set of numbers sent to someone is likely to be set aside to be "looked at later" or considered too much effort to figure out easily. Either way, material not read is certainly not effective.

Feedback. Feedback must be allowed for and encouraged to get the most out of communications endeavors. Feedback is the most overlooked aspect of communications efforts; this is true whether talking face-to-face or putting out a handbook. How many times have you been in a situation where everyone is anxious to say what they want to say? No one is listening to the other speakers. Or have you ever received an employee manual that left you with questions, but there was nowhere to direct those questions? The sender in both cases is overlooking feedback. Communications must be a reciprocal process to achieve its potential. You may not get the totally desired effect with feedback, but you certainly will not get the desired effect without it.

Subordinate-Initiated Communications. Research also supports the notion that communications efforts from subordinates are poorly handled. That is, people who are "below" on the totem pole don't get listened to very well. This is more than a motivational problem. If people at the top are not getting accurate information from people below, they have inadequate information on which to make decisions.

Executives, for instance, may hear what managers want them to hear, and managers may hear what supervisors want them to hear, and so forth. The result can be excessively rosy notions, poor data, or limited ideas and perspectives. It is especially important to remedy this condition in employee ownership companies. Everyone is an owner and everyone depends on the company getting and acting on good information and ideas. Some techniques to implement subordinate-initiated communications are:

1. *The Suggestion Box.* Boxes placed in accessible areas afford employees anonymity to say things they may not feel secure enough to say in any other forum. Responsible suggestions are sometimes obtained through this method. Management can get an idea of what is going on in the "shop." This practice also serves the valuable purpose of simply letting employees "blow off steam." This last use is in itself worthwhile. However, as one person put it, companies whose whole communications system is a suggestion box are themselves in need of suggestions.

2. *An Open-Door Policy.* The boss is available for employees to come in and talk. A number of smaller employee ownership companies have reported to us they have this policy. How effective this is is hard to measure. It is very difficult for an employee to take the initiative, walk past other personnel and into the boss's office, and complain or make suggestions. However, the symbolic importance of an open-door policy may outweigh the drawbacks.

3. *Participative Decision-Making.* This will be discussed in detail in the next section of this chapter.

4. *Conducting Questionnaire Surveys.* This method provides the company with information about employee attitudes about issues, and if handled properly can help to improve feelings of self-worth. However, a response should be provided with information about what was found and what can or cannot be done.

5. *The Grievance Procedure.* Most unionized and many non-unionized companies have a grievance procedure. It is a way for employees to register a complaint beyond their immediate supervisor.

6. *Communicating Across Boundaries.* Seek out ideas from employees and encourage employees at all levels to communicate freely with those people who need the information. "Going through channels" should be a rule with many exceptions, or perhaps not a rule at all.

Summary. Basically, communication research points out that to be effective communications must (1) have both parties trying to view a situation from the other's perspective, (2) employ varied media and be continuous, (3) provide feedback, and (4) provide multiple ways to allow effective subordinate-initiated communications.

A Survey of ESOP Company Communications Practices

We sent a one-page, 11-item survey to 83 NCEO employee ownership member companies in order to find out the specific ways in which companies are communicating with employees about their plans. We received responses from 42 companies. Of these, 39 have ESOPs, one is a worker cooperative, and two have stock purchase plans. The breakdown of the responses to the questionnaire from most-to-least-used communications methods is as follows:

Number of Companies	Communications Method
39	Annual account balance statement for each plan participant
39	Employee ownership plan discussed in initial orientation for each new employee
33	Informal conversations with employees about the employee ownership plan
30	Annual meeting for employee stockholders
29	Employee ownership plan described in employee handbook
26	Employee ownership plan regularly mentioned in company newsletter or company letter to employees
18	Small group meetings about employee ownership
17	Employee ownership plan described in slide show for employees
13	Employee ownership posters around the company
10	Employee ownership payroll stuffers
9	Employee ownership mentioned in company letterhead

1–8   Other efforts, including passing through dividends, bulletin boards, mentors, stickers, films, bonuses, open doors, open houses, information about payouts, and advertising.

We have several additional suggestions. They are a "what if" computer game, sending non-managerial employees to workshops and conferences, and participating in "Employee Ownership Week," an annual event initiated by the NCEO in 1987. We will discuss all of the above in detail, providing samples of some of the printed materials from some employee ownership companies.

Annual Account Balance Statement. Providing an annual account balance statement to the employee stockholders was the most-used communication method of the companies in our survey. This is a legal requirement in ESOP companies. The account balance statement is straightforward, usually providing for each employee the previous balance if there is one, employer contributions to the account for the year, the share of forfeitures if there are any, share of dividends if any, and any withdrawals from the account if that is provided for in the plan. The total account balance is usually shown in number of shares and dollar value. Some statements also show the original cost of the stock so the employee can see if the stock has increased or decreased in value. Some also give the employees the vested value of the stock in their accounts. Some companies provide the information in the form of a stock certificate facsimile. This, of course, reinforces the notion that the employee is a stockholder in the company. Figure 8.1 is an example of an account balance statement that resembles a stock certificate from Reflexite Corporation, a Connecticut manufacturer of reflecting materials.

Initial Orientation. Nearly every company has some kind of introductory meeting for new employees. Sometimes these are on an individual basis. This is usually the case in smaller companies. Larger companies may have an orientation meeting once a month, or once every few months. Almost all (39) of the companies responding to the survey reported that an introduction to the employee ownership plan is a part of these meetings.

In addition, many companies have employee meetings when the ESOP is established. A company manager or the firm's lawyer may present the details. At the Lambert company in Ansonia, Ohio, after the initial presentation, employees were asked to write anonymous questions on note cards. These were then all answered in a subsequent meeting. Tim Johnston, the company's vice-president, reports that there were a lot of good questions, questions employees felt were too sensitive or too basic to ask in public. However this meeting is handled, the presentation needs to be simple and straightforward, not complex or promotional.

In some companies employee stock ownership is part of the core of the company culture. Employees are told this initially and it is reinforced continually. At other companies stock ownership is part of a package of benefits with

Figure 8.1
ESOP Account Balance Statement

REFLEXITE CORPORATION
Employee Stock Ownership Plan

To _____

Social Security No. _____

In accordance with the provisions of our Employee Stock Ownership Plan, your account has been credited as follows for the year ended _____

	SHARES	DOLLARS
COMPANY STOCK ACCOUNT		
Your balance from last year	_____	_____
Employer contributions this year	_____	_____
Total employer contribution	_____	_____
Your share of forfeitures	_____	_____
Your total account balance	_____	_____

	SHARES	DOLLARS
TOTAL VESTED VALUE		
Current cost per share	_____	_____
Vested amount	_____	_____
Total vested market value	_____	_____

This certificate is for your records only and does not represent a negotiable security.

Used with permission from Reflexite Corporation.

no significance beyond that of other benefits. But whatever role the concept of employee ownership plays in your company, tell the employees what that role is. If it is an integral part of the company culture with shared company information, say that; if it is to be solely another benefit, say that. Neither approach, nor any degree in between, is right or wrong. What is right is providing honest information about the stock ownership plan; what is wrong is falsely raising expectations about stock ownership to get more out of the employees.

Informal Conversations with Employees About the Ownership Plan. The president at Fastener Industries, a weld fastener manufacturer in Berea, Ohio, spends much of his time walking around the company talking to the employee-owners. So does Harry Quadracci, president of Quad/Graphics, a Pewaukee, Wisconsin, printing company. He is a common sight on the floor, just letting everyone know he is accessible.

Delta Electronics, in Alexandria, Virginia, has an open-door policy and "depends more on informal discussions to spread the word than on printed material." Allied Plywood has an open-door started by the founder that is still carried out under the new president. Employee ownership is not the only topic of discussion in walking around or open-door efforts. But these efforts deliver the message that employees' ideas and opinions are appreciated and desired because they are part owners.

Another area of informal discussions is among employees themselves. They do discuss the notion and act as agents among themselves to have their peers conform to ownership behavior.

Annual Meeting for Employee Stockholders. Many of the companies invite the employee stockholders to an annual meeting. As depicted in the 1950s TV series "Hazel," annual meetings were pretty stuffy affairs with little effort to have stockholders actually participate in the affairs of the company. Though even the stuffy meeting may be inherently more interesting to employee-stockholders, some companies have gone beyond the head table and hard-back straight-chair format. The chief executive officer (CEO) and chief operating officer at Leslie Paper in Minneapolis visit each company location once a year. All stockholders and their spouses are invited to the presentation and discussion event. This is followed by a dinner party.

Of course, there is no restriction on meeting more often than once a year. Bofors, a printing company in San Mateo, California, meets semi-annually. Large charts are used to present operational and financial information to the employee stockholders. However, to avoid "leaks" the information is not reproduced for distribution. Pheoll Manufacturing in Chicago and HunterLab, a color measure instrument manufacturer in Virginia, both hold quarterly stockholder meetings. Landmark Savings in Pittsburgh works discussions of their ESOP into every possible group meeting.

These kinds of meetings with this kind of information presented to employees are not held in conventional companies. But the companies that hold employee stockholder meetings and provide them with sensitive information report that they have not regretted it. In fact, many of them relate that the company has benefited from the employees knowing and understanding the company's financial situation and the reasons for the operating methods and practices.

Employee Ownership Handbook. Over two-thirds of the responding companies reported that they provide an Employee Ownership Handbook. A Summary Plan Description (SPD) must be provided to employees in ESOP companies and is often in a handbook format. Guidelines for preparation of an SPD are available from the Department of Labor. Figure 8.2 is a copy of the cover and an excerpt from Weirton Steel Corporation's SPD. Weirton's SPD measures 7 ½" × 5" and is, as you can see from the Table of Contents, very straightforward. It covers everything from definitions to a detailed description of Weirton's ESOP to ERISA rights and is in non-technical language.

SPD's and handbooks are like rules of the game for Monopoly. Few people actually sit down and read them first. They read them as they need them. A brief, easy-to-read brochure might, therefore, be a good introductory supplement.

Company Newsletters. Many companies publish in-house newsletters as a means to keep employees informed about business and social events. The frequency of the newsletters generally varies from weekly to quarterly. Some are typeset and multi-colored; others are simply typed and reproduced. Typesetting an eight-page, single-color newsletter would cost about $300–500; reproduction costs would range form $0.20 to $0.40 per copy in most places. A typed, photocopied version, of course, would cost much less. Whatever format you might use, content is more important than style.

Newsletters provide a means to let employees know about trends in the industry, what their fellow employees are doing, developments in the company, and how their employee ownership plan works. A typical company newsletter might include a story about a new product the company is marketing, an article on how a new market development (a change in trade laws, for instance) will affect the company, a piece highlighting an employee's community service work, and a column about some aspect of the ESOP. The ESOP column might be based on questions employees submit. Occasional features might look at the company's history, in-depth stories on various aspects of the business, business educational material, stories about employee ownership elsewhere, and so forth. Finally, the newsletter might contain a column written by employees or containing employee comments. Figure 8.3 shows the front page of a newsletter from the Burns and McDonnell Company, a Kansas City engineering firm. This issue focused on the company's new employee ownership plan.

Small Group Meetings. Nearly half of the survey respondents said that they hold small group meetings with employees about employee ownership. Simply holding such meetings is a way of communicating to workers that the company is serious about the employee ownership plan and is interested in involving them in company affairs. But more than that, the meetings provide another forum for exchange of information. The meetings can help put into perspective

Figure 8.2
Weirton Steel Corporation Employee Handbook Cover and Contents Pages

ESOP

EMPLOYEE STOCK
OWNERSHIP PLAN

WEIRTON STEEL CORPORATION
"Your Stock in Weirton Steel"

EMPLOYEE HANDBOOK

Used with permission from Weirton Steel Corporation.

Table of Contents

Figure 8.3
Burns & McDonnell Newsletter Cover

Illustration 8.3

FOCUS

January 31, 1986

IN THIS ISSUE:

P.O. Box 173
Kansas City, MO 64141
Telephone: (816) 333-4375
Telex: (910) 771 3059 BURNS MCDKSC

Burns & McDonnell
ENGINEERS - ARCHITECTS - CONSULTANTS

We're All Partners Now

"Intangible assets: the experience, education, and capabilities of our people at Burns & McDonnell and The C.W. Nofsinger Company...there's no reason why anyone but ourselves and our clients should profit from them. They're ours. And now the company is ours. We bought it; we bought the future...it's all ours."

--Newton Campbell

On January 15, Newt Campbell and Dave Ruf stood near the windows on the 82nd floor of the Sears Tower in Chicago, America's tallest building. They had just finished months of tough negotiations with Armco for the repurchase of Burns & McDonnell, resulting in a 100 percent employee-owned firm.

The repurchase of Burns & McDonnell is perhaps the most significant chapter in the history of our 88-year-old firm. The sequence of events that led to closing the deal began about a year ago, amidst rumors that Burns & McDonnell might be included in Armco's planned divestment of units outside its core steel-making business.

Newt Campbell had been talking with Brian Lewis, a principal of the Coxe Group, management consultants specializing in serving consulting engineering firms.

"Brian mentioned to us that a management/employee ownership was the preferred way for an engineering consulting firm to be structured," said Newt. "We didn't think seriously about it then--as far

as we were concerned, we were still firmly a part of Armco."

Not long after that, however, Armco announced that its entire Professional Services Division, including Burns & McDonnell, was to be divested.

Because of Burns & McDonnell's very successful performance, Armco was reluctant to divest Burns & McDonnell--but the decision was necessary to generate cash and improve Armco's overall financial condition.

The Winds Were Right

Our course was set. The management and employees would propose to buy back the firm that was purchased by Armco in 1971.

Recent legislation that had been introduced by Senator Russell Long of Louis-

► See Partners, Page

After closing the deal with Armco in Chicago, Newt Campbell returned to Burns & McDonnell to address the new owners.

Used with permission from Burns & McDonnell.

the expectations and roles of everyone concerned and, perhaps, clarify what those roles and expectations should be.

Like the suggestion box, small group meetings may be less intimidating than large meetings. At small meetings people would often be in a group with their immediate peers, with whom they are accustomed to interacting and who could act as a support group. Specific examples of small group meetings, especially in the context of small decision-making groups, are discussed in the next section of this chapter.

Films or Slide Shows. Reading materials and meetings are very useful, but some employees will be more interested in visual material, such as a film or slide show. Short films are especially useful but very expensive. Professionally produced 20–30 minute films will cost $10,000 to $100,000 or more. Films will probably be primarily of interest, therefore, to larger companies, particularly those that have multiple sites. Ideally, these films should be shown in small group settings with someone there to answer questions or develop themes. Weirton Steel has taken this idea one step further by having 85 television monitors placed around the plant to show a weekly in-house news program about Weirton and the steel industry. The well-produced ten-minute program is not fluff. Problems in the company and the industry are openly discussed.

A less-expensive alternative is a slide show. These can be professionally developed for a few thousand dollars. A few generic slide shows are also available. The slide shows provide a basic introduction to ESOPs, and need to be shown in the context of a presentation at a meeting.

Posters, Payroll Stuffers, Letterheads, Advertising, and Other Reinforcers. Posters and payroll stuffers specifically for your company can be developed. Bofors, a California printer, helped design and printed a poster with employee ownership company logos displayed for Employee Ownership Week 1989 (see Figure 8.4). Production Management Companies developed their own series of stickers. The Lowe's Companies and S. S. Pennock Company are among the firms that incorporate employee ownership in their letterheads, both to remind their employees and their customers that they are employee-owned (see Figure 8.5).

Advertising can be a particularly effective way to promote employee ownership to customers and employees. Employees will see the ads in the newspaper or trade journals (ads can be reproduced and distributed or put up as posters), and customers may comment on their ownership plan. A survey conducted in 1987 indicated that shoppers like the idea of buying from an employee ownership company.

Annual/Periodic Reports. Public companies, of course, issue annual and other reports. Employees as shareholders are entitled to receive these reports. Providing training to the employees about how to read and understand technical and financial information would help make those reports more meaningful.

"What If" Computer Game. A most important question with which employees are concerned is "How much will I get when I leave?" This question

Figure 8.4
Employee Ownership Week Poster

Figure 8.5
Employee Ownership Letterhead

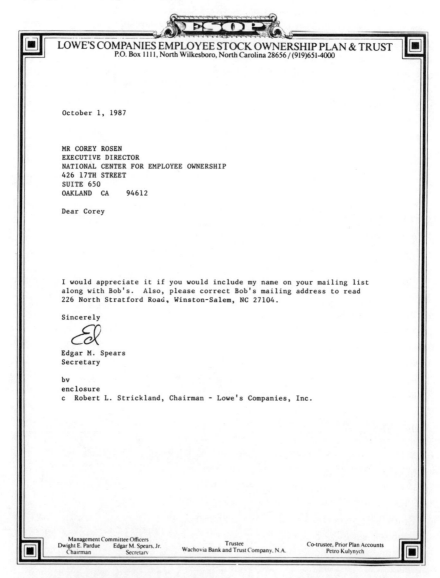

ESOP

LOWE'S COMPANIES EMPLOYEE STOCK OWNERSHIP PLAN & TRUST
P.O. Box 1111, North Wilkesboro, North Carolina 28656 / (919)651-4000

October 1, 1987

MR COREY ROSEN
EXECUTIVE DIRECTOR
NATIONAL CENTER FOR EMPLOYEE OWNERSHIP
426 17TH STREET
SUITE 650
OAKLAND CA   94612

Dear Corey

I would appreciate it if you would include my name on your mailing list along with Bob's. Also, please correct Bob's mailing address to read 226 North Stratford Road, Winston-Salem, NC 27104.

Sincerely

Edgar M. Spears
Secretary

bv
enclosure
c Robert L. Strickland, Chairman - Lowe's Companies, Inc.

Used with permission from Lowe's Companies, Inc.

cannot be answered with certainty, of course. Stock price varies based on a number of factors. And the amount an individual receives upon leaving the company also depends on a number of additional factors such as tenure, salary, vesting, forfeitures, allocations, and so on.

However, computers can help address the question. You can create a simple computer program using spreadsheet software that many companies already have. Program into the computer a variety of alternative scenarios, varying the company's rate of contribution to the plan, employees' salaries, stock appreciation rates, and rates of forfeitures for unvested shares. Then you can show employees how to use the program to enter their own salaries and try different assumptions about each of the other variables. If someone on your staff is a programmer, the process can be greatly simplified by creating a special program that just asks employees to enter various numbers.

Either directly on the program, or on instructions you give out, you can explain to employees what various realistic assumptions might be. Employees can then get a range of numbers about how much they might accumulate after "x" number of years. While it is hoped that number will be motivating to them, there is another benefit as well. The process you are having the employee go through is very much the kind of business projections you, as a manager, probably go through as well. With a little effort, you can use this "what if" game as a way to teach employees about business, and about how their efforts can result in dramatic changes in their own ESOP accounts.

Obviously, this approach will not work for every company. It does require having someone set up a program. And you need enough terminals around the company to make it practical.

Send Non-Managerial Employees to Conferences. Many management people have gone to an employee ownership conference or workshop and come back excited and motivated. Why not let employees have that experience? That is just what Dimco-Gray in Ohio decided it should do. In its first two years of being an employee ownership company, Dimco-Gray sent dozens of its non-management employees to a variety of employee ownership meetings. They came back enthused and full of ideas, and shared this with their co-workers. The result was a much broader appreciation of how employee ownership works and how employees can help make it work better. No matter how effective management may be in communicating, employees are going to be more credible to their peers. Sending all these people was expensive, but the company has no doubt it was an excellent investment.

Employee ownership conferences are not the only important meetings. Clay Equipment sends non-management employees to trade shows to find out what the competition is doing and what they can learn from it. Sixteen employees go each year, reporting back to their peers on a variety of nuts-and-bolts improvements the agricultural equipment maker can use. Clay president Cal Schacht says there is another benefit, too, in that employees come back very aware of just how tough the competition can be.

Participate in Employee Ownership Week. The first employee ownership week was organized by NCEO in 1987, and was such a success it has become an annual event. The week was created to encourage companies to celebrate their employee-owners. Over 200 companies participated in 1987 and that many or more in 1988. In 1989 that number more than doubled. There are all sorts of things companies can do. HealthTrust, with 30,000 employees in 103 hospitals around the country, found the week an ideal way to focus its efforts to communicate its new ESOP in a coordinated way. Dan's Supermarkets in North Dakota had a special employee ownership week sale, and featured its employee owners in radio ads during the week. M. W. Carr in Boston arranged to have Senator Edward Kennedy (D. MA) visit the company, with a media entourage trailing along. Bliss-Salem in Ohio, as did dozens of other companies, invited the press to tour the company and write a story.

These are just a few of many examples. There is no special formula, other than to share information and to have fun. Many companies create a special employee committee to design the week, giving them a budget of their own. Local media are often invited to join in, since few things make people feel as special as seeing a story about them in the paper or on the evening news. Amid all the work you need to do to explain valuation, allocation, leveraging, and all the other technical ideas, it's good to let your hair down once in a while and just have a good time.

Reinforcement Is the Key

All of the ideas just presented are aimed at providing explanations of how employee ownership works. Our research has shown that companies need to go beyond these basics, however, to really have the employees identify with and internalize the idea of ownership.

Like going to church on a holiday, an employee ownership plan need not be a one-time or even annual event. It is, we hope, a day-to-day way of running a company. Reinforcing the notion of ownership can be the norm, whether it is through visual reminders like posters, regular meetings, employee participation groups, plan descriptions, newsletters, or just the everyday interactions between manager and non-manager employee-owners. A constant and varied flow of communications is essential, but it cannot be propaganda; it must be the sharing and seeking of useful information and ideas.

The variety of all the things suggested here may seem intimidating. There is obviously a lot that can be done. Some of these ideas involve substantial time and expense. Our purpose is not to scare people off, however. Find the ideas that work for you, and that fit into your time and financial budget. Then carry out those ideas with tenacity. Ultimately, a good communications program is defined less by the sophistication of its production than the sincerity of its commitment.

THEORY "O," THE OWNERSHIP STYLE
OF MANAGEMENT

Over the last decade, Quad/Graphics, the Wisconsin printing firm described earlier, has grown at a compound annual rate of 50% per year. W. L. Gore Associates, a Delaware-based high-tech manufacturer, has grown at about 40% per year during the same period. Weirton Steel Corporation is the most profitable integrated steel maker in the United States, even though its former owner, National Steel Corporation, wanted to close it down. Virginia Textiles started in a warehouse in 1977 and by 1985 had sales over $12 million.

These companies have something more in common than enviable financial performance. They are each exemplars of what we call the ownership theory of management. In these companies, it is not enough to enrich jobs and treat people more respectfully (as in Theory "Y" management), nor is it even enough to set up a consultative, participative management style (as in Theory "Z"). Valuable as these theories may be, they still envision a distinction between employees and employers. In "Theory O" companies, there are only "partners" or "associates" or "fellow owners." People, managers and non-managers, treat each other like the owners they all are. It is assumed that everyone has ideas and talents that should be used fully, that the people who know the most about something should be the ones making decisions about it, and that every employee has a responsibility to make a contribution.

The particular ways in which each of these companies puts its ownership theory of management into practice differ greatly from company to company. Strong leaders at each company have looked at their own situations and pursued what seems appropriate, often changing and experimenting with new ideas that reflect their and their companies' personalities. The essence of their experience is both simple to describe and hard to do: treat people like owners. The success these companies have had, however, suggests the effort may well be worthwhile.

Of course these companies are particularly good examples. Not every company can expect the kinds of returns these four have had from their management styles. But the empirical research makes it very clear that just sharing ownership, in itself, will produce only some of the gains in corporate performance of which employee ownership is capable. The companies that really outshine their competitors are those that combine the financial rewards of ownership with more employee involvement in decision-making, especially at the job level.

The companies described in this chapter may also go further in implementing "Theory O" than many firms will be able to do. Our research and experience suggest, however, that even small steps are worth taking. To start taking those small steps is a sometimes confusing and uncertain journey. The vast body of research on employee participation, job enrichment, human relations, and related fields provides some guidelines, but the best advice comes from the lessons and experiences of employee ownership companies themselves. As a result of looking carefully at all of the companies we had information about we came up with eight principles that successful employee ownership companies enlist. We call this set of principles "Theory O," the ownership style of management:

The personal commitment of the person at the top of the organization is essential.

A set of written values embodying your commitment to employee ownership is an important starting point.

Symbols of how everyone is treated as an owner are important.

The people who have the most expertise about an area should be the ones making decisions about it.

If employees are to participate in decision-making, they need training to develop the necessary skills.

Information should be shared not just from the top down but from the bottom up as well.

Participative decisions take more time to make but less time and effort to implement.

There are no pat formulas for implementing the ownership theory. What works for one company may not work for another, or even for the same company at a different stage of its development.

Lessons from Employee Participation Research

Most of this section will focus on specific things that certain employee ownership companies do. There is, however, a large body of research and experience with employee participation programs in non-employee ownership companies that is worth considering briefly.

For simplicity, throughout this chapter we will define employee participation broadly to include any efforts to give more employees more authority to make decisions affecting their work or their company. Examples of employee participation would include small group meetings, employee committees, task forces, a job enrichment program aimed at giving employees a broader job definition and responsibility, statistical process groups, having suggestion boxes, board representation, and so forth. In the last decade, these kinds of programs have become very popular, in large part in response to the perception that similar efforts in Japan have greatly increased productivity there.

The logic behind employee participation appears compelling. Employees today are more educated than ever before and, surveys show, are demanding more personal fulfillment from work than did workers a few decades ago. One way to offer this is to create jobs with more employee participation. This should help attract and retain better people, improving productivity by improving the workforce. Costs should be cut as well by reducing the expense of training new employees. At the same time, employees have ideas and experience that traditional hierarchical management approaches may fail to use effectively. Once involved in participation programs, employees may find that the ability to have more say and to improve the quality of their work will make them more motivated to work harder or smarter.

Many things seem plausible in theory that do not work out so well in practice, however, and employee participation programs often fall into that category. There have been hundreds of studies of the effect of employee participation on employee attitudes and corporate productivity. The results have failed to show a clear relationship. In many cases, participation programs are set up along with many other changes in management and labor relations practices, and it is impossible to sort out what causes what. Where studies have been able to focus just on participation, results have been ambiguous. Some programs seem to work; others do not.

There appear to be several reasons for this. First, employee participation programs, even if initially successful, tend to be short-lived. Programs are sometimes set up to resolve particular problems, and lose their impetus once the problem is solved. Second, management people frequently feel threatened by programs that give more authority to employees. Third, workers often feel resentful if they help improve productivity but do not receive some financial compensation for their efforts. Fourth, many programs are poorly thought out, asking workers to participate in areas where their expertise is limited, or they are not given adequate information about the issues they are asked to help resolve. Other programs may be limited to issues that have more to do with work amenities (dress regulations, break schedules, lunchroom facilities, etc.) than productivity questions. Finally, some programs lack solid support from top management. Without that, mid-level managers and other employees may believe the programs are not permanent and that their ideas will not be taken seriously, and they are probably right.

Even with these drawbacks, however, there are, as we have seen, compelling reasons to try to make employee participation work in employee ownership companies. Our research has very clearly shown that the most participative employee ownership companies have growth rates 11 to 17% per year higher than the least participative companies. Moreover, employees in the most participative companies were significantly more satisfied with their work and their ESOP, were more committed to their company, and were more likely to stay with their firm than workers in the less participative companies. The experience of the most participative employee ownership companies helps provide a guide to making an employee ownership plan work.

Lessons From Employee Ownership Companies

Most material on employee participation tends to be at a high level of generality. While this has its value, it can also be frustratingly vague. What most management people need are specific examples of what other companies have done. In giving these examples here, we are not proposing that companies simply copy what others have done. Instead, the examples are meant to be suggestive, helping people conjure up their own ideas about what would work best for them. The examples will be presented in the context of Theory O.

Principle 1: The Personal Commitment of the Person at the Top of the Organization Is Essential. One of the ironies of successful employee participation programs is that for them to work they often need a strong leader to provide a role model. While the goal of employee participation is to get more people more involved in decision-making, very strong, determined leadership is often needed to overcome the natural resistance people will have to this change. Moreover, if the top person is not committed to employee participation, people below will invariably become frustrated and give up. Leslie Paper Company in Minneapolis was founded in 1894 and had grown to 200 employees by 1969. At that time Jim Leslie, whose grandfather founded the firm and whose father was president, came to the conclusion that unless the company changed, its future would not be bright. The company was "an inbred family operation," he said, "heavily controlled from the top." That paternalistic structure bred "dependency and cynicism and many of the independent thinkers and innovators left." The company had lost money for the preceding three years. Leslie decided to give his father an ultimatum: sell him the company, or he would leave. His father agreed, and Jim Leslie took over in 1972, at which point he turned around and sold the company to its employees through an ESOP.

Leslie changed more than ownership. Employees were now asked and expected to take more responsibility. Truck drivers, for instance, came up with different routing schedules that increased productivity 40%. Warehouse employees began their own safety inspections, cutting insurance costs in the process, and devised new work schedules that cut the need for overtime. Employees suggested that employee health care benefits be broadened to include prevention, and two staff people were hired to develop a corporate "wellness" program. Employees have full voting rights on their stock, all employees are called "partners," and the theme of the company has become "The Power of Partnership."

While it may seem that Leslie was simply abdicating, in fact he was creating a very effective strategy. With the same number of employees, sales have increased at a compound annual rate of 18% per year, with productivity up 476% in the last decade.

Polaroid Corporation recently appointed an employee representative to its board of directors with not only the blessing but the encouragement of CEO McAllister Booth. The woman appointed is director of market research and development and is one of only three inside directors joining Mr. Booth and the chairman. A nominating committee of 15 employees was chosen out of a group who were identified by the senior managers as having a broad base of knowledge about and trust from their co-employees. A meeting was called for all employees who might be interested in sitting on the board. The duties and responsibilities of a director were explained at this meeting. Some 75 serious contenders remained in the pool after the meeting. These people were interviewed by the nominating committee who finally came up with three finalists whose names were submitted to the board for the final selection. Marian Stanley was chosen.

Principle 2: A Set of Written Values Embodying Your Commitment to Employee Ownership Is an Important Starting Point. Developing a set of guiding values and committing them to paper may seem little more than an exercise in platitudinous banality. Indeed, for some companies, that is all it is. Value statements sometimes are more a function of public relations imperatives than a genuine expression of deeply held corporate commitments. But value statements can be much more than this. If a company develops the statements through discussions with managers and employees, the statements can reflect a consensus of what the employee-owners hope to achieve. Even if the statement is created entirely by management, it can serve as a reminder to everyone that there are certain basic principles that should guide everyone's actions. The key, of course, is to remember to live up to what the statement says. This requires that the statement be realistic, not setting goals so high that they cannot be reached.

Value statements typically include guidelines for corporate ethics. In an often cynical society, these statements may be viewed skeptically. Our experience with many employee ownership companies has been, however, that the leaders of these companies often do have a deeply held set of standards and that these standards really do guide their actions. Cynicism aside, people can be moved by appeals to a higher sense of purpose, and value statements can be part of that effort. North American Telephone, a Tampa, Florida, telecommunications firm, has one of the best value statements we have seen. It is reproduced as Figure 8.6.

Principle 3: Symbols of How Everyone Is Treated as an Owner Are Important. Much like the written set of values, establishing symbols of a company's commitment to employee ownership may seem like an empty gesture. If done with sincerity, however, the symbols can remind people that they are owners, and should be treated and act as owners. There are many ways in which companies establish these symbols. Many firms eliminate status perquisites, such as executive lunchrooms, parking privileges, or different dress codes for managers. It is difficult to maintain an atmosphere in which people are told that they are fellow owners, that their ideas are valued, and that everyone should be pulling together when some people are treated distinctly differently from others.

Advertising can be another important symbol. By stressing that a company is employee-owned on its stationery, on its equipment, or in its commercials, employees are reminded that theirs is a special company. Customers may start expecting more from employees as well, creating another valuable reinforcement of the ownership culture. Another potentially powerful symbol is what

Figure 8.6
Value Statement from North American Telephone

The North American Telephone Declaration

As the first employee-owned and operated long distance and full-service telecommunications company in the world:

We will develop a corporate attitude that will survive the fiercest competition, maintain aggressive growth, and assure quality service for every single North American Telephone customer.

We will provide better service than any competitive company, win and keep our customers through merit and integrity, not through sales promotions or empty promises.

We will measure our success by the number of satisfied customers rather than the number of accounts; listening intently to our customers will be our yardstick, responding to what what we hear is our mandate.

We will make a significant positive economic and social contribution to the state of Florida by creating and selling unique products that focus on the special needs of Florida business.

We will reward our employees who strive for excellence, who dedicate themselves to improving service and whose performance attains established goals.

We will operate with fairness, kindness, integrity, efficiency and effectiveness to create a work environment where employees enjoy their work and which could become a model for other workplaces.

We will always remember that superior performance leads to superior profits and results in superior service for everyone. We are Partners in Progress.

---

employees are called: "partners", "associates," "employee-owners," "managers," and so forth. As with all of these symbolic gestures, however, unless they are backed up with the content they imply (really treating people as associates, for instance), the symbols can cause more cynicism than motivation.

At Scully-Jones, a Chicago manufacturer, the sign outside the company proclaims "employee-owned," and inside the employees paint their own machines the colors they want. The cover of the Herman Miller Company's 1985 annual report reads "Meet the Owners." A picture of every owner (employee) is then featured on page after page, all 3,000 of them. Herman Miller is one of the nation's leading manufacturers of office furniture and is regularly recognized for its innovative designs. To reinforce the notion that everyone is part of the Miller "family" (a term used frequently among employee ownership companies), president Max DePree urges employees to become "tribal storytellers," relating to new employees and to customers how the company's highly participative, open culture works. All offices are designed so that everyone has some natural light, and one-fourth of each Miller facility is given over to plants and other green space. All of this helped the company increase its revenues from $40 million in 1973 to $400 million in 1983.

Each company can find symbols appropriate to it. Apart from the other efforts described in this book, the symbols are empty; along with them, they can be powerful reminders.

Principle 4: People Who Have the Most Expertise About an Area Should Be the Ones Making Decisions About It. Of all the lessons, this one is the most central. While it seems only a sensible way to organize a company, it is something few companies actually follow. There are a number of reasons for this. Managers, for instance, have an understandable need to demonstrate their competence over a wide range of issues and may feel compelled to exercise their authority even when a subordinate may know more about a particular issue. Conversely, some subordinates may be reluctant to assert their greater knowledge if it means appearing to upstage their superiors. Moreover, some employees may feel "Why should I tell them a better way to do it? I won't get anything out of it." Even when managers want to involve employees more, they may be hampered by a system in which employees are not given enough access to information or training to be able to make more decisions. The typical company is organized as a pyramid, with information flowing up or down through several layers of managers and supervisors. Just as in the childhood game of "gossip," by the time the information reaches the the top, it often becomes very distorted, especially if lower level people want to shield their superiors from bad news. Thus even if higher level people might have the competence to act on an issue, they may not have the most accurate information. The costs of not equating expertise and authority are obvious. The companies described below are all incorporating this most fundamental principle into their way of managing their companies.

Polaroid Corporation, which increased its ESOP holdings to 14% in early 1989 bringing to 20% the amount of the company owned by employees, has a long history of employee involvement. It has had an Employees Committee since 1946, less than 10 years after the company was founded, which represents employees' interests at all levels and in all areas of the company. The committee is comprised of 25 workers who are elected by their peers.

Along with increasing the ownership share, the company has decided to increase the employee participation activities to help create an "ownership culture." Employees are being involved in discussions about what can and should be done to institute more participative management practices. Establishing hourly and salaried cross-company teams to review financial performance is one of the ideas brewing. This practice will do two things: it will help different work groups see how they can help contribute to the bottom line, and it will help solicit ideas from those who are in the production area—the people, of course, who are closest to the product.

Fastener Industries, a 145-employee manufacturer of industrial weld fasteners in Ohio, is another company with exceptionally well-motivated employees. In fact, Fastener has among the highest job satisfaction, ESOP satisfaction, and organizational commitment scores of any employees we have surveyed. The company became employee-owned in 1981 when an ESOP was used to buy out the stock of the family that had owned the firm since 1905. Richard Biernacki, the company's treasurer at the time, became president.

Biernacki firmly believes that "the worker owns the place and expects to be involved. You respect him and you want him involved. You know he knows his job best and he can save you a lot of problems." When the ESOP was set up, Biernacki insisted on full voting rights for the employees, though not required by law for private companies. Employees elect the board of directors and Biernacki notes that if they do not like what he is doing, he could be "on the street in 30 days." That makes his job a little harder, he notes, but the extra effort is important. It holds his feet to the fire: "When you make a decision, you have to have your reasons, and have done what was fair."

While workers want to know what Biernacki does and why, Biernacki wants to know what workers think and put that to use. At the shopfloor level, there are monthly meetings between plant managers and workers. When new machinery is purchased, the employees who work on those machines are consulted. Every employee meets with Biernacki in groups of 11 every six months. Anything can be and is discussed, giving workers an opportunity to make their views known and Biernacki a chance to know what is going on on the shopfloor. He also spends much of his time walking around the plant, soliciting workers' opinions.

This combination of ownership and decision-making pushed down to the lowest levels possible helped Fastener maintain its employment during the recession of the early 1980s, a time when many of its competitors were going out of business. After the recession, the company returned to very healthy profitability.

When it comes to profits, few companies outshine Quad/Graphics, the Wisconsin printer. The company's over 4,000 employees print hundreds of magazines, including *Newsweek, U.S. News, Inc., Time,* and many others. Founded in 1971, the company set up its ESOP just a few years later. The plan now owns 20% of the stock. Since the mid-1970s the company has grown at an astounding 50% compounded annual rate.

What really distinguishes Quad/Graphics, however, is its distinctive and highly effective management style. All of the workers at Quad are "partners," an apt term. Partners are expected to participate in decision-making at several levels. Employee peer groups, for instance, set disciplinary standards, and can even fire people. Partners created the Quad/Ed training and education program described later. A group of employee truck drivers developed a profit center, arranging for backhaul loads on previously empty returning trucks. Press crews are autonomous, with crew leaders responsible for keeping records. The crews have almost total authority for cost containment, quality control, and customer relations, and have a say in hiring, firing, and work schedules. Managers are expected to be coordinators, not order givers, helping partners use their skills to take as much responsibility as they can. The idea is that Quad people know their jobs best and should be encouraged to take responsibility for them.

Quad founder and president, Harry Quadracci, believes this is the only way to run the company. When the drivers came to him to propose the backhauling operation, for instance, Quadracci said "I don't know anything about driving an 18 wheeler. I'm not going to find your loads." But he gave the truckers the authority to find them, and they did. Like many Theory O managers, Quadracci seeks out opportunities to describe his company's philosophy. In a recent Quad/Graphics annual report he said:

Our emphasis is not on the numbers, but rather on people who are caring and sharing in common values and attitudes; people who have stretched their minds and broadened their horizons . . . and people—ordinary people—who have achieved this extraordinary result through the Quad philosophy of people helping people to become more than they ever hoped to be.

Principle 5: If Employees Are to Participate in Decision-Making, They Need Training to Develop the Necessary Skills. The responsibility employees assume at companies like Quad and other highly participative firms must be backed up by appropriate training. Otherwise, employees will either be asked to do less than they really could do if they did have training, or won't be given training and will be asked to do more than they are ready to do.

Quad/Graphics solves this problem with its Quad/Ed and mentor programs. According to Quadracci, new employees are in "boot camp." For the first year or so, partners (employees) have a mentor to help guide them with their job and acculturate them to Quad's way of operating. Quad/Ed, located in a former school bought by the company, features classes in all aspects of printing and the printing business. Quadracci himself teaches the introductory class. It is only after employees are thoroughly trained that they move out of their initial probationary period and assume all the responsibility that partnership implies.

Weirton Steel, the largest industrial employee-owned company, which, as of 1988, made a public offering of 15% of its stock, has based its operating philosophy on employee participation. When the employees bought the company in 1984, a new CEO, Robert Loughhead, was brought in largely because of his commitment to participative management. From the outset, the company began organizing employees into employee participation groups. The groups consist of 10–12 workers and a facilitator with exclusive Employee Participation Group (EPG) responsibility. Weirton's management has not measured their impact, but believes the groups have saved millions already. For example, one EPG developed a technique for preventing imperfections in the casting of flat rolled steel.

Group participants are encouraged to go through a three-day training session to help teach them how to operate in a decision-making group. The training sessions are now part of the orientation for new employees at Weirton. At the end of each training session the company and union presidents speak to the class to congratulate them, an important symbol of the program's central role at Weirton.

Principle 6: Information Should Be Shared Not Just from the Top Down but from the Bottom Up as Well. As stated earlier, communications must be a reciprocal process. Participation groups like those at Weirton, the small meetings Rich Biernacki holds with employees, and the time spent on the shop floor by Quad/Graphics' president Harry Quadracci all provide information to management from employees. Avis, though 100% employee owned through an ESOP, is in size and structure comparable to many of the large public ESOP companies. With 12,500 employees it is the second largest ESOP company in the country and has multiple locations.

Initiation of a systematic, all-encompassing participative management style was all part of the package when Avis was bought by the ESOP in September 1987. ''Here we are with this wealth of knowledge from employees who have been doing the same job for some time. They know more about how to do their jobs than we [management] do'' is how Avis CEO Joseph Vittoria felt. And he has been supported in that belief by the suggestions, ideas, and information coming out of the set up at Avis along with the ESOP.

The formal structure is that one or two employees from each work area at a site are elected by their peers to represent the group at a monthly EPG meeting. This means the groups are comprised of between 10 and 12 people. People from the monthly meeting group are selected by the group members to attend quarterly zone meetings; again, representatives from the zone meetings are sent to a semi-annual regional meeting; the process culminates in representatives from each region attending an annual meeting with top management at World Headquarters. Representatives at each level report back to their respective groups about what went on at the meetings.

Topics for the meeting range from how to run the meetings better to very sophisticated ideas about improving company performance. All monthly meetings are always at 2:00 p.m. on the first Thursday of the month. This is done to emphasize the point that the company is serious about this idea, and to help insure that the meetings are an integral part of company operations. They are important, and time must be scheduled to hold them. However, the company underlines that participation is not just meeting once a month, but must be a daily occurrence. The purpose of the meetings is to share, focus, and take action on the ideas people present through their representatives.

Participative management was intended to be and has proven to be more than a rhetorical exercise. In the two years since Avis became employee-owned, operating profits are way up, market share has increased, and service complaints are way down.

Many suggestions have been made and implemented, contributing to the improvements cited here. Some of them are:

- ''Ready spaces'' were made more available for walk-in customers.
- A list of bilingual employees was put together in the customer service department to help non-English speaking customers.
- ''Employee Swap Day'' was begun in which employees in the field change jobs for a day with World Headquarters employees to learn to better appreciate the work of others.
- Customers are notified about articles left in the vehicles rather than waiting for the customer to contact the company.
- Non-smoking cars are now provided.
- A system was devised to avert car theft and vandalism.
- Gas island curbs have been reshaped so that there is less tire damage.

Is it working? Yes. More dollars have been earned and more dollars have been saved in real terms than before the transition to employee ownership and participative management. But more than that, employees are making it happen, and they know that they are the ones making it happen. As one 18-year employee said about the participative efforts and the effect they are having on the employees,

Most of the things we've presented to them, they've acted on. Even when they don't they get back to you. It makes you feel good when there's some response. I see in the people I work with that they're more highly motivated now. Before, they used to let little things slide. Now they feel it's coming out of their pockets.

Principle 7: Decisions Take More Time to Make but Less Time to Implement. One of the greatest barriers to the establishment of a participative decision-making system is the belief that it takes too much time to make decisions that way. Managers conjure up visions of endless meetings with everyone insisting on getting in their views and little getting decided. These problems can occur. But the experience of many ownership theory companies is that once these decisions are made, much less time and effort are needed to implement them, and they are carried out with more enthusiasm.

This is really just common sense. People rarely like to be told what to do. If a manager simply says ''do this!'' it is not likely that an employee will act with enthusiasm. If the manager takes the time to explain why ''this'' needs to be done, the employees may respond better. But, as research indicates, if employees have a role in the decision, even indirectly, then they will be more likely to see the decision as ''their own'' and thus need less persuading to act accordingly. The same theory explains why totalitarian systems need huge internal police forces and democracies rarely do. The dictator can make decisions very fast indeed; it is getting people to carry them out enthusiastically or even at all that is the trick.

How this will work out from company to company depends on the nature of the workforce. Some employees are more internally directed than others and less likely simply to take directions. Questionnaires can get at this issue, but many managers will already have a good sense of how their employees will react. Our point here, however, is that participative decision-making should not be ruled out simply because it can be time consuming, because considerable research has shown that whatever is lost in making the decisions may be more than made up in carrying them out. Another benefit is that the quality of the decision is often enhanced.

Probably no company goes further in involving employees in decisions than Springfield Remanufacturing Corporation. Springfield set up an ESOP in 1982 when International Harvester decided to divest the division. John Stack engineered the buyout using an ESOP because he wanted to share the responsibility and was gladly willing to share the wealth.

Sharing seemed to be the elixir needed. In those first years of employee ownership, sales grew 40% per year, debt-to-equity ratio went from 89:1 to 5:1 and the share value increase from $.10 to $8.45. Then in December 1986, General Motors, a primary customer, decreased a sizable contract. Here they were doing all the right things and prospering as a result and ready to relax somewhat, then this happened. It's like doing your exercises faithfully, eating a healthy diet, and filtering your water only to be hit by a GM truck. Anyway, this decrease by GM meant another sizable cut—this time in personnel. One hundred people would have to go or the company would have to generate a substantial amount of new business. Stack agonized. The numbers said they had to go. How could he ask any more from a group that had given its all already? Either decision on his part would have met with cynicism and resistance. Then it dawned on him. Sharing was at the core of the company's philosophy. Why wasn't he sharing this? Let the people affected make the decision. So that is what he did.

All 350 worker-owners showed up at a town meeting. They were told that if the people were kept, bonuses would be smaller, a lot smaller. Also, if people were retained, and they were not able to get new business, maybe twice as many would have to go. So there were losses to be had either way, and there were risks. The worker-owners listened, they considered, and they decided. They decided to "go for it"—to try to generate 50,000 hours of new business and keep everyone working. And they did it. They ended up adding $2 million in sales, even with the $8 million GM loss and increased the workforce by 100 people. Stack could have said "off with your heads" and that would have been that except for dealing with demoralized people. Instead, he said "put on your thinking caps" and he got to deal with devoted people.

Principle 8: There Are No Pat Formulas for Implementing the Ownership Theory. What Works for One Company May Not Work for Another, or Even for the Same Company at a Different Stage of Its Development. In Greek mythology, the robber Procrustes would stretch out his victims or cut off their legs to make them fit his bed. While we would not suggest that modern-day consultants selling formulaic approaches to employee involvement are Procrustean robbers, they may be stretching a point to suggest that there are pat solutions to getting people more involved in their companies.

If there is one very clear lesson the ownership theory companies have taught us, it is that what works for one company will not necessarily work for another. The characteristics of the workforce, the size of the company, the nature of the business, the preferences and personalities of managers, and many other factors make each company unique. A good participation consultant can help a company develop its own approach, although many of the companies discussed here were able to create their own plans.

To many managers contemplating the kinds of issues discussed here, all this may seem intimidating. There is so much to consider and so much to do to make a program work. And just getting a good plan is not enough. The best plan in the world will fail if the key people carrying it out are not comfortable with the idea of employee involvement. But this is, we believe, too pessimistic a view. Getting employees more involved does not require that everything be done at once. A company can take a few small steps at first, going on to bigger things as people become more comfortable with the process. Some managers may resist change at first, but if they see that the new process is not as threatening as they imagined, their attitudes can change. Most importantly, we have found that the commitment of top management to treat people as owners is ultimately more important than the particular structures used to implement that approach. So keep trying. The results should more than justify the effort.

CONCLUSION

Many people are drawn to employee ownership, especially ESOPs, for practical reasons. And there is certainly nothing wrong with that. According to ESOP consultants we surveyed, about 40% of those setting up plans do so only to get the tax benefits, while about 53% are motivated both by tax benefits and a belief in the concept. Only 7% would set up a plan without the tax benefits. We have had any number of people call us or come through our door who say the ESOP is the answer to their dreams. It provides a way for them to get their money out of the company without draining or liquidating the company, which they didn't want to do but saw no other way until they heard about the ESOP. It has provided a borrowing mechanism that can be the difference between a healthy cash flow and a negative one. And, again practically speaking, it provides a direct and easily usable way for a company to share ownership under the most favorable tax conditions for all parties. There are some who use a form of employee ownership simply because they like the idea of shared ownership. Whatever the original impetus for having an employee ownership company, the company must be managed, and it must be managed somewhat differently simply because there are more stockholders to consider. There are stock allocations, vesting, distribution, and forfeitures to handle. These technical issues are usually guided by state and federal laws. This chapter is about guidelines also. These are guidelines used by the most successful employee ownership companies in monetary as well as human areas. As we stated at the beginning, there is strong evidence that following these guidelines will enhance corporate performance. There is also strong suggestion that these guidelines contribute to "moral capitalism," which is just as valuable as "capital capitalism."

NOTES

1. *Report on Wealth* (Washington, DC: U.S. Congress, Joint Economic Committee, 1985).

2. Ravi Batra, *The Great Depression of 1990* (New York: Simon & Schuster, 1987).

3. Barbara S. Romzek, "Personal Consequences of Employee Commitment," *Academy of Management Journal,* 32:3 (September 1989): 649–59.

4. Corey Rosen, Katherine J. Klein, and Karen M. Young, *Employee Ownership in America: The Equity Solution.* (Lexington, MA: Lexington Books, 1986).

5. Ralph G. Nichols, "Listening Is Good Business," *Management of Personnel Quarterly,* Winter 1962, p. 4.

9

ESOPs and the 1989 Budget Reconciliation Act: The Impact on Public Companies

DAVID M. BINNS

The employee stock ownership plan is largely a creature of statute. And, since ESOPs are by far the most common form of employee ownership in the United States (discounting stock options, which in most cases are limited only to a few select management employees), the growth over the past 15 years of employee ownership can be largely attributed to the federal tax laws that have been structured to encourage the establishment of ESOPs.

Although the same could be said of any qualified employee benefit plan since the passage of the landmark Employee Retirement Income Security Act legislation in 1974, it is even more true for ESOPs, which have been greatly enhanced through subsequent legislation. Indeed, since the passage of ERISA, 17 different pieces of legislation have made changes to laws affecting ESOPs and most of these changes have resulted in improved tax incentives for companies establishing ESOPs. Any change to these ESOP incentives would therefore have important ramifications for the future development of ESOPs.

This is particularly true for publicly traded companies that have established or are considering the implementation of an ESOP for their employees. Although most publicly traded firms established tax-credit ESOPs in the 1970s (PAYSOPs or TRASOPs, the tax incentives that are no longer available), the development of full-scale ESOPs of any significant size, leveraged or non-leveraged, has largely been confined to closely held corporations. That is, until quite recently.

For a variety of reasons this changed dramatically in 1989 when more than $20 billion worth of ESOP transactions were completed, most of the value of which was attributable to large multi-million-dollar transactions involving publicly traded corporations. Although the motivations and circumstances of each of the public-company ESOP transactions that occurred in 1989 were certainly distinct, it is safe to say that the existence of ESOP tax incentives, in particular the lender interest exclusion and the tax deduction for ESOP dividends, as well as the ability of the ESOP to address several different corporate objectives simultaneously, was critical to these companies' decisions to establish such a plan. Now, with ESOP laws changed once again in the 1989 Budget Reconciliation Bill, the obvious question is what impact these changes will have for ESOPs in public companies.

To put the recent changes in context it is worth noting briefly why public companies have recently been engaging in a "rush to ESOPs," as some observers have described the phenomenon. What has happened to make ESOPs more attractive to public companies, seemingly all at once? Will the dynamics that have resulted in so many new public-company ESOPs continue in the future?

The simplest explanation of why public companies have relatively recently made the move to ESOPs is that the financial markets have only just recently begun to promote ESOPs to any significant degree. There are several reasons that may account for the public market's hesitancy to experiment with employee ownership. Though the key ESOP incentives have been in place since 1984 (the deductibility of principal debt repayments since 1974), there were very few public companies with significant levels of employee ownership. More traditional public corporations and their advisors were undoubtedly concerned about negative accounting requirements for ESOPs and their potential deleterious impact on earnings per share, and uncertain of the political climate surrounding ESOPs. In addition, ESOPs were somewhat arcane and perhaps a bit idealistic sounding for the hard-knocks world of big business.

Soon after the passage of the new ESOP incentives in the 1984 Tax Reform Act, the original proposals for what eventually became the 1986 Tax Reform Act surfaced and cast a cloud over every tax incentive, including those for ESOPs. This undoubtedly further delayed much serious consideration of the ESOP concept. It wasn't until the 1986 bill finally passed and it became clear that ESOPs not only survived tax reform but were enhanced in attractiveness that the financial community began studying ESOPs in earnest. It then took some time for them to convince their corporate clients of the benefits of ESOPs and to structure ESOP transactions to address both their financial and employee benefits needs. By the end of 1988 enough ESOP transactions had been completed, and enough motivations were evident to establish ESOPs, that ESOPs were positioned to become the hot financial technique of 1989.

One of the key developments that changed the dynamics of the public-company ESOP market was the change in the 1986 bill that allowed a tax deduction for ESOP dividends used to repay ESOP debt. Traditional dividend-paying companies were able to use the cash flow benefits of this ESOP incentive to great advantage and the practical implications of this became quickly apparent.

Another key market innovation that helped to make ESOPs more attractive to public companies was the use of convertible preferred stock for the ESOP. Convertible preferred stock, which pays a higher and more predictable dividend than common, was developed as an attractive means of maximizing the benefits of the dividend for ESOP debt repayments. When combined with a repurchase of common stock, the ESOP convertible preferred stock was anti-dilutive as well, another key attraction for public companies. This type of ESOP was often combined with an existing 401(k) plan whereby the company match to the employee salary deferrals was made in the form of company stock contributed to the ESOP. These "KSOPs" allowed ESOPs to be integrated into the overall employee benefit structure much more easily.

All of the above reasons made ESOPs more practical from a financial perspective for public companies. All that was needed was a spur to action. That spur was provided by a judicial decision upholding an ESOP as part of a takeover defense and subsequent congressional action that threatened some of the key ESOP incentives mentioned above.

When the Delaware Chancery Court upheld the Polaroid Corporation's ESOP despite the fact that its creation was associated with defending the company against a hostile takeover attempt, many public companies concerned with takeover protection quickly followed suit by establishing ESOPs of their own. By establishing a large enough ESOP so that corporate insiders could control 15% of the stock outstanding, Delaware corporations could enjoy greater takeover protection under a state law that requires an 85% ownership stake in order for owners to be able to sell assets of a corporation after a change in control. By putting stock into the presumably friendly hands of employees (or the ESOP trustee) these corporations felt they were adding another layer of takeover protection.

The rush to ESOPs began with the Polaroid decision and picked up speed when rumors began to circulate that Congress was considering legislation to cut back ESOP tax incentives to stem the tax losses associated with ESOP deductions. With so many large public-company transactions taking place, congressional estimates of the potential tax revenues lost due to the ESOP tax incentives were sharply increased. The rumors became reality on June 6, 1989, when House Ways and Means Committee Chairman Dan Rostenkowski (D. IL) introduced legislation to repeal the ESOP lender interest exclusion. Matching legislation was soon introduced in the Senate.

That congressional action hardly slowed things down, however. During the next month nearly $10 billion worth of new ESOP transactions were consummated, nearly all in large public companies. The action didn't slow until July 10 when Congressman Rostenkowski introduced a budget proposal that recommended repeal of the ESOP dividend deduction as well as the repeal of the lender interest exclusion. An amendment sponsored by Congressman Beryl Anthony (D. AR) subsequently led to a compromise, setting an over 50% ESOP ownership threshold for interest income exclusion, and retaining the dividend exclusion for all companies.

It was several months later when the 1989 Budget Reconciliation Act was finally passed by Congress and signed into law by the president, and the legislation clearly portends significant changes for ESOPs and will have a major impact on the market for ESOPs among public companies. The most apparent impact of the bill is on the availability of the ESOP lender interest exclusion. By requiring that any ESOP transaction result in the ESOP owning a minimum of 50% of the company after the transaction is completed in order to qualify for the lender interest exclusion, Congress effectively removed this incentive as a factor to consider for all but a handful of public companies.

Most public-company ESOPs own between 5% and 15% of the sponsoring corporation's stock. Many own less than that and only a few own as much as 20% of the stock outstanding. When one considers the 50% ownership test, very few public companies would qualify. Indeed, of the several hundred publicly traded companies that have established ESOPs, fewer than five are more than 50% ESOP owned. And despite the attractiveness of the ESOP lender interest exclusion, very few public companies will be in a position to take advantage of this incentive even if they wanted to. The reasons for this are fairly obvious. The cost of financing an ESOP transaction would be too costly for most companies to bear and the debt load required would be too disrupting to the market for the company's shares. In fact, most of the recent public-company ESOPs have been "shareholder neutral," meaning that the company bought back shares from the market equivalent in value to the shares issued to the ESOP, and that the net cost of the new ESOP was not borne by the shareholder. Not to do so would risk seeing shareholder complaints or perhaps a sell-off of the shares and a drop in the market value. In addition, in virtually every instance obtaining a 50% ESOP stake could be done only at the expense of changing the funding of other employee benefit plans, a choice most large corporations would be unwilling or unable to make. And, for those companies concerned about takeovers, a 15% ESOP is sufficient for such purposes, and there is little incentive—lower interest or not—in increasing the ESOP's stake.

Although Congress declined to limit the market for ESOP loans as had been proposed, making it possible to issue publicly traded bonds to raise money for ESOP financing as the IRS had previously ruled, the 50% threshold for the lender interest exclusion makes the existence of such a market questionable at best. As a result, lower interest rates obtainable due to the ESOP lender interest exclusion will largely be limited to the closely held market (which should continue to be vibrant) and to the occasional transaction involving an ESOP leveraged buyout of a public company or to the few firms who can reasonably obtain a 50% stake for their ESOP.

Even without the lender interest exclusion, however, public companies are still likely to be attracted by ESOPs as long as dividends on ESOP debt remain tax deductible. The evidence for this is clear from the number of companies establishing ESOPs in June 1989, despite the likely repeal of the lender interest exclusion. And, in general, the tax treatment of ESOP dividends remains suitably attractive for public companies to consider establishing new ESOPs or expanding their existing ones.

Unlike with the lender interest exclusion, Congress established no minimum threshold for an ESOP to qualify for the dividend deduction. Congress did place additional conditions on when the ESOP dividend deduction applies, specifically requiring that the deduction on ESOP dividends used to repay ESOP debt is only available on shares acquired with an ESOP loan (for shares acquired after July 10, 1989). There will be no restriction on dividends passed through in cash to plan participants.

This limitation will be less advantageous for companies looking to maximize tax savings by converting pre-existing plans containing employer securities to an ESOP in order to take advantage of the ESOP dividend deduction. But for those firms looking to increase the level of employee ownership, for whatever reason, this should present no significant hurdle to new ESOP activity.

Much of the ESOP activity in the future will be determined by the overall health of the economy, the volatility of the stock market, the continued pressure of corporate takeover activity, the federal legislative and regulatory environment, particularly issues relating to fiduciary requirements involving ESOPs. Perhaps most importantly, the success of those ESOPs that have already been established in terms of both providing benefits to employees and in helping to improve productivity and stabilize ownership patterns in public companies will have a major impact on the future development of ESOPs. Because ESOPs are a relatively new phenomenon among public companies, the question of just how well they work is yet to be tested to any significant degree. To the extent that these ESOPs prove to be successful, other companies are likely to follow suit.

Tax issues aside, there are other signs that interest in employee ownership will continue to grow among large public companies. These firms are increasingly becoming familiar with the uses of ESOPs for corporate strategic purposes, whether as a means of selling or acquiring subsidiaries, restructuring employee benefit plans, or shoring up takeover defenses.

ESOPs are gaining support on the political front as well. Treasury Secretary Nicholas Brady has recently issued a five-point economic plan to encourage U.S. businesses to focus on long-term profitability and to lower the cost of capital. One of Secretary Brady's five goals is the promotion of ESOPs. With the active support of the government, the role of ESOPs could very well increase in importance.

The increasingly competitive international business arena requires companies to look for means of competing more effectively. The growing research indicating that employee ownership can help improve productivity, particularly when combined with effective employee participation programs, is also attracting a great deal of attention. Although the decision to establish an ESOP often comes from the financial department, it is the human resource development department that is likely to have a growing role with employee ownership in the long term.

Many of the large public companies have divisions located in other countries where interest in employee ownership is on the rise. Some companies, having already established ESOPs for their domestic employees, are actively seeking means of establishing employee stock ownership plans for their foreign-based employees as well. If foreign governments continue to promote employee ownership legislation, this phenomenon could accelerate.

Predicting developments in the public market is no sure thing, but it does appear that ESOPs are here to stay and will continue to grow among public companies. Just as surely, ESOPs in these companies will be affected by regulatory rulings on accounting issues, fiduciary standards, securities standards, or other issues. Future legislative proposals will undoubtedly affect ESOPs, as will the prevailing market conditions. Ultimately, ESOPs will be judged by their success in creating employee wealth through ownership.

Some of America's most well-known corporations have established ESOPs. It remains to be seen how well they perform when their largest shareholder group is their own employees.

10

The Development and the Future of Employee Ownership in the Publicly Traded Corporation

JOSEPH R. BLASI

INTRODUCTION

In this chapter the slow development of employee ownership into a major phenomenon in the publicly traded corporate sector will be followed. Data are just becoming available, and this chapter constitutes an initial analysis of evidence, trends, and impressionistic material from various sources. The main goal is to help the reader think through how we got where we are, and what the main issues are. The author plans to present a systematic analysis of all the evidence in the near future.

GROWTH AND DEVELOPMENT

A Phenomenon of Privately Held Corporations: At First

Employee ownership has largely occurred in privately held companies, either as a result of transfers of ownership in such firms, or transformations from public to private corporations, or spinning off the subsidiaries or units of public corporations as closely held corporations. Let's briefly review the different kinds of ESOPs so that we can place the development of meaningful ESOPs in publicly held firms in the proper context.

First, tax-credit ESOPs were set up and funded by a tax credit related to the corporation's investment tax credit. They were generally not responsible for more than 5% of employee ownership in companies, and they frequently excluded unionized or rank and file lower paid employees from their plans. They have been eliminated from the tax code. Second, non-leveraged ESOPs create employee ownership through a company's contribution of stock or cash to an ESOP trust for which the corporation receives a tax deduction. Most companies are unable to create substantial percentages of employee ownership in this manner in a short period of time because they simply do not have that kind of cash available or because contributing large amounts of treasury stock to an ESOP trust would heavily dilute existing shares. Third and most important, leveraged ESOPs create employee ownership by using borrowed money to purchase existing shares or newly issued shares. As noted earlier in this book, the corporation gets substantial and multiple tax deductions in such a transaction that can create significant amounts of employee ownership in a very short period of time. The bottom line is that leveraged ESOPs constitute the most meaningful ESOPs in the publicly traded corporate sector. Nevertheless, data will also be presented on various forms of employee benefit trusts where substantial employee ownership has resulted without the use of leverage.

Until 1987, the best estimates from the U.S. General Accounting Office research were that transfers of ownership in privately held firms to ESOPs— usually to cash out a retiring founder, family owner, or majority stockholder— accounted for 59% of all leveraged ESOPs and 35% of all non-leveraged ESOPs. These data are based on a sample of ESOPs where the GAO surveyed managers.

In order to shed further light on this question, the GAO also identified the trading status of all the ESOPs it was able to discover through its review of Internal Revenue Service records as of 1983. Privately held ESOPs were clearly the majority. When all non-tax-credit ESOPs identified in the GAO sample up to 1983 were taken into account, 89.9% were set up in privately traded corporations and 10.1% were set up in publicly traded corporations. But it is interesting to note that the impact of public- and private-corporation ESOPs on federal tax expenditures has actually been the opposite. It is estimated that from 1973 to 1986 tax credit ESOPs used up more than 90% of such tax expenditures while the balance was used up by non-tax-credit ESOPs, which were mainly in privately held corporations.[1]

The Slow Ascendance of Employee Ownership in Public Companies

The situation has been changing and public-corporation ESOPs have been in ascendance. In 1974 employee ownership was rare in public companies. Employee ownership certainly was a gradual development in U.S. society. After World War I Congress was looking for ways to help industry attract and hold workers. The Revenue Act of 1921 gave the first tax-favored status to stock-bonus and profit-sharing plans; five years later, the same status was accorded pension plans. Even so, in 1939 there were only 659 such plans of all types in the United States.

During World War II, however, government wage and price controls prompted employers and unions to develop jointly various types of plans in order to retain and compensate workers without causing inflation. In 1947 the Supreme Court upheld a National Labor Relations Board ruling requiring employers to bargain in good faith about the terms of retirement benefit plans. Plans numbered about 25,000 by 1954, just over 100,000 by 1964, and over 400,000 in 1974, just after Congress passed the Employee Retirement Income Security Act, which more carefully defined and regulated the various approaches to worker investment and retirement security.

A surge in the development of retirement plans followed this law. In 1986 there were about 1 million worker investment plans in the country. A U.S. company is not required to establish a retirement plan, but if it does it must abide by federal regulations. Organized labor had a major part in the proliferation of retirement plans by demanding them in bargaining after the war and pushing hard to make them consistently available in all firms it represented. Many non-union firms mimicked the retirement plans at union firms—which were usually defined benefit plans—and set up the same type of plans or savings plans, stock bonus plans, profit-sharing plans, or 401(k) plans where the firm got employee contributions and/or tied the retirement to the performance of the company.

Defined benefit pension plans and defined contribution pension plans essentially allow companies to set up tax-sheltered investment trusts with employee and/or company contributions. To encourage the employer to contribute, the earnings on these investments, as well as the contributions themselves, are not subject to corporate tax.

In the defined benefit plan, the company is required by law to contribute enough funds to allow the trust to generate sufficient assets to pay a predefined benefit, which is insured by the Pension Benefits Guarantee Corporation. With such a plan, it is not always possible to predict what the capital requirements for employee benefits will be over time. In the defined contribution plan, the company commits only to making certain contributions to the plan; the employee benefit depends on the company contribution and the investment performance of these contributions. This tax-exempt trust, like all retirement-plan trusts, is regulated by the IRS and the Department of Labor. Each account is credited with its share of investment return over time, including any increases or decreases in the market value of the investments.

Defined contribution plans are often referred to as capital-accumulation plans because that is what they allow workers to do. In addition to ESOPs, they include profit-sharing plans, which base the contribution on profit—although they are no longer required to do so under the 1986 tax law—and distribute cash to workers in cash plans or invest profits in a trust in deferred plans, stock-bonus plans (which distribute stock to workers and do not base the contribution on profit), money-purchase pension plans (where the company makes fixed contributions not based on profit), thrift or savings plans (where employees contribute a predetermined portion of earnings to an investment account, and the employer matches these contributions), and 401(k) plans (where employees channel part of their salary before income taxes to an investment trust and the employer can and usually does make a contribution also).

Defined contribution plans are not insured by the Pension Benefits Guarantee Corporation, but they are all legal trusts regulated by ERISA and they operate as employee investment funds that are held in a combination of stocks, bonds, cash instruments, and real estate. They are also a fairly recent phenomenon. There were only 39 profit-sharing plans in 1939. By 1956 there were about 2,000 defined contribution plans, most of which were profit-sharing plans. They then began to increase rapidly through the 1960s and 1970s as new types of plans were introduced. Defined contribution plans are cheaper, easier, and more predictable in costs, and simpler for companies to administer than defined benefit plans.

Defined benefit plans are more often found in medium and large companies, while the defined contribution plan is more common in smaller firms. Instead of increasing the benefit levels of defined benefit pension plans—widely viewed as one of the great outcomes of labor organizing since the 1950s—many companies are supplementing or even replacing such plans with defined contribution plans. Data indicate that 60% of workers in defined contribution plans are in companies with defined benefit pension plans. Four-fifths of the Fortune 500 firms sponsor along with their defined benefit plan at least one defined contribution plan, commonly a deferred profit-sharing plan, a 401(k) plan, or an ESOP, in that order of frequency.

The Changing Structure of Ownership of Employee Benefit Trust

The role of employee ownership in this development was always thought to be minimal. As noted, in the early 1970s Congress was unaware of substantial employee ownership by employee benefit plans. Commentators such as Peter Drucker predicted that it was employee ownership of stock in corporations in general and not their employer's company that would represent the true historic development at the bottom of the growth in equity holdings of employee benefit trusts. Drucker predicted tremendous growth in corporate stock holdings by these plans to 50–60% of all corporate stock by 1985 and to 67% by the end of the century.[2] In fact, Drucker was proven completely wrong. Partly because of poor performance of the stock market in periods of the 1960s and 1970s and partly because of risk aversion, these plans began to diversify and their holdings of corporate stock did not grow so dramatically. In fact, in 1983 worker ownership of non-employer stock was 15.23%, far below what Drucker predicted. Table 10.1 shows how various kinds of corporate stock ownership were spread among different kinds of employee benefit plans.

The significant change was more in the structure of the holdings in employee benefit plans and not so much in their quantitative growth as Drucker predicted. For a variety of reasons, as we shall see, employee benefit plans began to take

Table 10.1

Corporate Stock Ownership and Employee Benefit Plans, 1983

Total stock outstanding in 1983	Percent of Total	Dollars (in billions)
Employer and non-employer stock owned through pension funds of all kinds	18.4%	$395.87
Employer stock owned by employees through benefit plans and other arrangements	3.9%	$ 83.26
In private pension plans:		
Defined benefit plans	.2%	4.3
Defined contribution plans other than ESOPs	2.1%	45.18
ESOPs	.87%	18.72
In other arrangements (stock purchase and stock option plans)	.70%	15.6

Sources: Data on non-ESOP arrangements from Douglas Kruse, Rutgers University; ESOP data from U.S. General Accounting Office

larger and larger positions in the stock of the employer corporation. Unions and individual workers, whether union or non-union, had nothing to do with this development. Non-ESOP employee benefit trusts were almost exclusively controlled by corporate managers or their appointed trustees, who were usually corporate officers (or the same managers) or bank trust departments. Investments in these plans' assets were typically handled by professional institutional investors who had little or no interest in pension socialism, employee stock ownership, unions, employee representation, or the worker involvement impact on corporate governance.

It is clear that this pattern was well under way and would have occurred even without the encouragement of the Employee Stock Ownership Plan in congressional legislation beginning in 1973. A large proportion of this employee ownership was not through ESOPs and did not involve leveraging, which the law generally proscribes for employee benefit plans other than ESOPs, but was through passive retirement vehicles. By 1981 employee-investment funds were among the top stockholders in 69 of the Fortune 500 companies and attained close to 20% ownership in 11 cases. Much of the growth was in profit-sharing and employee thrift plans.

General Trends in Various Benefit Plans

We can examine the different types of benefit plans investing in employee stock separately.

Through Defined Benefit Plans. Federal law prohibits defined benefit plans from putting more than 10% of their assets in employer stock; this ensures that risk can be shared among a number of investment vehicles. Currently, no figures are available on how many defined benefit plans own stock in their own companies, but the maximum investment could be no more than $65 billion. If investment managers invest in employer stock at the same rate they invest in all stock—43% of all assets in corporate and union-sponsored plans in 1985— total defined benefit plan investment in employer stock is more likely $28 billion. Indeed, the evidence suggests that defined benefit pension plans are investing far less in their own company's stock: the figure is only about $4.3 billion.

Through Defined Contribution Plans. Capital accumulation plans depend on investment performance for their success, so companies and workers have generally avoided massive investment in their own firms. In addition, employees generally do not have the savings to invest in such plans. Nearly 70% of the participants in defined contribution plans had their benefits wholly financed by the employer. But a slight trend toward investment in employer stock is discernible. Figures for participation of U.S. employees in various defined contribution plans are based on the most recent (1985) Department of Labor national survey of establishments employing more than 50, 100, or 250 employees, depending on the industry. Some 24% of all employees in such firms were in employee stock ownership plans, although this number fell to 2% when the tax-credit ESOP was excluded. It is estimated that the total assets of defined contribution plans held as worker ownership of the stock of employer companies is about $45 billion or about 2.1 percent of all corporate equity.

Profit-sharing plans are the predominant form of defined contribution plan. In 1983 they accounted for about 350,000, or over 60% of all defined contribution plans. An average 22,000 new plans have been established per year throughout the 1980s: 18% of employees in 1985 had profit-sharing plans, while cash plans covered 1% of all employees, with 3% in combination plans in medium to large firms. Deferred plans covered 14% of all employees. Indeed, they have accounted for half of all the retirement plans established since the passage of ERISA in 1974. Until the 1986 Tax Reform Act, deferred-profit-sharing plans were tax-exempt trusts with the employers' contributions based on the company's profit. They are more prevalent than plans that give a cash share of profits directly to workers.

A number of very large companies invest about 40 to 100% of their profit-sharing plans' assets in their own stock, yet this still does not add up to much. Best estimates are that the plans account for the greater part of the $25 billion, or 1.2 percent of the corporate equity that is probably held by all defined contribution plans.

Thrift (or savings) plans involve payroll-based employee savings with company contributions directly related to the amount saved by the worker. Just over one-fourth of all employees in medium and large firms participated in such plans, which were more prevalent among white-collar workers (36% versus 17% of blue-collar workers). The plans allow for the employee to choose from a set of investment alternatives. There are less than 10,000 such plans in the country; they tend to be concentrated in some very large firms, some of which have put together sizable portfolios of worker investments. Just over 40% of the plans require that the company's contribution be invested in company stock, effectively turning those contributions into a stock bonus plan. Among nine different alternatives for worker investment, 54% of these plans include stock in the employer company. The DOL study found that, nationwide, companies usually require half of the participants to invest the company's contribution in employer stock.

These plans have not spread throughout the economy or had a substantial impact. They are based mainly on savings, which most employees do not possess in abundance, and they tend to exclude hourly workers, who constitute the bulk of the workforce.

Salary-reduction or 401(k) plans came into being in 1978, when Congress allowed employees to make contributions to these plans from their paychecks before income taxes but after social security taxes. Companies can match these contributions. This favorable tax treatment has led to the conversion of many thrift plans to 401(k) plans. These are the fastest growing type of defined contribution plans in U.S. corporations, and they are sizably invested in employer securities. One survey showed that 73% of a sample of major U.S. companies had 401(k) plans and suggested that they were becoming an increasingly dominant form of defined contribution plan. Some 37% of all white-collar employees and 14% of all blue-collar employees are eligible to participate in such plans, although some studies indicate that only one-third of those who are eligible actually participate.

Some data are available on investment in company stock by 401(k) plans as a whole. One survey indicated that 51% of 401(k) plans had an investment option for company stock. Also, 16% of all employees in salary-reduction plans had their contributions invested through profit-sharing plans, and 68 percent through thrift plans, both of which use employer stock.

Stock-bonus plans provide benefits without a cash outlay. The company contributes stock, often its own, to the tax-exempt trust. The plans are not, however, required to own stock in their own companies. Stock-bonus plans are the most unpopular type of defined contribution plan; excluding ESOPs, which are a special kind of stock-bonus plan, they probably number fewer than 1,000, or less than 0.33% of all defined-contribution plans. Only 1% of all employees in medium to large firms are in these plans.

Direct stock-purchase plans encourage direct employee ownership of stock through voluntary purchase. They are not supported by extensive tax incentives, although a 1984 Hewitt Associates study suggested that, of the 40% of Fortune Directory companies with such plans, as many as one-quarter enjoy some tax advantages under Section 423 of the Internal Revenue Code, as long as the plan is offered to virtually all employees. Sponsoring corporations often make no contribution other than to offer stock at a discount price and provide a payroll-deduction mechanism and reduced brokerage fees.

In 1983 one out of three American shareholders, or about 12 million people, were participating in such plans. Over 10 million individuals reported to the New York Stock Exchange that they first acquired stock this way. For five million of these individuals—about 12% of all shareholders—this is the only stock they own. Evidently, despite the popularity and state support of stock ownership through various retirement benefit plans, direct stock ownership plans remain the more common approach to employee ownership. The vast majority of these plans, however—almost 90%—own less than 5% of their companies' stock. Yet, although company stock owned by employees through these plans amounts to only about 0.70% of all stock held by households, and figures for both stock-purchase and stock-option plans indicate participation by only 3% of all employees in medium to large firms nationally, direct stock-purchase arrangements have created a substantial amount of employee ownership even though they have fewer tax incentives than the other plans discussed.

Stock-option plans, which tend to be strongly management oriented, are the major means of putting stock into employee hands according to New York Stock Exchange estimates. The Internal Revenue Act of 1964 provided some favorable tax treatment for these plans—called incentive stock-option plans—for both companies and employees, although they have come in and out of U.S. tax law over the last three decades. When Congress reinstated these plans in 1981, it acknowledged the value of employee equity, saying they "will provide an important incentive device for corporations to attract new management and to retain the service of executives who might otherwise leave, by providing an opportunity to acquire an interest in the business (Blasi, p. 14)." No estimates are available of how much employer stock was gained through stock-option plans.

The Trend Is Growing

One of the most puzzling aspects of this trend is the perception that all employee ownership is in ESOPs and that deferred-profit-sharing trusts—the most popular kind of defined contribution plan—are about profit sharing and not stock ownership. The main reason is that most of what researchers call profit-sharing plans are in fact deferred-profit-sharing trusts that have sizable amounts of employee ownership of employer securities. Of the approximately half million profit-sharing plans in the United States, 96% are deferred-profit-sharing trusts. An additional 3% are a combination of a deferred trust and cash profit sharing. There are various ways to estimate how much employee ownership is actually being masked as deferred-profit-sharing plans. The crudest estimate is based on the total amount of employer securities held by ESOPs and deferred-profit-sharing trusts. In 1983, ESOPs held almost 0.90% of all corporate stock outstanding in the United States. Deferred-profit-sharing trusts held 1.2%. In fact other defined contribution plans, such as savings plans and 401(k) plans that are both payroll-based savings plans with employer and employee contributions, held 0.90%.

Thus, deferred-profit-sharing trusts were responsible in 1983 for 25% more employee ownership than ESOPs in total. If all defined contribution plans (excluding ESOPs) are counted, they are responsible for almost 2.5 times more employee stock ownership than ESOPs. Because the evidence suggests that publicly held firms have a sizable prevalence of plans other than ESOPs providing company stock ownership, a good proportion of this phenomenon is probably due to such firms.

Several more specific studies indicate that private and public-company deferred-profit-sharing trusts actually hold substantial assets in employer securities. As noted above, various estimates based on public-company surveys indicate that 12–20% of public companies have deferred-profit-sharing plans. Plans with over $10 million in assets tend to hold 34% of those assets in company stock; 19% of the Fortune 1000 firms have profit-sharing plans that hold 10% or more in company stock. About 50–70% of large manufacturing and non-manufacturing firms have savings or thrift plans. About 40% in one sample required investment in employer stock, while company stock is offered as an investment option in many 401(k) plans. Just over 50% of these plans had an investment option for employer securities.

Aside from the 1,500–2,000 ESOPs that own a majority of their corporation's stock, the GAO estimates that 91% of ESOPs own minority stakes. One way to consider the real extent of the employee ownership of deferred-profit-sharing trusts is to ask how small it has to be to surpass the employee ownership in ESOPs. If only 2% of the half million deferred-profit-sharing plans— namely, 10,000 companies—own more than 20% of their employers' securities, then these trusts represent a larger number of companies owning sizable employer securities stakes than the whole ESOP phenomenon, which in 1989 included about 10,000 firms. This author estimates that no more than 4,000 of those ESOPs own 25–50% of their companies' stock.

More systematic data will probably conclude that the distinction between "profit sharing" and "employee ownership" is not as large as previously thought, at least inasmuch as ESOPs are thought to be the only significant mechanism for employee ownership. This bias is aggravated by the fact that different research camps and associations exist to study the so-called two phenomena. This is especially true since both ESOPs and deferred-profit-sharing trusts provide the economic incentive to employees after a long period of employment. Only comparisons between cash profit-sharing plans or perhaps deferred-profit-sharing plans without employer securities and ESOPs really segment the two types of employee involvement.

In conclusion, these are indications that the spread of employee stock ownership in non-ESOP employee benefit plans has been continuing to grow. More systematic data will be required on this in the future, but the general trend is becoming clearer and clearer as more data come in.

The ESOP Catalyst to Employee Stock Ownership in Public Companies

Employee ownership of employer corporation stock does not equal ESOPs, which are simply one vehicle for employee ownership. ESOPs have been both increasingly relevant to expanding employee stock ownership in the publicly. traded sector and increasingly irrelevant as public corporations have used a variety of vehicles. This is not to say that the establishment of ESOPs did not significantly change the dynamics of the evolution of employee stock ownership in the public corporate sector. It did in several crucial ways.

First, ERISA mandates that defined employee benefit trusts generally cannot invest more than 10% of their assets in employer securities except ESOPs, which are to invest primarily in employer stock. Depending on the proportion of the total assets of the employee benefit plan of any corporation to the total value of equity of that corporation—a proportion that was typically low—this rule made it difficult for significant employee holdings to develop in many companies. Deferred-profit-sharing trusts that by charter were intended to invest mainly in employer securities and the combining of various benefit plans could be used to circumvent this rule, but the intent of Congress to actively prevent sizable employee ownership of employer corporations for the purpose of protecting the independent investment status of pension plans was crystal clear to all concerned.

Second, the amount of employee ownership in these cases was mainly a function of company retirement security commitments to employees and limits on the tax deductions companies could get for contributing to such plans. ESOPs allowed companies to make it a function of how much leverage they could handle and provided them greater flexibility (i.e., tax subsidies) to handle more debt comfortably. Under ESOPs, corporate financial transactions became an important motive in the benefit decision. ESOP law and special dispensations under ERISA changed all of this. An ESOP acts like an employee benefit plan under ERISA but it can serve a substantial corporate finance purpose. This change was underlined by Congress' actively encouraging the use of leverage to establish employee ownership in ESOPs and by Congress' increasing the maximum tax deductions for contributing to ESOPs to 25% of the W-2 income of all participating workers in the plan versus lower limits for other employee benefit plans. When additional tax incentives created in 1984, such as unlimited deductibility of dividend payments on ESOP stock and lower interest rates on capital to leveraged ESOPs as a result of bank deductions on their interest profits, are added to this basic deduction, companies can get tax deductions well in excess of 25% of the W-2 compensation of participating employees. (See Chapters 2 and 3 and Appendix I and II of Blasi for a detailed analysis of these issues. Chapter 3 explains how earlier corporate finance disadvantages for public companies to adopt ESOPs became corporate finance advantages as a result of changing market conditions and changing tax incentives.)

This development occurred slowly and quietly and cuts itself into two periods: the 1974–84 period in which ESOPs were a minor phenomenon in public companies and the 1985–89 period in which ESOPs became a major phenomenon in public companies.

Generally speaking, before 1984, employee ownership appeared in public companies in insignificant to modest amounts, not as a result of leveraging but as a result of slow gradual investment of employee savings or pension funds. The plans already were mainly passive investments where employees themselves had little governance power either because of the size of the plan or because the stock was usually voted by institutional trustees. It was rare to have a company's employee ownership discussed in the press just as it was rare to have a company's pension investment discussed. They were investments and holdings not necessarily of strategic importance to the company.

The New Trend in Employee Ownership in Publicly Held Corporations

It may be counter-intuitive, but we can now state conclusively that even without ESOP legislation, employee ownership was slowly taking a modest position in the public corporate sector from the end of World War II to the early 1980s. From 1984 to 1989 several factors would significantly alter this slow rise and create an atmosphere of legitimacy and business as usual about employees owning large segments of major U.S. corporations. These factors are:

1. The legitimacy of slow growth and absorption of corporate employee ownership since World War II

2. Employee benefit tax incentives (pre-ESOP)

3. The growth of capital accumulation plans as a reaction to union demands for defined benefits and a desire to tie retirement security to corporate performance

4. Experience of publicly held corporations with substantial employee ownership through divestiture of units

5. The emergence of the ESOP in some publicly held corporations and the role of leveraging in employee ownership brought by the ESOP

6. Special 1984 tax incentives that removed barriers to ESOP diffusion

7. The role of ESOPs in large leveraged buyout transactions at the time leveraged buyouts became a tool for public corporate managers

8. The creation of employee ownership as a corporate finance strategy

9. The takeover era and the need for takeover defenses, especially as a result of the Polaroid decision

Many observers would favor one or two of these factors as their explanation, but an understanding of all of them is important to comprehend the substantial changes that have gone on in employee ownership in the public corporate sector.

1. *Growing Legitimacy of Employee Ownership in Public Corporations.* The first factor was the slow growth itself, which we have documented above. While researchers and the public were not paying attention, corporate managers and workers realized that their companies had substantial employee ownership and it did not hurt the company. The impact of this factor is not to be minimized. Corporate America is quite allergic to change, and here is a case where the very structure of corporate America began to change without resistance. Indeed, as we shall indicate later, the governance and power aspects of the employee ownership that emerged significantly neutralized the power of ownership.

2. *Pre-ESOP Employee Benefit Tax Incentives Set the Stage and Solidified the Commitment of the Government.* Over several decades Congress has consistently created a connection between employee investment funds for retirement security and tax incentives. It is widely recognized that these tax incentives are necessary to our retirement security system and are unlikely to be significantly changed. Once employee benefit plans became a legitimate and growing mechanism for employee ownership of companies, companies realized that they were essentially being paid to establish employee ownership because of the tax subsidy. That is vastly different than other kinds of corporate innovations or workplace innovations, and the author believes that it explains why corporate officials mainly concerned about the bottom line would consistently entertain the idea of employee ownership throughout the late 1980s.

3. *The Unexpected Growth of Capital Accumulation Plans.* These plans were an alternative to union demands for defined benefit pension plans and the preference of plans that tied retirement security to corporate performance. After the war and throughout the 1950s and 1960s, the cultural definition of a good job frequently meant one that had a good pension, usually a defined benefit pension plan where the workers knew exactly what they would get when they retired. The push for defined pensions became a central goal of union negotiations in the large manufacturing industries in the country. Also, many larger and more established non-union firms offered the same benefits to their employees as a way to keep unions out.

Unfortunately, the competitive pressures of the late 1970s and early 1980s and the concern about regularly expected wage and benefit increases among corporate officials led to a dramatic reversal of this trend toward assured pensions just as many in the public perceived it to be customary. The weakening of the expectation for assured pensions began slowly. Companies with defined benefit pension plans stopped making regular adjustments for inflation. On the one hand, corporate financial officers started to complain publicly about their inability to predict retirement costs with defined benefit pension plans. On the other hand, corporations sought to "raid" over-funded defined benefit pension plans when the market outperformed their expectations. Non-union companies began offering capital accumulation plans to their employees, which had the potential at least to provide greater returns than defined benefit pension plans. And companies, union and non-union alike, started to talk about tying retirement security funds to the performance of the company. The data provided above about the slow development of employee stock ownership in these various capital accumulation funds is evidence of this. The results of these various stresses can be seen in Table 10.2.

These data are based on a dataset consisting of publicly traded corporations. The implications are unmistakable. Employees covered by defined benefit pension plans have undergone a 12.5% decline while employees covered by ESOPs have more than doubled. Employees covered by profit sharing plans have increased by almost one-third. It is not possible from these data to tell definitively how many companies replaced defined benefit plans with capital accumulation plans or how many companies used capital accumulation plans to supplement defined benefit plans wherein inflation adjusters were cut out. Indeed, many firms do have both types of plans. The general conclusion is what is important: there is a transformation going on in how retirement security is provided to American workers. This transformation has not been fully recognized or featured in the popular press, and it is just beginning to be discussed in scholarly publications. No matter what one's attitude toward it may be, capital accumulation and investment plans tying retirement security to the stock performance of the employer or other companies is playing an increasing role in the pension system, whether as a replacement for existing benefits or as a supplement to existing benefits. Defined benefit plans, which also depend on the investment in stocks, bonds, and other investment media are also partly dependent on the performance of other companies. The key difference is that the employer is required in a defined benefit plan to increase the contribution to the plan in order to pay out benefits according to a prearranged formula. The ultimate performance of the underlying companies really does not determine the level of the benefit.

4. *Experience of Publicly Held Firms with 100% ESOPs in Divestitures of Unwanted Units.* Many corporations were able to get first-hand experience with the employee ownership idea in this manner. It gave them a safe way to explore the concept, learn about it, apply it, and watch its operation with little risk to the parent corporation.

Divestitures of units of publicly traded corporations to ESOPs became a phenomenon in the United States throughout the early and mid-1980s. The Weirton Steel divestiture by National Intergroup became a familiar story on the evening news. But it was mainly this incidental use of employee ownership by these companies that caught public attention. Nevertheless, by 1986 a sizable number of public companies had set up modest employee ownership plans in another major move in that direction.

Table 10.2
Growth of Deferred Profit Sharing Relative to Defined Benefit Plans and ESOPs, 1980–86

Numbers in 000's		1980	1981	1982	1983	1984	1985	1986
All profit-sharing	Participant estimates: high	10,098	10,713	11,764	13,010	14,261	16,166	17,068
	low	9,447	9,948	10,893	11,872	12,782	14,223	14,953
	Percent of employment (a)	12.8%	13.2%	14.6%	15.7%	16.1%	17.5%	17.9%
Non-thrift profit-sharing	Participant estimates: high	7,994	8,055	8,716	9,741	10,436	11,772	12,869
	low	7,554	7,627	8,195	9,024	9,572	10,626	11,582
	Percent of employment (a)	10.2%	10.1%	11.0%	11.9%	12.1%	13.1%	13.9%
Defined benefit	Participant estimates: high	30,250	30,125	30,089	28,467	29,242	29,760	29,018
	low	25,549	25,422	25,274	24,105	24,845	25,229	24,374
	Percent of employment (a)	34.5%	33.8%	34.0%	31.9%	31.3%	31.0%	29.2%
ESOPs	Participant estimates: high	5,009	5,175	6,464	9,582	11,190	12,076	12,122
	low	4,682	4,927	5,996	8,980	10,160	10,705	10,722
	Percent of employment (a)	6.3%	6.5%	8.1%	11.9%	12.8%	13.2%	12.8%
Private wage and salary workers in economy (000's)		74,013	75,289	74,430	75,522	79,327	81,356	83,488

"High" participant estimate represents total participants in plans, and contains some double-counting of workers in multiple plans. "Low" participant estimate represents total of participants in largest plan in company.
(a) Represents the low estimate of employees in plans divided by total private wage and salary workers.
Calculated from Form 5500 tapes, adjusted for small plans with information from Daniel Beller.

5. *The Role of Leveraging in Developing ESOP Employee Ownership in Public Corporations.* By 1986, as a result mainly of ESOPs, employee ownership became a frequent phenomenon among publicly traded corporations. Most of the companies, while public, were still relatively small and not represented among the group of the largest U.S. corporations.

6. *The Role of ESOP Tax Incentives.* The 1984 ESOP tax incentives were key to the rapid growth of employee ownership in the late 1980s. In Chapter 3 of Blasi I discuss the serious corporate finance problems faced by publicly held companies in the pre-1984 period in considering the adoption of a leveraged ESOP. The main barriers were the impact of issuing new shares to leveraged ESOPs on share value dilution, dividend income, and control of existing shareholders, as well as some accounting problems in reporting the leveraged ESOP. The details of these barriers are too extensive and technical to be covered here, but the upshot was to make the ESOP decision advantageous for only a select number of companies that could plan their way around these various problems and barriers. In 1984 Congress added tax incentives that increased ESOP tax deductions significantly and helped to offset some of these barriers.

7. *The Role of Large Leveraged ESOP Buyouts at the Time LBOs Became a Tool for Public Corporate Managers.* A series of large LBO deals that took public companies private in the mid-1980s—both before and after the new tax laws—helped educate the financial community about the usefulness of ESOPs in large companies. The specific names are less important than the fact that many of these transactions—Parsons, Raymond International, U.S. Sugar, Blue Bell, Dan River—involved very large ESOP LBOs in the hundreds of million dollars range. While many of these transactions were controversial for a variety of reasons, their appearance signaled that ESOPs and employee stock ownership and leverage had entered the U.S. market for corporate control in full force. This perception was only encouraged as corporate managers watched employee groups use leverage to purchase large companies such as Weirton Steel Corporation and to make offers for other firms such as United Airlines (UAL), which was first discussed in 1986. The implication was that ESOPs are different from the quietly installed employee benefit plan that owns some company stock. They are capable of operationalizing large, even huge, transactions. Certainly, this phenomenon and the public perception of it tracked the tremendous growth in ESOPs and their coverage in the press during the 1985–89 period.

8. *The Creation of Employee Ownership as a Corporate Finance Strategy.* The main reason for establishing employee ownership is no longer setting up passive employee benefit plans for modest tax deductions. Some companies, such as Lowe's and E-Systems, are dedicated to the idea of being partly employee-owned and partly owned by public shareholders. Some companies, such as Harcourt Brace Jovanovich and Ashland Oil, used employee benefit plans as a source of capital in a takeover situation in order to stabilize the companies' ownership. Some companies such as Michael Baker Corporation bought out a

major stockholder with an ESOP but remained public. Others such as Marsh Supermarkets combined the ESOP with a stock buyback program, and some, such as Pan Am and LTV, became employee-owned as a result of negotiations in concession bargaining with unions—in the Pan Am case—or as a result of concession bargaining and bankruptcy reorganization—in the LTV case.

But the clear difference is that these ESOPs have emerged as more substantial shareholders with higher visibility and more central importance to the strategic purposes of the corporation. Generally, the employee benefit purpose of the ESOP is integrated with a corporate finance or strategic purpose and the existence of the employee stock ownership as a passive retirement security vehicle is secondary to its strategic importance to the company. By the late 1980s employee ownership plans also emerged as important takeover defenses, as described later in this chapter and elsewhere in this book.

The employee benefit plan has emerged from many of these events as a new source of power if it is viewed as investment capital, worker equity, and part of corporate strategy. The central financial distinction motivating these developments is the fact that capital in an ESOP can be primarily invested in company stock whereas capital in other employee benefit plans is usually tied up in other investment media outside the company. The argument goes that the ESOP provides a benefit, innovative corporate financing, worker equity, and needed capital for ongoing corporate operations all at the same time. Labor observers have argued that such tactics represent a utilization of tax breaks and loopholes in pension law not envisioned by Congress, and that the retirement benefits of employees now become synonymous with the value of the ESOP stock they receive, creating undue risk. Companies, such as Phillips and Ashland Oil, which used ESOPs as major new corporate finance tools, would then alter their existing benefit plans.

The end result of these new experiments is broader-based than most management and labor leaders realize. The employee benefit plan has quickly become a crucial factor in business decisions, especially acquisitions and mergers, even in friendly takeovers, and the substantial increase of sizable ESOPs in public companies truly put employee ownership on the takeover agenda.

9. *The Takeover Era and the Need for Takeover Defenses, Especially the Perception of the Polaroid Decision, Influenced the Rapid Rise of ESOPs.* By the mid-1980s, the ESOP takeover potential was only partially realized. A series of court cases and conflicts ended in contradictory results. All that changed with the advent of a change in Delaware corporate law and the Polaroid decision by the Delaware Chancery Court. These events would be key because many large corporations are located in Delaware and the state's behavior on corporate control issues sets the standard for other states.

Delaware corporate law says that in certain types of takeovers the raider must gain more than 85% of the target company's disinterested (non-management owned) shares in a tender offer or the offer cannot be consummated. The law does not say that an ESOP holding a large block of the company's shares is automatically an entrenchment tool for management or a legal defense. A legal defense depends on the structure of the ESOP. If it allows employees to vote on the tender offer, it must be counted as part of the disinterested block.

Beginning in the 1987–88 period, public companies began setting up larger ESOPs through leveraged transactions as a reaction to the ESOP takeover defense tool offered in Delaware law. In the winter of 1989, the Delaware Court upheld the Polaroid ESOP as legal in the first strong challenge to this tool. Subsequently, the number of sizable ESOPs in public companies rapidly expanded. A partial list is in Chapter 2 of this book (Table 2.1).

In general, ESOPs, even in public companies, have tended to de-emphasize both formal ownership rights for workers and informal employee involvement. Regarding formal ownership rights, most of the ESOPs cited do have voting rights, but as leveraged ESOPs, employees may get only the right to vote or direct the tendering of shares allocated to them as the loan is paid off. In effect, in a mythical $1 billion ESOP owning 100% of a company that was set up using a loan that is being paid back over 10 years, only after the sixth year do employees actually have voting control of the company if, as is usually the case in private firms, a management-appointed trustee votes the unallocated shares (i.e., shares not allocated to employees' ESOP accounts because the underlying leverage or debt has not been repaid). It only slowly provides employees with the control over that voting block. Ultimately that happens only after many years, and, by that time, the stake can be diluted. Companies were often concerned because institutional trustees are required by ERISA provisions to do what is beneficial to the beneficiaries of the trust. Frequently, it is thought, it is safer for an institutional trustee simply to tender the shares if a premium can be gotten for the employees.

By the late 1980s, however, public companies were allowing employees to vote and direct the tendering of all shares in the ESOP. That way, they hoped, they could bypass the perceived obligation of the trustee to accede to a higher bid.

Polaroid exemplified some of these changes, while going further than normal practice. Polaroid make a commitment to enter into a partnership with its employees. Its ESOP was indeed set up close in time to a takeover attempt, and it clearly had an anti-takeover intent as a supplementary motivation. But Polaroid's ESOP allowed employees to vote all the shares in a tender offer, prescribing that unallocated shares would be voted in proportion to allocated shares. The company provided for a third party that would confidentially tabulate such votes. In addition, Polaroid had a history of communicating lots of company information to employees. It has employee involvement programs and a 23-person elected non-union Employee Committee that is involved in a deliberative role about company decisions.

A key reason why the judge upheld the Polaroid ESOP was that she determined that employee ownership was integrated into the labor-management relations strategy of the company and was thus likely to increase productivity.

As noted elsewhere in this volume, research has strongly suggested that employee ownership is likely to increase productivity when combined with opportunities for employee involvement.

THE NEW TREND IN PUBLIC COMPANY EMPLOYEE OWNERSHIP: WHERE IS IT HEADING?

We have seen that employee ownership has undergone rapid development since 1974, which has now resulted in a new trend that is characterized by fast growth, close ties to companies' strategic corporate finance decisions rather than simply their retirement security decisions, and a centrality to the takeover phenomenon. In addition, we have examined impressionistic evidence that while ESOPs are clearly the most publicized dominant vehicle of employee ownership, it is reasonable to assume that scores of publicly traded companies with and without ESOPs have sizable employee stockholdings in their deferred-profit-sharing trusts, savings or thrift plans, 401(k) plans, and employee share-purchase plans.

Let's consider several key questions. How did this all happen? What will be the characteristics of this sector? What will be the impact on productivity? What will be the impact on the market for corporate control? What will be the impact on corporate governance? What will be the impact on public policy? Only initial hints to the answers to these questions can be given because sufficient information from enough firms is not yet available to go beyond these remarks.

How Did This All Happen?

While comprehensive data on the subject are not yet available, it seems prudent to conclude that this new trend was not intentional but was an interaction between events taking place in the worlds of government tax deductions for employee benefit plans, corporate perceptions of the costs and flexibility of employee benefit plans, the growth of debt, the acceleration of the market for corporate control, the elimination of many takeover defenses in public corporations, and changing attitudes about employee ownership in general. All these factors are continuing to evolve in the directions that facilitated these changes in employee ownership in the U.S. economy.

Several guesstimates can be imprudently suggested. First, at the current growth rate of several hundred percent every few years in sizable employee ownership plans in public corporations, employee stock ownership of employer companies through varieties of vehicles will be a major economic phenomenon by the year 2000. It would be reasonable to see 20–30% of most public companies in the hands of their employees with much larger stakes in many companies as a result of the combinations of employee ownership from the different vehicles and plans. Second, it would seem that some of these factors will clearly accelerate. For example, it is likely that the engine of employee stock ownership will get a big energy boost because of the continuing reduced commitment of public companies to defined benefit plans at the same time that the baby boom generation requires more and more stability for its retirement security. Simply put, it is hard to imagine a cheaper way to fund such benefits than through company stock, which at least allows the company to use the capital until it is paid out. Obviously, this will raise very serious questions of risk, but one's moral judgments on the phenomenon and the fact that it is a decisive trend must be differentiated. Third, combined with institutional ownership of public corporate stock by pension funds, it is reasonable to assume that direct and indirect employee ownership of stock may in fact constitute the largest shareholder in many public companies in the future and many companies may find that these interests own a plurality of their stock.

What Will Be the Characteristics of This Sector?

The author's crystal ball indicates some surprising directions. This worker-owned sector will be largely non-union. Unions will probably be no more than 10% of the private-sector workforce by the year 2000. The author estimates that less than 10% of employee-owned firms are largely (more than 50%) unionized today. This will present an interesting anomaly: workers will own a lot of U.S. companies just when their representation in these companies will be at its lowest ebb. Certainly, employee ownership will co-exist with unions in some long-standing unionized public companies. Weirton Steel, which is a New York Stock Exchange company largely owned by a mostly union ESOP but partly owned by public shareholders, is a prime example. Labor relations are more cooperative in this type of company. For example, if the UAL take-over by its employees is completed, the company may go public again, and a similar situation may be in effect there. But will employee ownership become the basis of a new kind of worker representation of U.S. companies, one that is based on entrepreneurial and employee interest combined? Given all the changes that have taken place, that is a possibility especially because the nature of ESOP tax laws gives greater incentives the larger the number of participating employees. The employee ownership world rapidly moved from a situation where privately held corporations set up ESOPs excluding their union employees to one where publicly traded corporations set up ESOPS for substantially all their employees.

What Will Be the Impact on Productivity?

Based on previous research by The National Center for Employee Ownership and Michael Conte cited in Chapter 7 of this volume, one can expect that employee ownership will not negatively affect productivity. Hidden in all the data that ESOPs do not magically increase productivity is the important finding that they certainly do not hurt.

Corporate productivity is becoming the topic of competitiveness as policy makers, researchers, managers, and employees realize that the only way to compete in a global marketplace with the emerging Pacific Rim and "United States of Europe" super-markets and competitors is by making U.S. firms more productive. The only way the employee ownership that will be part of the U.S. corporate system can be converted to a productivity plus is by combining it with employee involvement in solving key productivity problems. To do this will require a change in the culture of these companies toward a Polaroid culture.

Polaroid set up an ESOP and funded it with employee pay cuts so that the performance of the company will be a large determinant of possible future wage increases. In this sense, it was like many public companies—as reported by Conte—that reduced benefits in setting up ESOPs. But Polaroid is way ahead of its time in combining its ESOP with an extensive employee representation committee that is involved in providing input on company human resource and strategic decisions. The company has developed a mechanism for employee board representation. It is redesigning assembly-line work in its manufacturing facilities to create a more team-oriented, problem-solving-oriented, and pay-for-performance approach, and the firm has expanded its culture of information-sharing so that its employees are regularly treated like owners. Even after it won its takeover battle, the company took steps to expand its ESOP to 22% of the firm.

One key aspect of the Polaroid human resources system is the protection of individual rights. The company has a grievance or fairness procedure that allows employees to take employee-manager conflicts based on individual events or company-wide patterns of perceived unfairness (similar to a class-action suit that can be anonymously argued) and argue these through ascending levels of informal and then formal bodies ending in mandatory outside arbitration. Interestingly enough, very few cases ever go to outside arbitration. The company has used this system to train managers and employees to solve their own problems.

This is significant because a corporation cannot expect employees to feel like owners and want to be involved if they perceive that their grievances get no sustained attention in a fair system. In effect, some forms of employee representation and problem-solving and conflict resolution will be necessary to developing ongoing employee involvement in productivity improvement. The employee ownership will create a common identification between the worker and the corporation. It will align the interests of shareholder and employee-owner and manager and co-worker, but it is only a potential for entrepreneurial involvement. A definite management commitment to change the labor-management relationship to one of fairness and involvement will be necessary to realize this potential.

What Will Be the Impact on the Market for Corporate Control?

Employee ownership may emerge as the preeminent solution to public corporations constantly changing hands, constantly besieged by short-term profit thinking, speculation, and greed. It may. Despite the coolness toward ESOPs and leveraged transactions in late 1989 and early 1990 in light of the events surrounding the UAL buyout and the junk bond and stock market problems, takeover defense ESOPs make good sense for public corporations, especially if they are set up quietly, before a raider comes on the scene, and before the stock of the company has been bid up to an unreal speculative level. These prophylactic ESOPs and employee-benefit-plan purchases will probably continue for some time. They almost guarantee companies will not be hauled into court for their ESOPs. They will always be a major source of employee ownership's growth in this sector. In the author's experience, they are limited mainly because many managers are afraid to have sizable employee stakes. Discussions with senior executives and investment bankers have provided impressionistic data that many managers simply do not believe that the serfs deserve to own part of the castle and they have feudalistic attitudinal barriers to considering significant employee ownership. In effect, they would rather throw the dice and lose control of the firm than develop a real employee partnership.

So lots of boards and senior managers consider employee ownership only when the takeover attack is about to begin. At least this behavior needs to be recognized for what it is: imprudent and contrary to whatever lessons the historical and legal record of ESOPs in public companies has to teach us. Nevertheless, this behavior will probably continue. At present, corporate America perceives the message of the more permissive Polaroid decision as meaning that any ESOP set up in a takeover is OK. Our analysis indicates that these individuals have really not read Judge Carolyn Berger's opinion carefully. Her opinion is heavily conditioned on the unique features of Polaroid that we have recounted. It is likely that in the near future a management entrenchment ESOP will come along that will be put to the test again in the Delaware court. This will happen only if corporate managers who use ESOPs do not follow the Polaroid/Delaware model.

That model has two criteria: (1) employees get a real choice in a tender offer and management has the confidence in giving them that choice because it has made a commitment to a culture of partnership and ownership; and (2) shareholder value gets maximized because the ESOP is not set up in a way to dilute shareholder dividends or control, but rather is set up in a context of various methods to increase productivity and make the firm more competitive. In the Polaroid case, as noted, management coordinated the ESOP with a stock buyback to avoid dilution of dividends and control to shareholders and support the stock price. The ESOP was also part of a cultural re-orientation of the company.

If the Polaroid model is not followed by enough public companies, a restrictive opinion is almost certain by the Delaware court. The impact of such an opinion, depending on its severity, would be to safeguard only prophylactic ESOPs and not reaction ESOPs set up in the midst of a takeover battle.

What Will Be the Impact on Corporate Governance?

One observer of this scene recently predicted that employee-manager battles will be the result of a new public corporation of the future with sizable employee stakes. Other observers of the corporate scene have said that ESOPs in public companies will actually prevent the maximization of shareholder value because they may initially dilute shareholder control and dividends when they are set up, they may result in a decrease in stock price because arbitrageurs and institutions sell the stock of the company since they view the ESOP as a barrier to a sale at a break-up price, and they ultimately result in entrenching the current ownership structure thus reducing the chances of any future sale.

There is little truly objective evidence on which to base an evaluation of these claims. Most employee ownership stakes to date have not had employee votes because they were set up in employee benefit plans without voting rights attached to the stock or because they were set up in leveraged ESOPs where unallocated shares were to be voted by trustees under the pre-Delaware law expectations of how such ESOPs would function. Some initial data by researchers purporting to prove that share prices decline after the introduction of ESOPs are not conclusive because the researchers did not control for other explanations for the share price to go down.

On the other hand, no clear evidence exists for the counter-claims. Indeed, most public-company ESOPs have not resulted in improvements in economic performance according to Conte's research, and most are not likely to result in such improvements based on the fact that so few public companies take the human resource management steps necessary to achieve these ends after they introduce employee ownership.

It is too early to predict an employee ownership utopia in the public sector or the end of the takeover frenzy due to ESOPs or the joint governance of companies by employee representatives and management and outside directors. What can be safely predicted is that the employee ownership phenomenon in publicly traded companies will begin to have observable effects on corporate boards, tender offers, takeover battles, labor-management relations, employee benefit and wage discussions, organizing campaigns, company reorganizations, and other events. Employee ownership is larger, more active, more recognized. It is growing, it is in the press, it is known, it is being debated, and it will figure in all these developments.

What Will Be the Impact on Public Policy?

Congress and the presidency will soon wake up to the fact that the deductions for all these employee benefit plans in the tax code are now closely tied into a major transformation of the U.S. public corporation and that any string they pull is likely to affect this dynamic transformation. This transformation will have to be managed from Washington because anything Congress or the president does or thinks about it will have the effect, either by commission or omission, of managing it and of changing it. The bottom line is that it makes sense for both Congress and the president to convene study panels to figure out what a responsible comprehensive national policy should be on this issue. Should the U.S. democracy encourage popular capitalism through employee ownership? Should public policy accelerate these developments? Should it be stopped? Should public policy encourage combining employee ownership with forms of productivity improvement to realize its competitive potential? These are the questions that will become unavoidable.

NOTES

1. The major source for this chapter is Joseph R. Blasi, *Employee Ownership: Revolution or Ripoff?* (Cambridge, MA: Ballinger, 1988).
2. Peter Drucker, *Unseen Revolution* (New York: Harper & Row, 1976).

Selected Bibliography

Benefits and Costs of ESOP Tax Incentives for Broadening Stock Ownership. Washington, DC: General Accounting Office, December 1986.

Blasi, Joseph R. *Employee Ownership: Revolution or Ripoff?* Cambridge, MA: Ballinger, 1988.

Blasi, Joseph R. and Douglas C. Kruse. *The Coming Revolution in Employee Ownership.* New York: Harper & Row, forthcoming 1991.

"Buying Out the Boss," *Forbes,* April 3, 1985, p. 56.

Conte, Michael A. and Jan Svejnar. "The Performance Effects of Employee Ownership Plans." In *Paying for Productivity: A Look at the Evidence,* Alan S. Binder, ed. Washington, DC: Brookings Institution, 1990.

Conte, Michael A. and Arnold Tannenbaum. *Employee Ownership.* Ann Arbor: Survey Research Center, University of Michigan, 1980.

Delahaut, P. "ESOPs as a Corporate Finance Technique: Possibilities and Limits Under ERISA." *Journal of Pension Planning and Compliance,* Spring 1988.

"Elements of a Good ESOP." *Mergers & Acquisitions,* 23 (July–August 1988):5.

Employee Stock Ownership Plans: Interim Report. Washington, DC: U.S. General Accounting Office, February 1986.

Employee Stock Ownership Plans: Little Evidence of Effects on Corporate Performance. Washington, DC: U.S. General Accounting Office, October 1987.

"Employee Stock Plans Playing a Bigger Role in Buyout Deals," *American Banker,* September 3, 1987.

"ESOP Defenses are Likely to Increase; Plans Not Seen as Full Protection from Takeovers." *Wall Street Journal.* April 6, 1989. p. A2.

ESOP Forms Manual. Jacksonville, FL: Corbel & Company, 1985.

"ESOP Gains as Anti-Takeover Defense," *Christian Science Monitor,* 81 (January 1989): 9.

"ESOPs and Section 401(k) Plans—A Marriage Made in Heaven?" *Tax Adviser*, 16 (October 1985):640–44.

Feldman, Jonathan and Corey M. Rosen. *Employee Benefits in Employee Stock Ownership Plans: How Does the Average Worker Fare?* Oakland, CA: The National Center for Employee Ownership, 1985.

French, J. L. "Employee Perspective of Stock Ownership: Financial Investment or Mechanism of Control?" *Academy of Management Review*, 12 (July 1987):427–35.

Harris, Anthony A., ed. *ERISA: The Law and the Code*. Washington, DC: Bureau of National Affairs, 1987.

Kalish, Gerald I., ed. *ESOPs: The Handbook of Employee Stock Ownership Plans*. Chicago: Probus Publishing Company, 1989.

Kelso, Louis. *The Two-Factor Theory: The Economics of Reality*. New York: Random House, 1967.

Kelso, Louis and Mortimer Adler. *The Capitalist Manifesto*. New York: Random House, 1958.

Kelso, Louis and Patricia Hetter Kelso. *Democracy and Economic Power: Extending the ESOP Revolution*. Cambridge, MA: Ballinger, 1988.

Ludwig, Ronald, Jared Kaplan, and Gregory Brown. "ESOP Portfolio." Washington, DC: Bureau of National Affairs, Tax Management, Inc., 1987.

"A New Way to Keep the Raiders at Bay." *Business Week*, January 23, 1989, p. 39.

Pruitt, Deborah. *Employee Participation Programs in Employee Ownership Companies*. Oakland, CA: The National Center for Employee Ownership, 1988.

Quarrey, Michael. *Employee Ownership and Corporate Performance*. Oakland, CA: The National Center for Employee Ownership, 1986.

Rosen, Corey, Katherine J. Klein, and Karen M. Young. *Employee Ownership in America: The Equity Solution*. Lexington, MA: Lexington Books, 1986.

Rosen, Corey and Michael Quarrey. "How Well is Employee Ownership Working?" *Harvard Business Review*, September–October 1987.

Rosenburg, Hilary. "Are ESOPs Headed for Trouble? Generous Tax Breaks Have Made These Plans a Big Hit With Corporations; But Many in Washington Think Things are Getting Out of Hand." *Institutional Investor*, 21 (August 1987):109.

"Should Your Company Adopt an ESOP?" *Management Accounting*, 70 (January 1989): 31.

Smiley, Robert W., Jr. "How to Fund for an ESOP's Repurchase Liability." *Journal of the American Society of CLU*, 14 (May 1987):62.

Smiley, Robert W., Jr. and Ronald J. Gilbert, eds. *Employee Stock Ownership Plans: Business Planning, Implementation, and Law and Taxation*. Englewood Cliffs, NJ: Prentice-Hall, 1989.

Sollee, W. L. "ESOP Diversification Rules Explained." *The Journal of Taxation*, July 1988, pp 22–23.

———. "Readily Tradable Equal to Public Traded." *Journal of Taxation*, 67 (November 1987):351.

"Substitution Stocks for Health Plans: ESOP Transfer Rising Cost of Benefits to Retirees." *American Banker*, 154 (April 18, 1989):6.

"Suddenly the Blue Chips are Red Hot for ESOPs: A Boon to Morale and Taxes, the Plans Can Be a Poison Pill Too." *Business Week*, March 10, 1989, p. 144.

''They Own the Place: Employee Stock Plans Come of Age as Morale Boosters and Takeover Tools.'' *Time*, 133 (February 6, 1989):50.

Yoffee, Michael. *Gainsharing and Employee Ownership*. Oakland, CA: The National Center for Employee Ownership, 1988.

Index

About the Editor
and Contributors

KAREN M. YOUNG is cofounder and associate director of The National Center for Employee Ownership, a non-profit membership research and information organization formed in 1981 in Oakland, California. Prior to that she served on the staff of the U.S. Senate Small Business Committee where she became interested in the concept of employee ownership. Ms. Young is author of *Beyond Taxes: Managing an Employee Ownership Company*, coauthor of *Employee Ownership in America: The Equity Solution*, and contributed to *Employee Stock Ownership Plans, Business Planning, Implementation, Law and Taxation*. She speaks and writes regularly on the subject of employee ownership. She holds a B.A. in English from George Mason University and an M.A. in Organizational Management from George Washington University.

DAVID M. BINNS is the executive director of the ESOP Association, a national trade association based in Washington, D.C. The ESOP Association represents companies with employee stock ownership plans and professionals involved in the ESOP area. A former congressional aide and public relations account executive, Mr. Binns has served in his current position at the ESOP Association since 1984.

JOSEPH R. BLASI is author of *Employee Ownership: Revolution or Ripoff?* which was written while he was a visiting researcher at the Harvard Business School and taught social studies at Harvard University. A frequent consultant on employee ownership and participation, he is now a professor at the Institute of Management and Labor Relations at Rutgers University. He is co-author of *Taking Stock: Employee Ownership at Work.*

RICHARD S. BRAUN is a principal of the valuation advisory firm Houlihan, Lokey, Howard & Zukin, Inc. He is a frequent speaker and writer on ESOP topics and is currently chairman of the Valuation Committee of the ESOP Association. He is a graduate of Harvard Business School.

MICHAEL A. CONTE received his Ph.D. from the University of Michigan and has since concentrated on employee ownership research. He served as a consultant to the U.S. General Accounting Office in its study of ESOP companies and has written extensively on employee ownership and participation companies. Dr. Conte is director of the Center for Business and Economic Studies at the University of Baltimore and has recently founded an Institute for Research on Employee Ownership.

JACK CURTIS is a partner in the San Francisco office of Keck, Mahin & Cate, a Chicago law firm. He also served as counsel to the U.S. Senate Committee on Finance, a position that was created for him by then-Chairman Russell Long. In that capacity, he was responsible for the committee's work in the areas of ESOPs, ERISA, and other tax matters.

GIANNA DURSO is a Ph.D. candidate at Brown University. Previously she was a project coordinator at The National Center for Employee Ownership, where she edited *The Journal of Employee Ownership Law and Finance* and participated in studies on privatization through employee ownership and international applications of ESOPs. Ms. Durso received her B.A. from Princeton University.

CHESTER A. GOUGIS is an executive vice-president of Duff & Phelps Inc. and managing director of its wholly owned subsidiary, Duff & Phelps Financial Consulting Co. The subsidiary performs projects involving corporate valuations and financial policy consulting. Mr. Gougis holds a B.A. in economics from Harvard University and an M.B.A. in finance and accounting from the University of Chicago. He is a member of the Valuation Study Group and the ESOP Association.

LILLI GORDON is a Managing Director of the Institutional Voting Research Service. Ms. Gordon specializes in finance, industrial economics, and corporate governance. She has directed studies on issues involving managerial incentives, corporate financial structure, the structure of corporate claims, and the effects of shareholder voting. She has also performed extensive research on the mutual fund industry and co-authored a comprehensive study on the economics and regulation of mutual funds.

JENNY A. HOURIHAN is a vice-president in the Corporate Finance Department of Salomon Brothers and manages the ESOP Group. Since joining the firm in 1981, she has also worked in the Finance Utility Group, the Municipal Finance Department, and the Capital Market Group. She has structured ESOPs for Parker-Hannifin, McDonalds, Xerox, and Johnson Controls, Inc. Ms. Hourihan has an economics degree from Swarthmore College.

KENNETH W. LINDBERG is a partner at Hewitt Associates, where he has been for over 23 years. He has been on the ESOP Resource Committee since its founding in 1984. He is currently the firm's national practice leader of ESOPs for plan design and legal requirements. He also designs other types of plans intended to promote employee stock ownership. Mr. Lindberg is a graduate of Lake Forest College.

JOHN POUND is the senior academic advisor to the Institutional Voting Research Service and assistant professor of public policy, John F. Kennedy School of Government, Harvard University. Mr. Pound is a specialist in corporate control and governance. He has published on voting and corporate control in leading journals and advised private institutions, state governments, and research organizations on voting. He served as senior financial economist at the U.S. Securities and Exchange Commission.

COREY M. ROSEN is executive director and co-founder of The National Center for Employee Ownership. He has co-authored two books and over 100 articles on this subject. He received his Ph.D. in politics from Cornell and spent five years as a professional staff member in the U.S. Senate before co-founding NCEO.

MALON WILKUS is president of American Capital Strategies (ACS), an investment banking firm in Washington, D.C., specializing in ESOP-structured corporate transactions. ACS facilitates buyouts of corporations or subsidiaries in either private or auction transactions. From 1982 until January 1986, Mr. Wilkus was vice-president of Calvert Securities Corporation, a $2 billion investment management company. He is currently a director of The National Center for Employee Ownership and Co-op America.